Contents

Introduction

Native American women all too often have been overlooked in the history of the United States. Under the extreme circumstances that accompanied the diaspora of America's indigenous people in North America that all but wiped out Native American tribes and their traditions, brave and intelligent Native American women such as Sarah Winnemucca, Pocahontas, and Chipeta put their safety and the lives of their families at risk by taking on the roles of peacemakers, diplomats, and spokeswomen for their people. Many, through their actions, such as Sacajawea, Jane Timothy Silcot, and Kakeri Tekakwitha, proved detrimental or changed the destiny of their tribes. All these women, whose stories are told here, were caught between two cultures, yet many worked tenaciously to preserve the traditions of their tribes and teach others. Dat So La Lee, Frances Slocum, and Nampeyo achieved this through the arts of pottery and basketmaking; others such as Maggie Axe Wachacha, Lozen, and Gladys Tantaquidgeon accomplished these things through healing and magical traditions. The inspiring legacies of these wise women, who came from diverse backgrounds and who helped to form this country, are preserved in these stories.

Sarah Winnemucca Hopkins
1844–1891

$\mathcal{X}$

A Sparrow Among Eagles

In 1864 twenty-year-old Sarah Winnemucca, a Paiute Indian, stood on the stage of Henry Sutliffe's Music Hall in Virginia City as the audience rose, their applause thundering in an avalanche of praise. She nervously brushed her hands against her buckskin skirt, the swaying fringe revealing ornately beaded boots. Long, coal-black hair fell across delicate features as she turned to smile at her father, Chief Winnemucca, who stood stoically behind her.

Sarah and her father hoped their presentation would mend escalating tensions between white Nevada settlers and the Northern Paiute Indians, as well as garner enough food and clothing to keep the Paiutes from starving or freezing that winter. It was the beginning of a journey that would leave Sarah heartbroken, destitute, and ill as she attempted time and again to bring understanding and cooperation between two very different cultures. Not until long after her death would she be heralded as a peacemaker between the two races.

Sarah Winnemucca's birth in the summer of 1844 near the Humboldt River occurred just prior to the great influx of gold seekers crossing the desert plains to California. Captain Truckee, the Paiute chief and Sarah's grandfather, served as guide for parties heading west and considered the white man his friend and peer.

Her parents, Winnemucca and Tuboitony, named Sarah Thocmetony, meaning "shell flower." She spent her childhood beside her mother and other Paiute women and children traveling miles each day gathering roots, herbs, and wild seeds to flavor the fish, ground squirrels, and larger game caught by the men. Crunchy delicacies of roasted crickets and grasshoppers were favorite treats. Although they considered the Pyramid Lake region their homeland, the Paiutes were hunters and gatherers, not settling to farm but preferring to rely on the land for sustenance.

The Paiutes kept their past alive by relating ancient tales. The story of Cannibal Owl, who snatched naughty children, pounded them into pulp, and ate them, is a typical legend. When her father described the first white men he saw as owllike with scraggly gray beards and colorless, ghostly eyes, Sarah steadfastly believed she would be eaten if caught by one of these white apparitions.

Sometimes nightmares become reality. As white miners and settlers penetrated farther into their territory, Sarah's people learned to avoid the newcomers—encounters usually ended in tragedy for the unsophisticated Paiutes. One terrifying incident cemented Sarah's fear of the white intruders.

Sarah's mother, Tuboitony, and the other women were gathering seeds when a band of white men approached. As Tuboitony ran, little Sarah and her cousin lagged behind, unable to keep up with the fleeing adults. Rather than endanger the entire band, Tuboitony dug a trench in the sandy soil and ordered the two little girls into the ditch. She pushed dirt atop them and spread sagebrush over their heads to protect them from the sun. She then fled, leaving the girls to their fate. The sun rose higher and hotter before starting its westward descent toward a darkness filled with unknown terrors. Would the white men find them, smacking their lips as they stoked a roaring fire before pounding them to death? Or would marauding coyotes discover them first? Suddenly the girls heard rustling in the bushes and knew their fate was but a few feet away. In her book *Life Among the Paiutes: Their Wrongs and Claims*, Sarah described what happened next:

At last we heard some whispering. We did not dare to whisper to each other, so we lay still. I could hear their footsteps coming nearer and nearer. I thought my heart was coming out of my mouth. Then I heard my mother say, "T is right here!" Oh, can any one in this world ever imagine what were my feelings when I was dug up by my poor mother and father?

Captain Truckee ruled the Northern Paiutes wisely and compassionately. Having guided the whites into California, he understood they would soon wield more power than his people could ever muster. In 1851 he took a contingent of Paiutes to California to learn the white man's ways. Six-year-old Sarah, convinced she would be eaten by the dreaded white owls, cowered under a blanket as they crossed the Nevada plains.

After returning to their homeland, Winnemucca and Tuboitony sent Sarah and her younger sister Elma to live with Major William Ormsby, who ran a stage depot in Genoa, then part of Utah Territory. The Ormsbys taught the girls to speak and write English. In return, Sarah and Elma worked in the depot store, helped with household chores, and were companions for little Lizzie Anne Ormsby. The Ormsbys' kindness toward the two girls during the year they lived with them alleviated some of Sarah's doubts about white savages. It may have been during this time that Thocmetony acquired her English name of Sarah and her sister became known as Elma.

By the winter of 1858, the influx of white settlers had devastated the vast herds of wild game, fish, plants, and seeds that the Paiutes relied upon for sustenance. As bitter winds howled and snow drifted to towering heights, the Paiutes were forced to ask for assistance from Virginia City citizens—warm clothing and enough food to make it through the winter. But their pleas were ignored, and many froze or starved to death. The following winter brought little relief and even colder temperatures.

Old Captain Truckee, perhaps sensing his pending death, requested that Winnemucca and Tuboitony send Sarah and Elma to school in California to learn about the new world emerging around them. The San Jose school seemed amicable to the girls, but after only a few weeks white parents objected to their children sitting next to the Indians and insisted they leave.

White settlers, prospectors, and businesses now dominated the West. Virginia City boasted a white population of almost 15,000, and they wanted the Paiutes off the lush, productive land surrounding Pyramid Lake. The Natives were already restricted in where they could hunt and fish. Now the white populace wanted to determine where the Indians could live, pledging to provide food, clothing, and farming equipment if the Indians would stay within proscribed reservation boundaries. None of these promises materialized.

Winnemucca, now tribal leader after Captain Truckee's death, took the plight of his people to the citizens of Nevada. He walked onto the stage of Sutliffe's Music Hall that day in 1864 with Sarah, Elma, son Natches, and a handful of other Paiutes seeking assistance from the people of Virginia City. Sarah interpreted her father's words for the audience.

The Paiute group continued on to San Francisco and made their plea before an audience at the Metropolitan Theater. Sarah donned the expected attire—buckskin skirt trimmed with fringe and ornately beaded boots. She had quickly assessed the delight of white audiences when she romanticized her appearance, dressing as writers depicted Indians in western dime novels rather than in more traditional attire. Though the troupe was well received in San Francisco, their appeals were largely ignored.

In 1865, when Chief Winnemucca and his men were on a hunting expedition, a cavalry troop rode into the Paiute camp and accused the Indians of stealing cattle and slaying two white men. Refusing to believe the Indians' denial, the cavalry slaughtered thirty women, children, and old men. Sarah's sister Mary fled to the mountains to warn Chief Winnemucca and his men not to return. By the time the Mud Lake Massacre was over, Mary and Sarah's mother, Tuboitony, lay dead.

Conditions on Pyramid Lake Reservation became unbearable. The Paiutes were desperate for food and clothing. Tempers flared between the two races.

The summer of 1868 brought no relief for the destitute Paiutes. Sarah and Natches went to Camp McDermit near the Oregon border seeking assistance from the army. Recognizing her ability to speak several languages—English, Spanish, and various Indian dialects—the army hired Sarah as an interpreter. Natches, with the promise of protection and provisions for his people, was sent to bring in Chief Winnemucca. That July, around 500 Paiutes chose to relocate to Camp McDermit rather than starve to death.

Sarah believed her people could become productive farmers if taught how to plow and sow, skills they had not needed as hunters and gatherers. In a letter to Ely Samuel Parker, commissioner of Indian affairs, she offered her solution to the problem of feeding her people and respecting their needs:

> So far as their knowledge of agriculture extends they are quite ignorant as they never had an opportunity of learning but I think if proper pains were taken that they would willingly make the effort to maintain themselves by their own labor if they could be made to believe that the products were to be their own and for their own use and comfort.

Nothing came of her request for assistance, so in 1870 Sarah returned to San Francisco, where newspapers touted her as "Princess Sarah." But once again, false promises and undelivered goods were all the Paiutes received.

While she was still at Camp McDermit, First Lieutenant Edward D. Bartlett caught Sarah's eye with his dashing uniform, expert horsemanship, and happy-go-lucky lifestyle. Marriages between Native Americans and whites were forbidden in Nevada, so the couple traveled to Salt Lake City and wed on January 29, 1871. Unbeknown to Sarah, Bartlett had deserted his company. His fun-loving nature seemed to need the nourishment of copious amounts of liquor, purchased with money acquired by pawning Sarah's jewelry without her knowledge. The marriage was over within the year, although not legally dissolved until 1876.

In 1872 the Paiutes were relocated to the Malheur Reservation about 80 miles north of Camp McDermit. Resident Indian agent Sam Parrish and his wife were well liked, never demeaning the Paiutes' customs or needs; they also paid fair wages for work. When Mrs. Parrish opened a school, she and Sarah taught side by side. Under the supervision of Agent Parrish, the Paiutes accepted the confines of reservation living.

Unfortunately, life does not continue along straight and serene courses. Sam Parrish, never much of a religious man, was soon relieved of his duties, because the law insisted reservations be under Christian leadership. His replacement, former army officer W. V. Rinehart, bore ill will toward the Paiutes and soon ran afoul of the determined Sarah.

Rinehart blamed all the problems he encountered at Malheur on Sarah's insistent requests for fair treatment of the Paiutes. He refused to pay them for work they performed and withheld much-needed food and clothing. He closed Mrs. Parrish's school. Rinehart claimed Sarah was disloyal and purposely stirred up trouble. He threatened to put her in prison but, instead, banished her from the reservation.

In June 1878 a contingent of neighboring Paiutes begged Sarah to help their starving families. "You are our only voice," they pleaded. Realizing that assistance had to come from the highest power of the land, she decided to go to Washington, D.C.

Sarah made it as far as the Oregon–Idaho border, where the Bannock tribe, as destitute as the Paiutes, rallied against their oppressive Indian agent. With war pending, Sarah returned to her people.

Chief Winnemucca refused to join the Bannock uprising. In retaliation, the Bannocks held him and a contingent of his band hostage. When Sarah learned that her father was behind enemy lines, she vowed to bring her people to safety, offering her services as interpreter and scout to General O. O. Howard, commander during the Bannock War. Along with her brother Lee and his wife, Mattie, she set out across miles of treacherous, rocky terrain to rescue the Paiute prisoners, stopping only for fresh horses before heading out again. Nearing the Bannock stronghold, they quit their horses and, on hands and knees, crawled up the side of the mountain. Peering into the enemy camp, they found the Bannocks butchering cattle for an evening feast. The shadowy figures stealthily maneuvered their way through enemy lines to the imprisoned Paiutes, then led seventy-five of their people to safety. Over a three-day period, the triad rode more than 200 rough miles to bring the Paiutes home.

Sarah continued to serve under General Howard as interpreter and scout during the Bannock War, slipping in and out of enemy camps, stealing plans, intercepting Bannock war signals, and aiding in the capture of Bannock warriors.

After one particularly bloody fight, soldiers found a Bannock baby on the ground covered in dirt. The little girl was turned over to Sarah and Mattie, but knowing they could not care for the baby and continue to scout for the army, they entrusted her to two Bannock women prisoners. After the war, Sarah found the child's parents and reunited the family. The grateful couple named their daughter Sarah for her rescuer.

Sarah and Mattie were often called upon to hunt down fleeing Bannock prisoners. During one escapade across rock-hard ground, Mattie's horse slipped and tossed her brutally to the earth. Her injuries were severe, and Sarah feared for her sister-in-law's life.

By August 1878 the Bannock War was over. Because the Paiutes had not joined the hostile Bannocks, they assumed they would be allowed to stay at Malheur Reservation. The army, however, considered all Indians prisoners of war regardless of tribe. The Paiutes were ordered to Yakima Reservation in Washington Territory, a distance of more than 350 miles over treacherous mountain ranges. They would travel in the middle of winter clad in threadbare blankets and worn-out boots.

On January 6, 1879, fifty wagons started out across the mountains of Oregon and Washington. Elderly Paiutes froze to death and were left beside the road; children died in their parents' arms. Sarah watched a mother and her new baby die. Mattie struggled against unconsciousness in the back of a roughshod wagon.

The Paiutes were promised warm clothing, an abundance of food, and comfortable lodgings at the end of their journey. What greeted them after almost a month on the hard, bitter road was a hastily built, unheated 150-foot shed that let in cold winter winds and drifting snow. Firewood was nonexistent, and scant food was provided to the already emaciated group. The Paiutes were assured that wagonloads of warm clothing were on the way. With spring came the promised goods: twenty-eight shawls and a handful of fabrics. Everything else had been sold to the highest bidder before reaching the Indians. Mattie died at the end of May.

Sarah taught school at Yakima, but as soon as she received her pay from the army for her scouting and interpreting duties, she set out again for Washington, D.C. She was determined to secure aid for her people and to return them to Pyramid Lake. Her route was circuitous.

In November 1879 she went to see General Howard, who had not forgotten her invaluable help during the Bannock War. He gave her a letter of introduction to Washington officials. Stopping next in San Francisco, where her heroic deeds during the war had made her a celebrity, she took the opportunity to speak at Platte's

Hall. She told of her people's history, how Captain Truckee had welcomed white settlers and led them across the Nevada desert to the gold fields of California. She recounted the treatment received at the hands of Indian agents such as W. V. Rinehart, and then she detailed the horrible march to Yakima.

An 1879 article in the *San Francisco Chronicle* recognized Sarah's stamina and poise:

Sarah has undergone hardships and dared dangers that few men would be willing to face, but she never lost her womanly qualities. . . . She speaks with force and decision, and talks eloquently of her people. Her mission, undertaken at the request of Chief Winnemucca, is to have her tribe gathered together again at their old home in Nevada, where they can follow peaceable pursuits and improve themselves.

Chief Winnemucca, Natches, and a cousin joined her on her trek to Washington, D.C. There they met Carl Schurz, secretary of the interior, who promised to send supplies and suggested they return home to await the glut of provisions that would be forthcoming. Before leaving the capital of freedom, they toured the White House, where they met President Rutherford B. Hayes.

Yet Sarah's nemesis, Agent Rinehart, had already laid the foundation for her defeat in Washington by sending a barrage of letters to E. A. Hayt, commissioner of Indian affairs, disparaging her character, calling her a woman of low means, and accusing her of prostitution. Schurz may have become aware of Rinehart's accusations, for he reneged on his promises to send provisions to the destitute Indians.

Failing once again to obtain aid, Sarah's loyalty came under question by her own people. She had traveled between two diverse worlds for so long, experiencing the harsh existence of reservation life along with the comforts enjoyed in white settlements. Some of her people felt she had sold out for a more lucrative lifestyle.

Once again Sarah tried to find companionship and love in the arms of a white man. Fair-haired Virginian Lewis H. Hopkins, like Edward Bartlett, liked the action of gambling halls and saloons. Although he was five years younger than Sarah, the couple married in San Francisco on December 5, 1881.

The newlyweds enjoyed little wedded bliss. When Chief Winnemucca died in 1882, Sarah's brother Natches became Paiute chief, and she was once again asked to intercede on the tribe's behalf. She and Hopkins traveled east in 1883. On this trip Sarah met two sisters, Elizabeth Palmer Peabody and Mary Mann.

Elizabeth Peabody, considered the first woman book publisher in the United States, also owned a bookstore frequented by the literary elite of Boston. She arranged a series of lectures for Sarah, encouraging her to detail the history and culture of the Paiute people, to explain to America that the Indians had no land, no citizenship, and no government representation.

Elizabeth then urged Sarah to write down the history of the Paiutes. Sarah considered herself a poor writer but Mary Mann, widow of educator Horace Mann, offered to edit her work. The commingling of three compassionate hearts and minds resulted in Sarah's book *Life Among the Paiutes: Their Wrongs and Claims*, published in 1883 and thought to be the first book written by a Native American woman.

On April 22, 1884, Sarah spoke before Congress, petitioning for an allotment of land for her people at Pyramid Lake. Although Interior Secretary Schurz opposed the action, a bill was passed on July 6, 1884, giving each family 160 acres of Nevada land. It was not good land—that had been gobbled up by white settlers—but at least they would be back on home soil.

While Sarah counted on the money she received from her lectures and the sale of her book to provide funds for her people, Lewis Hopkins preferred to gamble away a good portion of her earnings. Very little was left by the time they returned to Nevada.

With her scant savings, plus the financial help of Elizabeth Peabody and Mary Mann, Sarah opened the Peabody Institute—a school in Lovelock, Nevada. She had always believed that education would bridge the disparities between the races, and said so in an article in the Winnemucca *Silver State* newspaper in 1886:

> *It seems strange to me that the Government has not found out years ago that education is the key to the Indian problem. Much money and many precious lives would have been saved if the American people had fought my people with Books instead of Power and lead. Education civilized your race and there is no reason why it cannot civilize mine.*

When Mary Mann died, she bequeathed her small estate to Sarah to help run the Peabody Institute. Sarah managed to keep the school open for a while but was soon inundated with financial woes. With her physical and emotional strength weakening, she was finally forced to close the establishment in 1888.

Ill, tired, and discouraged, Sarah went to live with her sister Elma at Henry's Lake on the Montana–Idaho border.

Sarah died in October 1891. She was only forty-seven years old. Although exhausted from years of fighting for her people, she had never quit. Her own words expressed her determination to return the Paiutes to the land of their ancestors: "When I think of my past life, and the bitter trials I have endured, I can scarcely believe I live, and yet I do; and, with the help of Him who notes the sparrow's fall, I mean to fight for my down-trodden race while life lasts."

Dat So La Lee

?–1925

❧

Washoe Basket Weaver

In 1978 four highly valued Washoe Indian baskets and a handful of arrowheads disappeared from the Nevada Historical Society Museum in Reno. The thief or thieves managed to grab the baskets from their display cases—each basket measured about 12 by 15 inches—and leave the building without being detected.

Two years later one basket was recovered in California and returned to the museum for a finder's fee of $2,500. In 1998 an art dealer in Tucson, Arizona, having procured three Washoe baskets, sent them to an appraiser in California. Not recognizing the baskets, the appraiser forwarded photos of them to an expert in British Columbia for attribution. Suddenly the Federal Bureau of Investigation was on the art dealer's doorstep in Tucson, wanting to know from whom and where he had purchased the baskets. The art dealer had no idea the baskets were stolen goods and voluntarily turned them over to the FBI. He was not charged with the theft and received $55,000 for returning them, the sum he had originally paid for the baskets.

The FBI turned the three baskets over to the historical society to ensure they would be properly cared for while agents continued their investigation. Reportedly, when the director of the historical society flew to Arizona to retrieve the baskets, he refused to put his treasured cargo in the baggage hold of the airplane for the return trip. Instead he purchased three additional airline seats so they would not leave his sight until they were back where they belonged. No one was ever charged with the theft of the baskets, which were said to be worth between $150,000 and $300,000 each.

How did a Canadian art expert, so far from the scene of the crime, recognize these valuable baskets? Dr. Marvin Cohodas of the University of British Columbia knew exactly who had created the three hundred-year-old baskets. As an authority on Washoe Indian basketry, he had no trouble recognizing the work of the woman who is recognized as the most renowned Washoe basket weaver—Dat so la lee. Where the baskets had been since their removal from the Nevada Historical Society Museum twenty years previously remains a mystery even today. The life of Dat so la lee is also somewhat of a mystery.

Born around the mid-1800s, Dat so la lee lived in and around the Carson Valley area and into the Sierra Nevadas, never far from beautiful Lake Tahoe. The Washoe (also spelled Washo) had neither chiefs nor leaders. Relying on the land for sustenance, they preferred to gather seeds, fish, and hunt wild rabbit and deer rather than farm the land. They never acquired horses to travel great distances. For the most part they lived peacefully with their neighbors, the Pomo and Maidu Indians in eastern California, and the Paiutes along the western border of what would eventually become the state of Nevada. Of the four main Nevada tribes—the Northern Paiute, Southern Paiute, Shoshone, and Washoe—the Washoe were the smallest in number. All these indigenous clans traded among each other, with the Washoe refining their talents as basket makers by incorporating the methods and intricacies of other tribes.

Washoe women made simple, unadorned baskets to hold the seeds and acorns they collected. Baskets lined with pitch held water. They cooked food by dropping a series of hot rocks into baskets filled with liquid, meat, and vegetables, then constantly moved the baskets back and forth to prevent them from burning. When the rocks cooled, they were replaced until the food was thoroughly cooked.

Little is known of Dat so la lee's childhood but, like all the Washoe, she certainly watched as white settlers spread across her native land. The rabbits and deer disappeared. Grass seeds and acorns, staples of the Washoe diet, vanished under the stampede of cattle and sheep or lay buried beneath the plow of industrious farmers. The Washoe became servants of the white populace in growing towns and campsites. They cooked, washed clothes, tended white children, and helped till the land, all for food they could no longer provide for themselves.

Dat so la lee learned the intricacies of making baskets, as did all young Washoe girls. When white settlers brought out their iron pots for cooking, however, many women abandoned ancient basket-weaving practices. Why spend days, sometimes months, creating a container that lasted only a few years when a big heavy pot did the same job and lasted almost forever? Few Washoe women continued to create the willow masterpieces. Many forgot their talents.

In the late 1800s Dat so la lee married Assu and had two children, neither of whom lived to adulthood. When Assu died, she may have married again, but there is little evidence of that union. She worked around Carson Valley washing the clothes of white settlers and tending to their children. And unlike most of her contemporaries, she continued to make baskets. Around 1888 she married master arrow craftsman Charley Keyser, part Washoe and twenty-four years her junior. At the same time, she took the American name Louisa Keyser—the third name she had acquired in her short lifetime.

When Dat so la lee was born, she received the name Dabuda, probably from her father, Da da u on ga la. When asked years later, she did not know her mother's name, and it's quite possible her mother died in childbirth. *Dabuda* may mean "young willow" in the Washoe language, certainly a fitting title for the yet-to-be celebrated weaver of baskets.

Around 1895 Dat so la lee was working as a laundress for Abram and Amy Cohn, second-generation owners of The Emporium, a clothing store in Carson City. The Cohns bought baskets from Indian tribes throughout the Southwest and California to sell alongside broad-brimmed hats, boots, and petticoats. When Abe saw the baskets his washerwoman wove in her spare time, he recognized her talent and encouraged her to spend more hours weaving and less time cleaning his clothes. Realizing that she might be his ticket to wealth and fame, he made her a proposition no poor Indian woman could ignore: In exchange for weaving her baskets solely for his store, he would provide her and Charley with a home, food, clothing, and medical care. Dat so la lee and Charley accepted Abe's offer, and a cloak of mystery fell over Dat so la lee's life.

The Cohns mastered the art of mythmaking, creating a fictional figure out of an ordinary Indian woman who only wanted to earn enough money to support herself and her husband. They wove stories of intrigue and romanticism around Dat so la lee and her unique form of basket weaving, hoping to entice more customers into their store.

Dat so la lee's baskets were derived from a combination of Washoe traditional weavings and Pomo Indian basketry. Her invention of the *degikup* (pronounced *day-gee-coop*) basket—a finely coiled container that started with a small, round bottom, ballooned in the middle, and then returned to a small opening at the top of equal size to the bottom—is considered to have renewed interest in Washoe basketry. This design gave her baskets a three-dimensional appearance. The word *degikup* refers to the small mouth-shaped rim.

She started each basket with a three-rod foundation made of willow twigs. She then sewed or wove around the foundation with simple, finely coiled stitches, measuring about twenty-five stitches per inch. Most of her baskets were finished in a self-rim with tapered stitches.

The background of her baskets was crafted from strips of pale-colored willow found just beneath the bark. Black stitching came from mature, brown fern roots that were dug up in spring, then buried in mud for several weeks until they turned black. In summer red bark was stripped from bunch trees, creating the red coloring of her designs. All these materials took days to dry, then were shredded and curled before curing. Lastly, they were cut into narrow strips ready to be woven into designs created from Dat so la lee's imagination. Some of her baskets took more than a year to complete.

Abe Cohn falsely claimed Dat so la lee acquired the *degikup* form of basketry from her ancestors—that this particular style was hers alone by family right. He also said she was the daughter of a chief and that the design on one of her baskets depicted the different levels of Washoe leadership, even though the Washoe did not subscribe to any form of hierarchy. According to Cohn, other weavers were forbidden to copy her style of basketry, and Washoe law deemed she could not weave the same design twice.

In actuality, Dat so la lee was the innovator and creator of the *degikup* style of basketry, and she often used the same design on different baskets. After 1900, as her construction techniques and designs grew in popularity, other basket weavers imitated her work. They wove to satisfy the demand for attractive, salable baskets, not to replicate ancient designs and imagery. Coloring was added to make the baskets more appealing to buyers and traders. Today the *degikup* basket is considered one of the most collectible forms of early Indian basketry.

Although Abe Cohn is credited with establishing Dat so la lee as a master basket weaver, Amy Cohn was the real creator of the Indian woman's fictional history. Amy wrote stories and gave lectures touting the intricacies of Dat so la lee's weaving, adding greatly to the myth surrounding the heavyset woman. Disregarding Dat so la lee's obesity, Amy invented a tale about her and Charley traipsing up and down the hillsides gathering tree limbs, roots, and bark to construct her unique baskets. She manufactured another story describing Dat so la lee sitting for hours splitting willow fibers with her teeth and fingernails, then smoothing the resulting threads with a piece of glass. "All day she sits patiently weaving these strands in-and-out," one of Amy's brochures read, "taking many moons to finish one of her rare and valuable *day-gee-coops*, or ceremonial baskets."

Sometimes Dat so la lee did sit in the window of The Emporium while passersby watched her interweave bundles of stripped willow and bark. Carson City newspapers announced the completion of each new *degikup* basket.

Amy invented stories about the baskets, giving them ritual significance even though they had none. She kept a ledger for each basket, indicating the date started and finished, a description of the design crafted on the basket, and the occasion for which it was made. All were numbered and titled. Statistics listed dimension, weight, and materials used. Even the weaving technique and stitch count were recorded. For years this ledger was the standard against which traders judged the value of Washoe baskets.

The Cohns sought to depict Dat so la lee as a product of the era before white settlers altered the Washoe lifestyle, before indigent Indians begged for handouts on the streets of Carson City. They wanted to present the image of a naive Native maiden working at her ancient craft; they believed this was what the white public wanted to see, not the reality of Washoe poverty. To give Dat so la lee a more romantic history, they changed her birth date by at least ten years, claiming that she was old enough to be one of the first Washoe to meet explorer John C. Frémont—considered the first white man to see the tribe in 1844.

Yet for all the liberties the Cohns took with Dat so la lee's life, they must be credited with bringing her basketry to the forefront of public attention, making her talent renowned among collectors worldwide. Abe and Amy Cohn freed the Indian artist from working menial jobs, encouraging her to create her legendary baskets and leave a legacy of artistry.

Dat so la lee really didn't need anyone to create a fantasy about her life or her ability to create magnificent baskets. And even though she was an uneducated Indian woman who signed her name with the palm of her hand, by the beginning of the twentieth century she far outshone other basket weavers in artistic ability.

In the summer of 1900, Amy took Dat so la lee to Tahoe City to display her baskets. That August she sought to expand her customer base by taking Dat so la lee to the California State Fair in San Francisco. And in September the Cohns and Dat so la lee exhibited baskets at the Nevada State Fair in Reno. Wherever they went, the big Indian woman attracted attention. Her fame was beginning to equal her size.

In 1903, in an effort to capitalize on an increasing national interest in western art, Amy opened a shop, the Biscoe, in Tahoe City. Every summer until her death, she took Dat so la lee to Lake Tahoe, where the big woman sat outside the store weaving.

Although Amy was socially active in Carson City, most of her time was spent in the company of Dat so la lee. The two women must have formed a sisterly bond on some level during the years they spent together. They traveled extensively in each other's company and certainly shared some moments of intimacy. Over the years Dat so la lee wove a set of miniature baskets, which she gave to Amy for her personal collection.

As the decades passed and Dat so la lee's fame increased, so did the size of her baskets. This may have been at Abe's insistence if he believed he could ask more money for her larger works. But it's also possible Dat so la lee made the decision to create these enormous baskets on her own.

Abe so overpriced Dat so la lee's huge baskets that he found few buyers. At one point he spread the rumor she was going blind in an effort to raise the value of her work. His largest sale came in 1914 when a Pennsylvania industrialist bought one of her baskets for around $2,000. Abe also thought he might capitalize on Dat so la lee's fame by opening a museum to display her work. He approached the Pennsylvania investor again about buying more baskets to fund his venture, but the man refused and the museum never materialized.

The tours they took throughout the West and the accolades Dat so la lee received for her basketry encouraged the Cohns to look to the East for more customers. In 1919 they bundled up Dat so la lee and a young Indian girl and headed for the St. Louis Industrial Exposition.

Dat so la lee sat on a stage dressed in a simple, large-patterned dress with a scarf atop her head. She worked on a basket while Amy told her listeners that the Indian woman before them was a Washoe princess and the only person allowed to weave these particular designs. To hear Amy tell it, after a Washoe–Paiute war, the victorious Paiutes forbade Washoe women from weaving baskets. But according to Amy, Dat so la lee secretly continued to weave, tossing the finished receptacles into the fire so she would not be discovered. By defying the Paiutes, said Amy, Dat so la lee became one of the few Washoe women to retain the knowledge of how to make the ancient designs. During these imaginative talks, Dat so la lee sat in the background, her head bowed, never uttering a word.

Amy died shortly after the group returned from St. Louis, and within a year Abe Cohn married again, much to the detriment of Dat so la lee and Charley. The new Mrs. Cohn saw no reason to keep the Washoe couple in such luxury, and their lifestyle declined under her care. No more pamphlets appeared lauding Dat so la lee's basketry. She did not weave as prolifically as when Amy was alive, and the baskets she created lacked the heart of her earlier designs.

Toward the end of her life, Dat so la lee suffered from what was then called dropsy (edema). She summoned a medicine man, but he was unable to help. She allowed a white doctor to treat her, to no avail. On December 6, 1925, Dat so la lee died in Carson City and is buried with her last unfinished *degikup* basket. She was around eighty years old.

Abe Cohn continued to peddle her baskets in his store but never realized the bonanza he had always anticipated from her artistry.

He died in 1934 with more than half of Dat so la lee's baskets still languishing on his shelves. His second wife, seeing no value in the old bundles of willow branches, sold twenty of Dat so la lee's baskets to the state of Nevada for a mere $1,500. Today some of the old washerwoman's larger baskets are worth hundreds of thousands of dollars each.

Dr. Marvin Cohodas, the art expert who recognized Dat so la lee's missing baskets in 1998, credits her with "originating the popular curio style of Washoe fancy basket weaving, both because she introduced the finely stitched, two-color *degikup* and because she inaugurated individuality and innovation for others to follow."

Today Dat so la lee's baskets can be found in the Nevada State Museum in Carson City and the Nevada Historical Society in Reno, as well as in museums across the country. As reticent as she was to speak in public, her voice can still be heard through the artistry of her work.

Kateri Tekakwitha
1656–1680

❧

The Lily of the Mohawks

Heart pounding, consumed with terror, the young Indian girl plunged headlong into the wild forest. Racing through the undergrowth, she leapt over fallen tree trunks and pushed frantically against the bare branches that sprang back against her scarred face. Stumbling over rocks, she blindly followed her two guides as they tore through the dense underbrush, just steps ahead of the fierce Indian chief who pursued them. At any moment the chief could catch up with them and force the girl to return with him to their Mohawk village home and his pagan way of life.

Suddenly she and her companions burst free of the forest and reached the swollen river. Flinging their canoe into the raging waters, they rowed frantically away, up that river and others, and across lakes. As the miles between Tekakwitha (pronounced *Tek'ak with'a*) and her pursuer lengthened, and she sensed she had eluded him, a great weight lifted from her spirit.

Finally she and the others reached the Christian settlement of Caughnawaga on the banks of the St. Lawrence River, not far from the city of Montreal in Canada. There she would be free to live a chaste and holy life devoted to her religious beliefs. Many would turn to her for help in their spiritual needs. In death she would bridge the gap between the white world and the Native American world as the first Native American to be declared "Blessed" by the Roman Catholic Church, one of the first steps to sainthood.

The forest that Tekakwitha and her companions had raced through was part of a vast, untamed wilderness that sprawled across New York State and was home to the five tribes of the powerful

Iroquois Nation: Mohawks, Oneidas, Onondagas, Cayugas, and Senecas. Her journey was the reverse of one her mother, Kahenta, had made many years before. Kahenta was an Algonquin woman who had been baptized as a Christian and who had lived at the Catholic Mission of the Three Rivers, among the French in Quebec. Kahenta had been abducted during a Mohawk raid of the settlement and carried off to become a slave in the Mohawk village of Ossernenon, near the present-day village of Auriesville, New York. Treated harshly by the women elders of the tribe, Kahenta had responded with a Christian spirit of compassion and tolerance, accepting her duties with quiet dignity and grace.

In time Kahenta's gentle nature caught the attention of the village war chief, Kenhoronkwa, who took the unusual step of marrying her, thus elevating her status from that of a slave to the wife of a great chief. The others in the village grew to respect her. They greeted with joy the birth of the couple's first child, Tekakwitha, in 1656, and her brother soon after. Tekakwitha's name is thought by some scholars to mean "she who puts things in order" and by others to mean "she who cuts the way before her."

Tekakwitha's early years were spent securely within her small family circle. The vast and seemingly endless wilderness that was their home offered a comfortable life for the Iroquois—abundant game for food; fertile soil in which to grow corn, squash, and beans; and rich, deep forests that provided berries, nuts, and fruits. As the daughter of a chief, her life was tranquil and protected. Her mother quietly taught her about the Catholic religion through prayers and cheerful stories of the saints that she herself had learned at the Catholic mission. She wished her children to be baptized in the Catholic faith, but knew it was impossible—her husband and the tribe would not allow it.

Although the Iroquois Nation was often at war with hostile neighboring tribes and had sometimes battled with the French, within their own tribe the Mohawks were a moral and spiritual people. They honored the Great Spirit, whom they believed watched the good acts of men and rewarded them. Through other religious ceremonies, they demonstrated their respect and gratitude for the natural world around them. They celebrated a feast to honor the maple trees and the sweet sap they provided. The Festival of the Green Corn lasted four days and demonstrated the tribe's respect for this nourishing and vital staple of their diet. Other religious ceremonies demonstrated their belief that the individual was an important and responsible part of the natural whole. Even at a young age, Tekakwitha developed strong religious convictions that were drawn from both the spiritual beliefs of her tribe and Catholic beliefs of her mother.

Tekakwitha was four years old when a smallpox epidemic swept through the tribe, killing her mother, father, and younger brother. She survived a bout with the disease but was left with a horribly scarred face and severely damaged eyesight. Smallpox had been imported into the Iroquois territory by the white man, and it had decimated other tribes as well because the Indians had no resistance to it.

An orphan, Tekakwitha was adopted by her father's brother, Iowerano, who became chief of the tribe in his brother's place. Iowerano and his wife had no children of their own. By adopting Tekakwitha they naturally wished to care for their niece, but they also hoped the girl would eventually marry, bringing into the family a warrior who would help to continue the family's line. Tekakwitha's Aunt Anastasia also moved into the family's lodge to care for Tekakwitha. Anastasia had been devoted to Kahenta. Now it was Anastasia's job to continue to instruct Tekakwitha in the Catholic religion and to keep the memory of the child's mother alive.

No matter their rank, all Mohawk children were expected to work alongside their elders for the good of the tribe. Even though she was the adopted daughter of a chief, Tekakwitha took her turn cutting wood for the fires and hoeing and weeding the crops in the fields. Because her eyesight was poor, she preferred to work indoors, pounding corn and preparing animal skins for clothing.

She was particularly skilled at using beads and quills to create elaborate designs. She also worked on the wampum belts and decorated clothing worn by other tribal members. But she did not readily join in the games and play with the other children of the tribe, preferring a more isolated life inside the lodge.

Throughout Tekakwitha's life the Iroquois Nation faced continuing hostilities with the French, and in 1666 the French again invaded their land, destroying three Mohawk villages, including Ossernenon. Tekakwitha and her family were forced to move to a neighboring area and build a new village, which they named Gandaouague. Peace terms were finally agreed on in 1667. The Mohawks agreed to allow the French priests, whom they called the "Blackrobes," into their villages to counsel and preach to their people.

The Iroquois were naturally suspicious of the Blackrobes. Other white men had sided with their enemies, had taken their lands, and challenged their religion. But as a sign of his willingness to cooperate peacefully, Chief Iowerano welcomed the Blackrobes into his lodge, offering them a place to stay in the village while they preached and tried to convert the Indians to Catholicism. Tekakwitha was fascinated by the priests' piety and kindness and their exciting tale of the birth of the Christ child. It reminded her of the ways of her mother, who had instructed Tekakwitha in the Christian virtues of humility, modesty, and charity. But she was too young to risk alienating her uncle, who did not approve of the Catholic religion, so she cared for the physical needs of the Blackrobes, bringing them food and drink, never mentioning her growing desire to pursue their religion.

The Iroquois way of life was not a gentle one. Rules of the tribe were strictly imposed. One of those rules was that young women must marry at an early age. Such strictures were designed to safeguard both the strength of the tribe and the well-being of the young women themselves. The young had to marry and produce strong, healthy children to continue the work of the tribe.

Marriage offered a young woman the protection of a strong warrior in a hostile world.

Marriage also conferred enhanced status on a woman. Unlike white women of the era, Iroquois women held important and influential positions in the tribe. Women were the undisputed leaders of the villages and longhouses. They voted on whether the tribes would go to war. A mother had even more voice in the tribe and could cast additional votes in the tribal conferences. It was the women who were charged with deciding the fate of captives during wars, and they could be merciless, inflicting horrible tortures.

But in her first open defiance of her tribe's laws and customs, Tekakwitha refused to even consider the subject of marriage. She announced that she wished to remain a virgin for her whole life, a preposterous idea, one far beyond the understanding of her family. Her aunts continually pressured her to accept one of the eligible young men of the tribe as a husband. Following custom, they invited a young warrior into their lodge for a meal. When it came time to serve him his food, they asked Tekakwitha to offer him the bowl, knowing full well that such an offer would mean that she was accepting him as her husband. Tekakwitha rose and left the house abruptly and did not return until the young man had left.

Her aunts were angry. Once a cherished stepdaughter, Tekakwitha now became an outcast, expected to perform the most menial chores, mocked, laughed at, derided by other members of the clan. She was suspected of harboring an aversion to the Mohawk men because of her Algonquin heritage and to the Mohawk and Iroquois way of life because of her mother's religious beliefs. There were rumors her mother had set her against marriage before she died. The entire tribe thought Tekakwitha had gone mad.

Tekakwitha was adamant in her refusal to marry, but she remained docile and compliant in all other ways. When the Jesuit priest Father Jacques de Lamberville again visited her village, she finally told him of her wish to be baptized in the Catholic religion. She also confessed to him the desire to remain a virgin for the rest of her life.

One can only wonder at Father de Lamberville's reaction to this confession by an eleven-year-old girl. He must have been delighted to have another convert to what he himself believed to be the one true religion. But he must have also been concerned about her welfare. Her open refusal to marry and to follow tribal custom had resulted in ostracism and punishment. Who knew what punishment would be inflicted on her for the adoption of Catholicism by this pagan society? He cautioned her against rashness, advising her to study and pray and to remain respectful of her uncle and her aunts.

Tekakwitha followed his instructions for nine years. During those years she prayed, studied, followed the tenets of the religion as best she could, and moved deeper and deeper into a spirit of religious mysticism. Father de Lamberville continued to instruct her and others in the tribe, including her Aunt Anastasia. In time her uncle and aunts withdrew their objections, even accepting her decision not to marry. Finally on Easter Sunday 1676, Tekakwitha was baptized and formally received into the Catholic faith. She was given the name of Katharine, or Kateri, in honor of Saint Catharine of Siena. She was twenty years old.

Christianity became more established in the tribal communities as the number of converts increased. But even as tribal leaders tolerated these conversions, they still expected their members to continue the Iroquois way of life and to contribute to the well-being of their own people. Tekakwitha's uncle was particularly concerned about converts leaving the tribe and taking away valuable members who were needed to maintain the community's strength and vigor. There were rumors of a settlement in Canada where converts to Catholicism could worship freely and live among Iroquois of their faith. As much as he loved Tekakwitha, he was adamantly against her leaving the tribe.

As a Catholic, Tekakwitha evoked hostility because she would not work on Sundays or on the church's feast days. She began to seek more time alone, moving into the forest to pray and meditate.

She withdrew from the activities of the young people of the tribe and avoided tribal celebrations, finding them heathen and cruel. The drunkenness and pagan activities of the tribe sickened her. Her devotion to the Blessed Mother grew, and she carried her rosary with her everywhere.

The community again began to lose patience with her. She was accused of speaking to her uncle in too familiar a fashion, of even perhaps having an immoral relationship with him. Both young and old began to taunt her, to make obscene gestures at her when she passed, and to contemptuously refer to her as "the Christian." Her religious conversion was making ordinary life within the tribe very difficult for her, and many members of the tribe did not understand such consuming devotion to an alien belief. Father de Lamberville began to fear for her safety and for her mental stability.

One day Tekakwitha's village was visited by the Oneida chief named Okenratariken, also known as Hot Cinders because of his explosive temper and strong beliefs. Hot Cinders was a highly respected chief who had converted to the Catholic faith some time before. His home was now the Mission of the Sault in Canada, but he often traveled throughout the Iroquois Nation spreading the doctrine of Christianity. Endowed with a natural eloquence, Hot Cinders described his Catholic beliefs in terms the natives could understand and also described the beauties of the Catholic Mission of the Saulte, where Christians worshipped freely in a joyful and prosperous community.

Accompanying him was another resident of the Mission of the Sault—or Caughnawaga, as the Indians called it—a relative of Tekakwitha's who was married to a girl who had been brought up with Tekakwitha in the same longhouse and who considered herself to be Tekakwitha's sister. This sister was also a Christian and wished to have her husband bring Tekakwitha back with him to the settlement at Sault St. Marie. Tekakwitha's Aunt Anastasia had already gone to live at the mission. Both Tekakwitha and Father de Lamberville believed she belonged with these relatives.

But they also knew that Tekakwitha's uncle would never agree to her leaving his home.

It seemed that providence smiled on Tekakwitha the day Hot Cinders and her brother-in-law came to the village. Her uncle was away signing a treaty with the Dutch at Fort Orange. Time was of the essence. They must move quickly to get her away as fast and as far as possible before her uncle returned. Tekakwitha packed quickly, bidding her aunts farewell. She and the others fled the village, racing through the deep forests in a frantic rush to freedom.

When Chief Iowerano returned to the village and found Tekakwitha missing, he was angry, and he probably felt betrayed by the favorite niece he had cared for after the death of her parents. He took up his gun, loaded it with three bullets, and set off to find her and bring her back. Halfway through the forest he came upon Tekakwitha's brother-in-law, sitting calmly on a log, smoking his pipe. But Iowerano had never met the man before, so he moved on, while Tekakwitha hid behind a tree, holding her breath. When they were certain Iowerano was gone, the three resumed their flight and finally reached the river. Hot Cinders gave Tekakwitha his place in the canoe and moved on to preach at another village. Tekakwitha and the brother-in-law sailed away to freedom. What became of Chief Iowerano remains a mystery. There is no record of him ever returning to his village.

A likely path the fugitives followed was up the Hudson River, on to Lake George, and across Lake Champlain. After three weeks of travel, they reached the settlement of Caughnawaga in the fall of 1677. Tekakwitha carried with her a letter from Father de Lamberville to the resident priests at the settlement, Fathers Cholonec and Chauchetiere. "You will soon know what a treasure we have sent you," he wrote. "Guard it well then!" Kateri Tekakwitha's new life had begun.

Tekakwitha was joyfully reunited with her Aunt Anastasia, moved into her home, and immediately began to study to receive her

First Communion. She attended two Masses each day. She carried her rosaries and prayed to the Blessed Mother. Finally on Christmas Day, 1677, she received Holy Communion for the first time. Father Cholonec described her early days at the settlement: "In a few weeks she stood out among all the other women and girls of the mission . . . in a short time a saint among the just and faithful."

But life at the Mission of the Sault was not without problems. Despite their Christian way of life, the Native Americans who lived at the mission kept many of their native practices, including going out on hunting expeditions, during which they left the mission for months at a time. Everyone was expected to take part in these expeditions. Tekakwitha drew the anger of the settlement when she refused to go because it meant long absences from Mass and the Sacraments. Once again it was suggested that she marry, and once again she refused, pledging herself to the life of a virgin and consecrating herself totally to the Blessed Mother. She and another Native American woman considered beginning their own community of nuns, an action that was discouraged by the priests of the settlement.

In the spirit of the Christian martyrs, Tekakwitha began a program of self-punishment that she continued until her death that she considered necessary as atonement for her sins. She walked in the snow without moccasins, slept on a bed of thorns, and fasted for days. She seemed determined to rise to a new level of holiness, using personal mortification as the cornerstone of her spirituality. After all her Native American upbringing prized and admired brave stoicism in the face of pain. Now she had a positive reason for suffering.

She again withdrew from the community, spending long hours in prayer, increasing her personal penance, even wearing an iron waist chain to increase her suffering. The villagers finally sensed that she was a soul apart and sought her counsel and guidance in spiritual matters. Finally the harsh life she inflicted upon herself began to take its toll, and her health began to fail. She was confined to her cabin, where she died on April 17, 1680. She was twenty-four years old.

Reports of Tekakwitha's saintliness spread almost immediately. Those who were present at her death told of a miraculous transformation of her features. The marks from her childhood bout with smallpox disappeared, and her skin lightened and became radiant. The Native Americans at the Sault Mission began almost immediately to call her "The Saint."

Hundreds of people came to her grave at Caughnawaga, Quebec, Canada, to pray. The ill came and asked to be healed. Many cures were reported. Several people told of personal visits by her after her death. Anastasia said Tekakwitha came to see her and was "radiant and lovely, carrying a shining cross." Father Cholonec reported that she visited him and asked him to paint her portrait. When the portrait was finished, it too was reported to be the source of miracles and cures of the lame and the ill. By 1695 there had been hundreds of claims of miraculous cures reported, and reverence for the young woman grew.

An example of such devotion was evidenced in a letter written in 1682 by Father Chauchetiere to a friend in France:

We cease not to say Masses to thank God for the graces that we believe we receive every day through her intercession. Journeys are continually made to her tomb, and the savages following her example have become better Christians than they were. We daily see wonders worked through her intercession.

In 1932 the accounts of her life that had been recorded by Father de Lamberville, Father Chauchetiere, and other missionaries contributed significantly to the documentation necessary for her to be canonized as a saint. In 1942 she was declared by the Roman Catholic Church in Rome to be Venerable, and private devotion to her was allowed. In June 1980 Pope John Paul II declared her to be Blessed, another important step in her journey toward sainthood.

Tekakwitha turned away from the pagan culture of her birth and lived in a world steeped in holiness and piety. Yet she exhibited enormous strength. She successfully challenged her community on several issues that were considered fundamental to the tenets of the group. Although Iroquois women had many rights within their communities, religious freedom and the choice to remain unmarried were not among them. Tekakwitha fought for her right to remain single and to worship as she chose. She endured ostracism, pain, and danger for the freedom to follow her Christian principles. She was the first Native American woman known to make a vow of chastity and to live a life of penitential spirituality. Her unflagging belief that it was the wish of God that she do so carried her from the relative obscurity of the Iroquois Nation to the very portals of sainthood—the first Native American to be so honored.

Today veneration of Kateri Tekakwitha goes on, as the case for her sainthood continues to be heard in Rome. At the shrine at Auriesville, New York, she is honored for her purity of faith and her devotion to God. Her feast day is celebrated on July 14. More than three hundred years after her death, devotion to "The Lily of the Mohawks" is alive and flourishing.

Maggie Axe Wachacha
1894–1993

Ƨ6

Healer, Teacher, and Beloved Woman

The mountains, huge and hulking, rose into ash-gray skies. Veiled in fog, their dark shapes all but disappeared in places, then revealed themselves through breaks in the smoky haze. These wild hills, thick with forests, lay hunched in the deep sleep of winter. Along the ridges, barren tree trunks reached stark and sharp into the clouded sky like quills from the backs of porcupines. Soon, when spring arrived, rushing rivers and singing creeks would tumble through the gorge. Small waterfalls would splash over the rocks and large ones would roar. But for now, the waters moved sluggishly, or lay still against the frozen ground.

The mountains bore the name Sha-cona-ge—land of the blue mist or blue smoke. The names of individual peaks were equally proud—Tu-ti, Unaka, Tsiya-hi. According to Cherokee legend, these hills and valleys had been formed by the wings of the Great Buzzard as he skimmed the surface of the wet earth long ago, when the world was new. The white people called this place "North Carolina's last frontier," and they called the mountains the Appalachians, the Smokies, or the Blue Ridge.

On the crest of one peak, almost hidden by fog, stood a line of horses. Their riders sat tall, watching and waiting. The snow-laden branches of the pine and cedar swayed, and the cold wind seemed to murmur the names of the seven Cherokee clans: Ani'-Wa'ya, Ani'-Kawi , Ani'-Tsi'skwa, Ani'-Wa'di, Ani'-Saha'ni, Ani'-Ga'tage'wi, Ani'-Gila'hi.

Ten-year-old Maggie Axe squinted into the distance. She belonged to Ani'-Wa'ya, the Wolf Clan, largest of the seven. As she stared through the haze, the men on horseback shimmered like ghosts. She blinked, and they were gone. They had probably never been there at all, Maggie realized. She knew large bands of Cherokee no longer roamed the hills in search of game. The United States government had removed most of them to Oklahoma more than sixty years earlier, in 1838. Thousands of the men, women, and children who were forced to make the trip west died from exposure and disease. They had truly traveled a "Trail of Tears." In Maggie's village, the old ones still talked about Tsali, who escaped into the mountains but later sacrificed himself and his sons so that hundreds of others would be allowed to stay in the land of their ancestors.

Shivering, Maggie pulled her thin coat tighter around her. To her ears came a familiar sound—haunting and lonely, strangely musical, barely audible as it floated on the wind. It was a single voice, rising and dissolving into the mist. Wa'ya was calling his friends, or perhaps claiming his territory. With a smile, Maggie turned and walked a well-worn path back through the woods. The mingled aroma of bean bread and coffee greeted her as she entered the one-room log house she called home.

Maggie's ancestors were among the Cherokee who managed to remain in the mountains of North Carolina instead of being marched to Oklahoma. They considered themselves fortunate, but their lives were never the same after the removal. As anthropologist Sharlotte Neely reported in her book, *Snowbird Cherokees: People of Persistence:*

> *During the first two decades of the twentieth century the role of the Bureau of Indian Affairs in Cherokee schools bordered on the dictatorial. White teachers became the norm and boarding schools the ideal. Children were beaten for speaking the Cherokee language and encouraged to adopt white cultural patterns to the exclusion of those Cherokee.*

The word "Cherokee" had no meaning in Maggie Axe's native language. Her people called themselves Ani'-Yun'wiya' meaning "principal people" or "real people." Historians have determined that the name "Cherokee" was probably a corruption of "Tsa'ragi" or "Tsa'lagi," words occasionally used among the Cherokee. In historical records, "Cherokee" is spelled at least fifty different ways.

Efforts to change the culture of the Cherokee were strong during Maggie's youth. In church, she was taught that the mountains and valleys were not formed by the Great Buzzard's wings but by God. Every Sunday, she listened eagerly to stories from the Christian Bible, translated into Cherokee. Maggie loved to hear about Jesus and His love, the miracles He performed, and the sacrifice He made. She quickly memorized Christian hymns. Yet she still felt connected to many of the old ways. At the age of ten, she began learning the skills of midwifery from her aunt and the art of herbal medicine from her grandmother.

For centuries, the Cherokee had used plants to cure sickness. Revered storytellers like A'yun'ini or "Swimmer" explained to each generation the reason for this tradition. The tale was also included in *Myths of the Cherokee,* published in 1901 by the Bureau of American Ethnology. The author was anthropologist James Mooney, who lived among the Cherokee during the late 1800s.

In the old days the beasts, birds, fishes, insects, and plants could all talk, and they and the people lived together in peace and friendship. But as time went on the people increased so rapidly that their settlements spread over the whole earth, and the poor animals found themselves beginning to be cramped for room. This was bad enough, but to make it worse Man invented bows, knives, blowguns, spears and hooks, and began to slaughter the larger animals, birds, and fishes for their flesh or their skins, while the smaller creatures, such as the frogs and worms, were crushed and trodden upon without thought, out of pure carelessness or contempt. So the animals resolved to consult upon measures for their common safety.

According to the legend, the animals decided the best way to control humans was to plague them with diseases.

When the Plants, who were friendly to Man, heard what had been done by the animals, they determined to defeat the latters' evil designs. Each Tree, Shrub, and Herb, down even to the Grasses and Mosses, said: "I shall appear to help Man when he calls upon me in his need." Thus came medicine; and the plants, every one of which has its use if we only knew it, furnish the remedy to counteract the evil wrought by the revengeful animals.

While learning the secrets of the medicine woman, Maggie lived where she had been born, in Snowbird Gap in Graham County. Her home was more than fifty miles from the Qualla Boundary of Swain County, where the vast majority of her tribe was located. Although the two factions of the tribe had much in common, they spoke different dialects of Cherokee.

Over the years, the main Cherokee Indian Reservation became a center for tourism, attracting thousands of visitors annually. Boxed in by the mountains, Maggie's community remained more isolated. At the same time, because Snowbird reservation lands were intermingled with white-owned lands, the Cherokee and non-Cherokee inhabitants interacted regularly.

Not much is known about Maggie's early childhood. According to tribal records, she was born to Will and Caroline Cornsilk Axe on September 16, 1894—in the Cherokee "Month of the Nut Moon." From interviews with Maggie and her family in 1991, writer Jennifer Ravi gleaned the following information:

The language always spoken in her home was Cherokee. She taught herself to write it at home when she was seven years old, using chalk or writing in the dirt. Sometimes her father read it to her and she would write it in chalk on a slab of slate rock. Her father told her that one day she would go to Cherokee and work, and this provided an incentive to learn. She attended a one-room, English-speaking school four months out of the year, when it was either too cold to work or when there was no work to be done. She stopped attending after the fourth grade. Her English began with the words "Jesus Christ," and the rest came easily from listening to people talk.

In an interview for the *Journal of Cherokee Studies* in 1987, Maggie described some of her memories of the past to Lois Calonehuskie:

I remember the livestock. There were about a hundred pigs when I first moved here. Now you don't see any pigs. Pigs and hogs were so fat. There were plenty of chestnuts back then. That's what they lived on. They belonged to everybody. When we needed some meat, we just butchered one. Cows were there, too. We had a fence around the house so the cows wouldn't come in the yard. Cows were loose until they made a law that you had to fence in your stock. They couldn't roam the mountains like they did before. Many pigs, cows, and sheep went wild or got eaten up by wild animals.

Maggie's dual career as a healer and midwife blossomed as she grew older. Using the age-old formulas and incantations she learned from her grandmother, she treated everything from headaches and broken bones to gallstones and diabetes. A drink made from the ginseng root was useful against headaches and cramps. Maggie always made sure to address the root as "Little Man, Most Powerful Magician" in the fashion of Cherokee priests.

As a midwife, Maggie assisted in the delivery of more than three thousand babies. During childbirth, tea made from the inner bark of the wild black cherry was often given to mothers to relieve their pain. Maggie regularly walked great distances, day and night, no matter what the weather, to help those who needed her.

In 1935, Maggie met and married Jarrett Wachacha. Twenty years older than Maggie, Jarrett was a member of the Deer Clan, Ani'-Kawi. He was descended from Wachacha, brother of Tsunu'lahun'ski or "Junaluska." Junaluska was credited with saving Andrew Jackson's life during the Battle of Horseshoe Bend in 1814. Nevertheless, he was exiled with his people to Oklahoma. Later, he walked back to Graham County, where he was eventually granted the right of citizenship and a tract of land. He is buried in a boulder-marked grave near Robbinsville.

When Maggie and Jarrett married, Jarrett already had a son named Riley, and Maggie had a daughter named Lucinda. Riley and Lucinda later married each other. In 1936, Maggie and Jarrett's daughter, Winnona, was born. The following year, Maggie took on yet another important role—Tribal Indian Clerk for the Eastern Band of Cherokee Indians. In 1987, she explained to Lois Calonehuskie how she got the job: "The former Clerk [Will West Long] said he couldn't write any more. I'd taught myself to write in the Cherokee language. . . . Back then they held the Council meeting for two weeks once a year in the fall. The meeting lasted three days, and it was all in the Cherokee language. No English was spoken."

Annual meetings were held thirty miles away in the town of Cherokee. It took Maggie and Jarrett, who was an elected councilman from Snowbird Township, two days to walk there. Starting out at three or four o'clock in the morning, they would spend the night at a friend's house and continue early the next morning. When they had the money, they rode the midnight train instead. Maggie's duties included transcribing the minutes of the meetings into the Cherokee Syllabary, the written language of the Cherokee. She held the position of Tribal Indian Clerk for more than forty years.

In addition to being a healer, midwife, and tribal clerk, Maggie was also a teacher. She taught Sunday School at Zion Hill Baptist Church and taught the Cherokee Syllabary to students in the

Robbinsville school system, at Tri-County Technical College, and in the Adult Education Program of Graham County. In this way, she helped preserve a heritage and language nearly lost during the years of forced acculturation.

Bill Millsaps of Robbinsville remembers Maggie fondly.

When I was little, my dad operated a country store and the Wachachas were regular customers. At age eight, I began learning the Indian Syllabary from Maggie and the Cherokee language from the family. To this day, I read and write Cherokee with much accuracy. I must admit that I've lost my ability to speak as fluently as I would like. Maggie was a medicine lady and has doctored on many folks, me included. She was a very unique person.

Millsaps particularly enjoys telling a story about the time he was having dinner with Maggie's family at her daughter Lucinda's home. The baked ham looked and smelled delicious, but Bill had a terrible toothache and couldn't eat.

They sent me up to Maggie's house. She went behind the smokehouse and came back with some sticks. She told me to boil them, take a spoonful of the liquid, and hold it against my tooth. It worked! Later, I asked some of her family what those sticks were. They started to giggle. Finally, one of them said "The sticks don't matter. It was the words she said over them." Now, I don't know whether it makes any sense or not, but I know my toothache went away.

Conjuring, the use of magic to influence people and events, has always been part of the Cherokee tradition. Even in the days of "enlightenment" that followed the influx of whites into the area, conjuring remained a viable approach to all manner of problems.

In fact, many of the most noted conjurers also served as ministers in the local churches. Sharlotte Neely, author of *Snowbird Cherokees,* heard the following explanation during a sermon at Buffalo Baptist Church: "Only Jesus can heal illness, accomplishing His purpose through physicians or 'conjure men,' whose duty it is to locate the plant or herb which will cure a particular disease."

The advances of medicine during the twentieth century have not been shunned by the Cherokee, but at times, the old remedies still seem to work the best.

In 1978, the joint council of the Western Band of Cherokee of Oklahoma and the Eastern Band of Cherokee of North Carolina bestowed upon Maggie Axe Wachacha the title of "Beloved Woman." As Gilliam (Gill) Jackson reported in *The Cherokee One Feather,* the title traditionally was granted to the widowed wife of the Principal Chief. Jackson went on to say:

One of the most important individuals in traditional Cherokee society was a "Beloved Woman" which was an honored title of a very aged, respected female who played an important role in the most solemn ceremonies of the Cherokee people. . . . In recent time the traditional role of "Beloved Woman" . . . has been bestowed upon a modern day woman, Maggie Wachacha. . . . She also has the distinction of being the only female in Cherokee history to have a Tribal Building named in her honor. Other Tribal Buildings have been named after Tribal Chiefs and war heroes.

In 1986, *Newsweek* magazine recognized Maggie as one of one hundred American heroes. That same year, she was one of five women to receive the North Carolina Distinguished Woman Award, presented by Governor Jim Martin.

By age ninety-seven, Maggie had given up clerking, midwifery, and healing, although people still came to her for herbal treatments. Jarrett had passed away seventeen years earlier in 1974, at age 101.

Maggie had come to prefer conversing in Cherokee, letting others translate to English if necessary.

Maggie's great-granddaughter, Carolyn, remembers her great-grandmother as a "happy, perky person" who made her own buttermilk butter and collected rocks shaped like familiar objects or animals. She was often seen working in her garden, sporting the red kerchief worn by many of the older Cherokee women. Her corn crib was always full.

In Maggie's final months, Carolyn often stopped by to check on her. She remembers hearing Maggie's voice singing softly in Cherokee from her bedroom. Carolyn had heard old people sing this way before. To her, it sounded like a song of parting, of preparing to leave this world. The song she remembers hearing is called "Sqwatinisesti Yihowa" ("Guide Me, Jehovah"). The chorus of the hymn is a simple plea: "Forever, forever, guide, direct and help me. Forever, forever, guide, direct and help me."

Maggie Axe Wachacha died on February 3, 1993, in the Cherokee "Month of the Bony Moon." At her funeral, Bill Millsaps and his wife, Wilma, sang two of Maggie's favorite hymns in Cherokee: "Oonelanvhi Oowetsi" ("Amazing Grace") and "Oowoduhadi-quinassv" ("A Beautiful Life"). Maggie is buried on a hillside not far from a house where she once lived. The small, deserted structure is almost completely hidden by the wild flowers and grasses of Snowbird Gap.

Standing beside Maggie's grave, encircled by the massive mountains, it is easy to understand the fierce devotion the "principal people" felt for this land and to regret the ruling that tore so many of them away. Today, Wa'ya's soulful howl is heard but rarely in this place. Yet sometimes ghostly men on horseback still appear along the highest ridge. They speak only Cherokee. They live close to the earth that was shaped by Great Buzzard's wings. And they will never be removed.

Pocahontas
1596–1617

❧

America's Princess

On an April day in 1613, Pocahontas walked the narrow plank leading onto the ship *Treasurer*, anchored in the Potomac River. She was accompanied by a Potowomeke chief, Jopassus, and his wife.

For more than three years, her father, King Powhatan, had forbidden her to have anything to do with the English settlers, and he'd sent her away from Jamestown to the far reaches of his domain. But she liked the English settlers and welcomed this chance to visit with Captain Samuel Argall and other Englishmen onboard the ship, which had sailed up Potomac River from Jamestown.

After the group had dinner, Jopassus and his wife took Pocahontas to the gunners' room of the ship, told her to wait a few minutes, and left her. Instead of returning, they disembarked with the copper kettle they'd been paid for luring her onto the vessel.

Time passed, and Pocahontas realized her companions were not coming back. Then the ship began to move. She was a prisoner.

Argall sailed with his hostage back to Jamestown, where Pocahontas was welcomed by settlers who had known her earlier and who appreciated all she had done to save the colony of Virginia. The colony's governor, Sir Thomas Gates, sent word to Chief Powhatan that he held Pocahontas. She would be reunited with her father when the chieftain returned the Englishmen he'd captured, along with tools and other goods stolen from Jamestown. He must also make permanent peace with the English, cease warring against neighboring tribes, and furnish the settlers with corn if he wanted his daughter back.

Powhatan returned seven captured English settlers and sent the colony one canoe of corn, saying he'd send more after the fall harvest. He continued fighting against other tribes, however, and attacked the outlying areas of the Virginia settlement. He made no further efforts to ransom his daughter.

Pocahontas was sent to live near Henrico, Virginia. Reverend Alexander Whitaker and the women parishioners of his church took charge of her, teaching her the English language and English ways. Pocahontas would eventually bring about peace between the colonists and Indians, but in an unexpected way.

The famous Indian maiden was born at the chief settlement of the Powhatan tribe, Werowocomoco, in 1596 or 1597. She was named Matoaka, which meant "Little Snow Feather." Pocahontas, her nickname, has been translated by the English as "Bright Stream between Two Hills" and by the Powhatans as "Little Wanton."

Pocahontas's father had become chieftain in 1570 and had taken the tribe's name, Powhatan, as his own name. The Powhatans were part of the Algonquian nation. Ruthless and fierce, Powhatans conquered neighboring tribes, slaughtering the men and taking women and children captive. The tribe practiced torture and dismemberment of their enemies. Coming from this savage background, it is amazing that Pocahontas was able to become friends with the English and convert to their ways.

Chief Powhatan, an absolute dictator, had many wives, each of whom usually bore him only one child. Nothing is known of Pocahontas's mother. Powhatan may have given or sold her to another warrior, even to another tribe. She may have died in childbirth. Pocahontas, born when Powhatan was about fifty, was her father's favorite daughter.

Pocahontas was eleven or twelve when the first three shiploads of white settlers arrived at Jamestown, but this was not the first European incursion into Powhatan's territory. In 1560 the Spanish had captured a young Powhatan and taken him to Spain, where they'd educated and baptized him, calling him Don Luis. In 1570 they returned to the Chesapeake Bay area to set up a mission. Once back among the Powhatan, Don Luis reverted to his Native American ways and murdered the members of the expedition. The Spanish retaliated by hanging some innocent tribe members.

In 1585 the governor of Roanoke Island burned several villages in the southern part of Powhatan's domain. In 1604, just three years before Jamestown was established, a group of white men attempted to kidnap several Powhatan youths to sell as slaves in the Caribbean. When Powhatan warriors fought back, the whites shot and killed a number of them.

Thus, Powhatan and his people had good reason to mistrust the newly arrived English.

Pocahontas undoubtedly watched as the white-skinned people began building a fort, a storehouse, and a crude church. The settlers were shorter than Powhatan men, and by the native's standards, strangely dressed. While most Englishmen had beards, long hair, and often mustaches, the Powhatan men were clean-shaven and cut all but a single strip of hair across the top of their heads. They scraped their faces and scalps clean with sharpened shells. The Powhatans wore light moccasins or went barefoot; the English workmen wore heavy boots. The whites were called "coat wearers" because they wore several layers of long-sleeved clothing in all but the hottest weather. By contrast, the natives usually wore only small leather aprons or breechcloths that covered only a scant area of the body. Women and men alike went bare above the waist.

Pocahontas was interested in the tools and gadgets the Europeans brought. The Powhatans hunted with bows and arrows and spears, and clubbed their enemies with tomahawks. The killing portion of all these weapons was made of stones painstakingly chipped to sharpness. The natives shaped canoes by setting fire to logs and burning out the center portion. The English, on the other hand, had knives, axes, and saws to build with. They had brought glassblowers to Jamestown and soon were fashioning serviceable containers. Masons built kilns and burned bricks to build houses, replacing the first wooden ones.

Above all, the English had guns. Powhatan and his warriors had seen the effect of these weapons and wanted to steal some for themselves. Pocahontas looked on all the activity and strangeness with the awe of a child.

Among the colonists was twenty-six-year-old Captain John Smith. Already a veteran of the Turkish wars, he had been captured and made a slave, but he'd managed to escape while awaiting ransom. Despite the mistrust and jealousy of some of the colonists, Smith was one of the eight men chosen by the English king to govern the colony. Although he arrived in Jamestown in chains because of a disagreement onboard the ship, he was soon freed when the charter box was opened and the king's wishes were made known.

Perhaps because of his military experience in foreign lands, Smith recognized the need to communicate with the Native Americans. When he saw the girl watching, he welcomed her, and by means of signs and objects began to learn a few Powhatan words and to teach her some English words. He also gave her some of the gifts the London Company, sponsor of the expedition, had sent along: glass beads and a bell.

Although Powhatan was impressed with the English guns, they were ill-suited for fighting in Virginia. Too long and unwieldy for moving through the woods, they were also heavy and inconvenient to load and fire. While an Englishman was pouring in powder and shot and tamping it down, many arrows could speed toward their target. In addition, the English suits of armor were too hot and uncomfortable to work in, so the colonists rarely wore them, making themselves vulnerable to arrows and tomahawks. Several settlers were killed, and those remaining were afraid to go far outside the fort to hunt or fish.

In late June two of the three ships that had come to Jamestown returned to England, leaving the colonists with scant supplies. Disease and brackish water took their toll. By the end of the summer, half the colonists were dead.

Pocahontas noticed the Englishmen's distress and persuaded some friendly Powhatans to bring the settlers corn (maize). Her half brother Pochins brought corn and fish. Smith later told Queen Anne that Pocahontas saved the colony from death and starvation.

Smith realized the colony needed more food than Pocahontas could provide, knowing that at any time she could be prevented from bringing anything at all. He set out with three companions in early December 1607 to explore the Chicahominy River area and to find other natives who might supply food.

At a point near present-day Providence Forge, Smith went ashore with several native guides, leaving the other three men in the canoe. Within a few minutes he was set upon by Powhatan warriors. Using one of his guides as a shield, he backed away, but tumbled into an icy stream and was captured. Two of his fellow colonists were killed; the third was captured, dismembered, and his body was burned at the stake.

Smith was taken as a captive from one of Powhatan's brothers to the other. Each ruled a portion of the Powhatan empire. He was marched to the Rappahannock chief, who was to determine if Smith had been the one who kidnapped tribe members in 1604. If the chief had so identified him, Smith would have been killed. Finally he was taken before the high chieftain Powhatan himself, bound and helpless, realizing he was about to become the next torture/murder victim. Two great stones were brought forth, and Smith was stretched out with his head lying on one of them. Warriors gathered with clubs to beat him to death.

Suddenly Pocahontas came out of the crowd, put her arms around her friend's head, and laid her head down on his. Powhatan honored a tradition and spared Smith's life. Smith was adopted into the tribe in a ceremony two days later, and then escorted back to Jamestown by twelve Powhatan warriors. Smith had promised Chief Powhatan several cannons at the fort, knowing the heavy weapons could not be lifted. He had also told the chieftain that the settlers were in Jamestown temporarily, taking refuge from the Spaniards.

Because she had saved him, Pocahontas was now, according to tradition, the guardian of Smith; his life was hers to do with as she wished.

Some historians have suggested that Pocahontas might have been disappointed that Smith did not marry her, but she was still a child by English standards. Others have said that Smith invented the story of his rescue. He was, however, the only survivor of the ill-fated exploration, and Pocahontas did spend a great deal of time in Jamestown during the next two years. Had there not been a special bond, Powhatan would undoubtedly have forbidden his daughter's relationship with Smith.

Pocahontas also often came to Jamestown to play with other native children, turning cartwheels, running races, and scampering about the settlement playing hide-and-seek.

Although still a child, Pocahontas was a princess who acted as a go-between for her father and the colonists. She reported to her father when a shipload of a hundred additional colonists arrived in January 1608, which contradicted Smith's claim that the settlers were only in Virginia temporarily. Powhatan sent for Smith and Captain Christopher Newport. When they went to see him, they took along a boy, Thomas Savage, who was to live with the Powhatans and learn their language; in return, a Powhatan warrior, Namontack, was to live at Jamestown.

Captain Newport traded far more liberally than Smith had, offering twenty swords for twenty turkeys. After Newport left, tribe members arrived with another twenty turkeys, but Smith refused to give them more swords. Smith took seven of them captive after they tried to steal the swords. Pocahontas was again the peacemaker, negotiating successfully for the return of the Powhatan warriors.

In the autumn of 1608, Smith was elected president of the council governing Jamestown. Food was plentiful, the church and storehouse were repaired, and things were going well.

When Captain Newport next visited Powhatan, he brought him a scarlet cloak and a European bed and other furniture. He also crowned Powhatan king of the Indians, despite Smith's objections. Smith thought all the generosity and elevation would make Powhatan more difficult to deal with, especially when the ship arrived with more hungry settlers late in the year. More food would be needed, and the growing season was past.

Smith was right. Powhatan now seemed more interested in fighting than trading, and when Smith tried to barter corn from the Nansemond tribe, he found that Powhatan had told them not to trade with the English. The chieftain seemed determined to get rid of the colonists. Before 1608 ended, Powhatan forbade Pocahontas to have anything to do with the English, or risk death. But she was twice more to aid the colony, putting her own life in jeopardy.

The situation at Jamestown grew desperate. The people were starving. Smith set off for Werowocomoco and talked with Powhatan, who was seated on his English bed surrounded by his wives and children, including Pocahontas. The two men argued about trade, weapons, and food. Refusing to disarm, Smith left before they could reach an agreement. Eventually Powhatan sent food to the barges and invited Smith back, but before the captain could leave the barge, Pocahontas arrived to warn him that her father planned to kill him at supper.

Meanwhile, despite Smith's instructions to the settlers to stay close to the fort, a group had gone hunting to Hog Island, their boat had capsized, and they had drowned. Richard Wiffen went to Werowocomoco to tell Smith of the tragedy. Powhatan warriors spotted Wiffen and were closing in to take him captive when Pocahontas grabbed him and hid him, sending the warriors searching in the opposite direction.

Smith strengthened the colony, but in July 1609, Captain Argall returned with news that the council had been abolished, a governor-for-life would soon arrive, and two of Smith's earlier enemies were returning to Virginia. Smith left Jamestown and began building a home farther upstream. He was on a boat carrying bags of gunpowder when it exploded, burning him badly.

Smith left Virginia for England in October 1609, and Pocahontas was told that he had died. Bereft of her best friend in Jamestown, she did not protest when her father sent her away to the northern reaches of his domain to live with his kin, the Patawomeke tribe.

The colony was thus without Smith and Pocahontas, two who had been responsible for the earlier peace and success. In an ambush later that year, Powhatan warriors killed sixty colonists. The remainder had little food, and that period in Virginia's colonial history is known as "The Starving Time." By spring 1610 only sixty remained of the 490 who had been in Jamestown the previous autumn. The survivors abandoned the settlement, boarded ships, and were sailing downriver on their way to England when the new governor, Sir Thomas Dale, arrived with food and determination.

Three years passed. The colony thrived and expanded, but the danger of attack always worried them. They thought if they could kidnap Pocahontas, they might force Powhatan to make peace. Captain Samuel Argall was sent in the *Treasurer* up the Chesapeake Bay to the Patawomekes. He bribed Jopassus and his wife to bring Pocahontas aboard the ship. The scheme worked, and the Indian princess was brought back to Jamestown.

Under the direction of the Reverend Alexander Whitaker and others, Pocahontas was taught Christianity. Although she could not read or write, she spoke English. She memorized portions of

The Book of Common Prayer, expressed her faith, and was baptized in the spring of 1614 with the Christian name of Rebecca.

While at Henrico, eighteen-year-old Pocahontas met a widowed farmer named John Rolfe, ten years her senior. Rolfe and his wife had been shipwrecked in Bermuda on the way to Jamestown in 1610. Both their newborn child and Mrs. Rolfe died before reaching Virginia.

Rolfe was interested in growing tobacco, and Pocahontas showed him how the natives cultivated the crop. He saw the attractive maiden not only at work, but at church as well. Rolfe fell in love with Pocahontas, despite their differences.

In 1614 Rolfe wrote Governor Dale, asking permission to marry Pocahontas. He detailed all the reasons against the marriage: her lack of education, her barbaric background, the long-standing taboo against a mixed marriage, even the Biblical admonition against marrying "strange wives." Still, he wrote, he was besotted with her. He assured the governor that the marriage would not be for carnal reasons only, but for the good of the colony and for the good of his soul.

Dale quickly agreed to the marriage. Perhaps this would be just the thing to heal relations between the two races. He accompanied Rolfe and Pocahontas on a visit to Powhatan, who sent two of his sons to meet them. Pocahontas told her brothers she was grieved that her father had been unwilling to give up his weapons to ransom her and that she liked the English so much that she planned to marry and stay with them.

To Dale's surprise, Powhatan gave permission for the marriage, but he did not attend the ceremony, held in Jamestown on April 5, 1614. He gave his daughter a necklace of freshwater pearls; her uncle gave her away.

The newlyweds lived on a plantation on the James River between Henrico and Jamestown. The land was a gift from Powhatan. They called their plantation Varina for a variety of Spanish tobacco Rolfe grew.

After his daughter's marriage, Powhatan made peace with the English that lasted the remainder of his lifetime.

In 1615 Pocahontas and John Rolfe had a son they named Thomas. In appreciation of all the good Pocahontas had done for the colony, the Virginia Company—a group of investors who financed colonization in Virginia—voted to give her and her son an annual stipend. The only person not pleased with this was King James, who declared that Rolfe had committed treason by marrying the daughter of a pagan king.

The following year the Virginia Company invited the Rolfes to visit England as a way to attract attention—and thus more settlers—to Virginia.

On June 12, 1616, the Rolfes arrived in England, accompanied by a group of Pocahontas's relatives. Her sister's husband, Tomocomo, had been instructed by Powhatan to cut a notch in a stick for every Englishman he saw. The poor man soon gave up, seeing the multitudes in England. John Smith wrote Queen Anne, persuading her to receive Pocahontas in gratitude for all the princess had done for Virginia. Pocahontas was also entertained by the Bishop of London, and twice had her portrait painted. The more familiar portrait shows her wearing an elaborate red and black Elizabethan costume and hat. Her coat is trimmed in gold, and lace surrounds her very fair face and hand. In the second she wears a simple skirt and embroidered blouse, her skin is tawny, and her features are more like those of a Native American. She is sitting with her arm around her son Thomas.

Everywhere the Rolfes went, Pocahontas was welcomed, feted, and praised. When Pocahontas began to suffer respiratory problems, the Rolfes left London for Brentford Inn. Here John Smith came for a very emotional visit. The two had not met for eight years, and Pocahontas had thought her captain dead. She scolded him for not sending her some word. She was now a stranger in his land as he had once been in hers, but the bonds forged years before had made them countrymen and kinsmen.

The Rolfes next visited John's family home, Heacham, so his family could meet Rolfe's wife and son. After a few weeks the Rolfes returned to the tiring London social scene and prepared to sail for Virginia. Pocahontas wanted to stay in England, despite the damp climate that kept her coughing, but Rolfe longed to be back in Virginia.

At Gravesend, while waiting for their departure to Virginia, in March 1617, Pocahontas became gravely ill and died. The cause may have been tuberculosis or smallpox. She was buried on the day of her death in the churchyard of St. George's Parish, far from her native land. She was only twenty or twenty-one years old.

The Jamestown colony might have failed without the aid of Pocahontas. Her marriage to an Englishman brought seven years of peace with the Powhatan tribe. She played a role in the future of Virginia as well, for through her son Thomas she became the ancestor of numerous descendants, including a First Lady of the United States.

Matilda Kinnon
"Tillie" Paul Tamaree
1860–1952

∂6

Tlingit Missionary and Leader

Under cover of darkness a young Tlingit woman crept out of a house in Victoria, British Columbia, and stealthily made her way along the dirt road toward the water. She carried her younger daughter and urged her older one to hurry quietly along with her. At the water's edge, her clansman waited in a small canoe. After handing over her few personal possessions and her precious daughters, the woman climbed into the canoe and started her long journey north.

Traveling only at night, and hiding during the day, the group covered 600 miles along the "Inside Passage" of Alaska, until they arrived safely in the land of the Stikeen-quan near Wrangell.

This escape allowed Matilda Kinnon and her older sister, Margaret, to avoid being sent to Scotland, where their father's family would have cared for them. Their mother, Kut-XooX, was ill with the "coughing sickness" (tuberculosis). Overhearing her husband's plan to send the children overseas, she vowed to find a way to return them to her own relatives, where they would be reared in the proper Tlingit tradition.

So Kut-XooX fled, taking her girls to her sister, Xoon-sel-ut, who was married to Chief Snook, of the Stikeen-quan. But soon after their arrival, Kut-XooX died. A potlatch, or community feast, was held to honor her life, and in a special ceremony, the two little girls were given Tlingit names. Matilda was given the name Kahthli-yudt. She came to be called Kah-tah-ah and was adopted by Chief Snook. Margaret was named Tsoon-klah. She went to live with her mother's brother in the nearby Tee-hit-ton village. After the naming ceremony, the "taint of white blood" was considered "wiped out forever," although as an adult, Kah-tah-ah (later named Tillie) always said that it didn't work.

Soon after her mother's death an important and prophetic event occurred in little Kah-tah-ah's life. She, too, became ill with the "coughing sickness." Snook, fearing she might die, took her to the shaman, Shquindy. Shquindy had long, black hair with one contrasting white lock over his forehead. It was neither combed nor cut, and he was very frightening. Snook laid Kah-tah-ah gently on the mat in front of the shaman and stepped back. After performing his healing rituals, Shquindy announced that Kah-tah-ah would recover, have children, and live to an old age; she would "do special work among her people and would be much loved by them." Then Snook took her home, where she recovered and grew strong.

Kah-tah-ah had a happy childhood as the beloved and privileged daughter of Chief Snook, who brought her up in the old Tlingit ways. When she was about twelve years old, a marriage was arranged for her with a Christian Tsimshian chief who named himself Abraham Lincoln. Snook did not want Kah-tah-ah to be married so young and sent so far away, and Kah-tah-ah certainly did not want to marry this man who was twenty-seven years older than she! But Lincoln sent many gifts to Snook requesting Kah-tah-ah as his bride. Also, Lincoln was Eagle clan and Kah-tah-ah was Raven clan, so the match would be acceptable. Traditionally, Tlingits are divided into two clans, Wolf/Eagle (or Eagle) and Raven. All members of a clan are considered to be brothers and sisters, so to marry inside the clan would be considered incest.

Snook decided to allow Lincoln to take Kah-tah-ah to Tongass, with the understanding that he would not force her into matrimony unless she agreed. The journey took three long weeks by canoe and when she reached her destination, she was even more determined not to marry the chief. A girl in the village told her, "We are Christians here, and we follow the white man's laws. So if you do not want to marry a man, no one can force you to do so."

The word circulated that Kah-tah-ah did not want to marry, and Lincoln called a council. He stated that if Kah-tah-ah announced before them that she did not want to marry him, he would release her from the marriage arrangement. Kah-tah-ah said "no" in front of the council and Lincoln was true to his word.

Kah-tah-ah then went to live with the Methodist missionary, Reverend Thomas Crosby, and his wife in Port Simpson. There she learned for the first time about the white man's God and Jesus. The Crosbys called her Sarah, not knowing she already had an English name, Matilda.

Kah-tah-ah was quick to relearn English, as it had been the language of her infancy. Even though she was busy, communicative, and appeared happy, she was very homesick. She even tried to escape, stealing away in a canoe one dark night, just as her mother had done many years ago. But the Crosbys sent rescuers to find her and bring her back safely.

In 1877 the first woman missionary to Alaska, Amanda McFarland, arrived in Wrangell. Although Snook still disapproved of the "white man's ways," he contacted Reverend Crosby and promised that if he sent Kah-tah-ah back to Wrangell, she would attend school with the "lady missionary."

Realizing how homesick their "Sarah" was, the Crosbys returned her to Wrangell, and she went to live in Mrs. McFarland's Presbyterian Home and School for Girls. She reclaimed her English name of Matilda Kinnon and was called Tillie.

At the school Tillie soon learned to read and write. Mrs. McFarland wrote to Sheldon Jackson, the Presbyterian missionary who later became Alaska's first General Superintendent of

Education, "Our oldest girl in the Home (Tillie Kinnon) has become a Christian, and expresses a great desire to be trained for a teacher. She is already quite a help in teaching the younger children. She is a girl of much promise and decision of character."

Reverend S. Hall Young arrived in Wrangell in 1878 and organized a Presbyterian church there. Tillie became his interpreter. On Saturday afternoons she would meet with him to hear the lesson for the following day's sermon, so she would be prepared to translate it. One afternoon Reverend Young read the story of the great flood to Tillie. She sat very quietly, with no comment. Finally, he asked, "Do you not understand the story, Tillie?"

She answered, "Yes, of course, I do. But if I tell this story to my people, they won't believe me. It rains here for forty days and forty nights all the time, and our land has never been flooded!"

In fact, Tillie found there were several biblical passages that would have been unbelievable to the Tlingit people. According to family lore, it wasn't unusual for the congregation to hear from Tillie a different Bible text from the one being taught by Reverend Young, who couldn't understand what Tillie was saying in her translation.

One day a handsome young Tlingit/French-Canadian named Louis Paul (Peyreau) stopped at Wrangell on his way home from the Cassiar gold fields. Tillie and Louis were attracted to one another immediately, and he ended up staying in Wrangell. Soon he joined Tillie's church, and in January of 1882, the couple married in a Christian ceremony performed by Reverend Young.

Snook was extremely disappointed that Louis did not come to him in the traditional Tlingit manner, bringing gifts in a symbolic show of respect for the bride's family. He further disapproved of the fact that Tillie did not have a proper Tlingit wedding. But, at least, Louis belonged to the Wolf/Eagle clan. Now Tillie Paul's missionary work began in earnest.

Six months after their wedding, the Presbyterian Board of Home Missions sent the Pauls, the first native couple so commissioned, to minister to the Tlingits living at the north end of the Inside Passage. The village of Klukwan was very remote and was accessible only by canoe. By the time winter came Louis had built a snug little log house, as well as a school. While Tillie taught at the school, Louis built the church. Bringing the gospel to Klukwan was a challenge. The people there still believed in shamanism and practiced witchcraft to cure illnesses. Still, as Tillie and Louis were both high-ranking in their respective tribes, they were received with hospitality in the village. Although these Tlingits were among the last to embrace the white man's culture, the Pauls wrote in an article for a national Presbyterian bulletin, "All the Indians say they were sorry a teacher did not come amongst them sooner; that by this time they would know more about God."

By the following summer their first child was due, and Tillie wanted to be near her family. They returned to Wrangell, where their first son, Samuel Kendall, made his appearance in August.

After Samuel's birth, the mission board sent the Pauls to Tongass at the south end of the Inside Passage, near Louis's family home. His grandfather, Yashnoosh, was greatly pleased to see him again and to greet his wife and new baby.

When the Pauls' second son was born with one shock of hair lighter than the rest, Tillie gave him the Tlingit name of Shquindy, after the old shaman, and the English name, William Lewis.

Tillie continued to teach school, to preach to the congregation, and to do all the work of a teacher and pastor. Louis supplemented Tillie's part-time missionary salary with hunting and trapping. Tillie and Louis were proud of the work they were doing and were happy and content.

Around this time, plans were being made to establish a "model" Christian town in which two tribes, the Cape Fox and the Tongass, would live together. An area south of present-day Ketchikan was being considered. In December of 1886, Louis Paul, Samuel Saxman, who was a government schoolteacher, and a native named Edgar, left in a canoe to survey the site and report on its suitability. They were never heard from again.

Tillie was devastated. She was left with two little boys, one of them just a toddler, and another baby was on the way. Without Louis it would be impossible for her to continue the missionary work in Tongass. Snook had died and she had no other close relatives.

Among her people there was an undercurrent of belief that the drowning had not been accidental. The weather had been clear and Louis was both an excellent seaman and swimmer. It was almost more than Tillie could bear. With all this weighing on her young shoulders, Tillie's baby son was born prematurely, but healthy. She named him Louis Francis Paul in honor of his father.

Tillie was at a loss as to how she was going to support herself and her boys. Dr. Sheldon Jackson was aware of Tillie's plight and invited her to join the staff of the Sitka Industrial and Training School, which he had started in 1878 for Tlingit students.

At first this would seem like the perfect answer for Tillie. But the tribes of Sitka and Wrangell had a long-standing feud; distrust of the Sitka people had been ingrained in Tillie since she was a small child. Nevertheless, Tillie took her boys and set out bravely for Sitka, determined to be a peacemaker in the Christian manner. This attitude served her well, and in future church disagreements, Tillie's mediating skills were often utilized.

Tillie Paul remained as a staff member at the school in Sitka for about seventeen years. During that time her accomplishments were legion.

An excellent seamstress since childhood, she was placed in charge of the sewing room. She organized and ran the laundry, even helping the older girls wash everything by hand one winter when the boiler failed to work and the water had to be heated over fires. When the boys' hospital was opened in 1890, she was the nurse. Her work there was so valuable that when the new infirmary was opened in 1926, it was named "Tillie Paul Manor" in her honor. At one point, when there was no one available who could play the church organ, Tillie taught herself to play and was soon accompanying even the most difficult hymns. She translated many of the standard hymns and scriptures into Tlingit. Additionally, she joined forces with her cousin, Frances Willard, and the two of them wrote the Tlingit language into English sounds and created a dictionary.

But even with her emphasis on Tlingit, Tillie knew English would be the language of the future. In Alaska, as in the rest of the United States, it was believed by educators that the white man's culture could only be taught using the white man's English, and native children were actually punished for speaking their own languages.

Bearing all this in mind, Tillie made the difficult decision to send her young boys to the Carlisle Indian School in Pennsylvania. This would mean a long separation, as it was so far away and travel was so difficult that the children would not be able to return for vacations, nor even for the summers.

Having seen the terrible effect of alcohol abuse on her people, Tillie joined with another staff member at the school to start a temperance organization. She was adamant about attending the group's weekly meetings, and walked the mile into town no matter the weather.

These prayer meeting services grew into the New Covenant Legion. The importance of this organization cannot be overemphasized. Begun as a temperance and prayer group, the organization also advocated other Christian works. Members distributed food baskets to the needy, fed and ministered to the sick, and worked to change some of the old customs that ran against the grain of church teachings. But most significantly, in 1912, the Legion's founders expanded the organization to become the Alaska Native Brotherhood (ANB). The ANB to this day has had an enormous effect on Alaska native people, working constantly for equality in land ownership, schooling, voting, and other basic rights. In 1920 Tillie organized an affiliated group, the Alaska Native Sisterhood, or ANS.

Tillie was a strong force in the Presbyterian Church and traveled extensively on its behalf. She twice traveled to New York City to attend the General Assembly and speak up for, among other things, the role of women in the church. In 1902 she was invited to address the General Assembly and—according to an article published in 1988, a copy of which is in the national Presbyterian archives—she was possibly the first woman to do so. She was also appointed a church lay worker and did work in both Kake and Petersburg, on Kupreanof Island, north of Wrangell.

In 1903 the Presbyterian Board of Home Missions sent Tillie to the Wrangell Presbyterian Church to "help heal a breach in the church there." Two years later she married an elder in the church, William Baptiste Tamaree, a Tlingit/French-Canadian, as Louis Paul had been.

It annoyed Tillie that even though she did much missionary work, her reports to the Presbytery had to be signed by a man in order for them to be "legal." Therefore, it was with joy that she was ordained an elder of the Wrangell church in 1931. She was the first woman to be so honored in the Alaska–Northwest Synod, and one of the first in the country after the General Assembly approved women as elders in 1930. She was one of the few workers to be given a fifty-year pin for missionary service.

Tillie could also be considered a civil rights activist. The Alaska legislature had given the right to vote to those who were U.S. citizens, which did not, at the time, include natives. In 1923 she encouraged her friend, Charlie Jones, to go to the polls. They were both indicted by a grand jury, Jones for "voting illegally" and

Tillie for "aiding and abetting illegal voting." Her son, William Paul, successfully defended Jones and the charges against Tillie were dropped. In 1924 all Native Americans were granted U.S. citizenship.

Tillie lived in Wrangell for the rest of her life. She and William had three daughters—but only one, Frances, survived. Tillie's oldest son, Samuel, remained in the eastern United States and she visited him whenever she could. When she was there, she had her feet measured and Samuel sent her new shoes every Christmas. William Lewis Paul returned to Alaska and became the first native lawyer in the territory. He married a white woman, Frances Lackey, who wrote a children's book based on Tillie's Tlingit childhood.

Louis Francis Paul became a newspaper editor in Petersburg, Alaska. He married Mathilda Jones. This caused quite a stir in both of their families, as they were both Raven clan. Two of Tillie's granddaughters, Nana Paul Estus and Marian Paul deWitt, tell this story from their parents' reminiscences:

> It was a rainy October night when Louis brought his new bride home to Tillie and William Tamaree. Tillie refused to let them in the house because they had broken an Indian law, which had had very serious consequences. In the old ways they would have been shunned and ostracized, even killed.
>
> Grandpa Tamaree, in one of the few times that he spoke forcefully to Tillie, chastised her, "You teach about Christian life and want our children to get an education and practice the white man's ways. That is just what Louis and Mathilda are doing!"

Matilda Kinnon Paul Tamaree died at her home in Wrangell on August 20, 1952. According to obituaries in the *Wrangell Sentinel* and the *Sheldon Jackson College* newsletter, *The Verstovian*, she was ninety years old. According to her granddaughter, Frances

Paul DeGermain, the family places her birth date as 1860, which would have made her ninety-two when she died.

Throughout her life Tillie Paul Tamaree maintained love and respect for both her old Tlingit culture and her new Christian life. She spoke out for the rights of women and Alaska natives. She was farsighted in her understanding that the "old ways" must adapt and incorporate the "new ways" if her people were to reach their full potential in society. She created a bridge between the old and new ways, that they might work together rather than have one supersede the other. As the shaman, Shquindy, had predicted those many years ago, she "did special work among her people and was much loved by them."

Reverend S. Hall Young wrote of her, "Tillie Paul Tamaree remains the most influential native woman in Alaska, the spiritual mother of her people, the example bright and shining of what Christianity can accomplish in a most difficult mission field."

Anfesia Shapsnikoff
1900–1973

✣

Attu Weaver and Aleut Culture Keeper

On June 3, 1942, Japanese planes attacked the U.S. military base at
Dutch Harbor on Amaknak Island, on the north side of Unalaska.
For two days bombs fell, and when it was over, thirty-five men had
been killed. In the village near the base, there were no casualties
among the local residents, who had taken refuge in air-raid shelters
as instructed. This attack came almost exactly six months after
the Japanese bombed Pearl Harbor.

On the sixth of June, Japanese forces invaded Attu, the most
western island of the Aleutian Chain, a mere 750 miles from
Japan. They captured forty-five Aleut natives and the government
schoolteacher, whose husband had died in the invasion. The
prisoners were taken to an internment camp in Japan.

Shortly thereafter, the U.S. Navy evacuated the residents of
Atka and burned their village to save it from Japanese occupation.
Next, the Pribilof Islanders were evacuated, as were the residents
of five smaller villages. The people of Unalaska knew that their
turn would come and prepared as best they could.

Several men from the community packed belongings from
the Church of the Holy Ascension. Father Dionecious removed
items from the altar while Anfesia Shapsnikoff's son, Vincent
Tutiakoff, kept a careful inventory of everything being crated.
Because Anfesia was a reader for the church, she was responsible
for packing the books and packed sixteen boxes.

The SS *Alaska* took the people from their homes. Each person
could carry only one suitcase of belongings. Family heirlooms,

photographs, and other items of irreplaceable value were hidden in their homes before the doors and windows were shut and locked. Reluctantly, Anfesia left behind the precious violin of her first husband, Michael Tutiakoff.

The ship deposited them in Wrangell, in southeast Alaska. From there they were moved to Burnett Inlet, a wilderness area between Wrangell and Ketchikan, where they found themselves surrounded by a forested world completely foreign from the wide-open landscapes of their homeland. There, they struggled to maintain their very existence in deplorable conditions. Many of the elderly died in that place, far from home. Although the Japanese troops were defeated the following year and there were no more hostilities in the Aleutians, it was three long years before the residents of Unalaska were returned to their island on April 22, 1945. Their homecoming was not a joyous one; they found their homes uninhabitable and ransacked, their valuables pilfered, and their church damaged.

"When we came [back] to Unalaska," Anfesia recalled, "we were happy and we were sad at the same time. Some of the homes were already deteriorating, windows broken, doors kicked in, personal belongings were gone. It made you feel like crying whenever someone got to go inside of their homes." The Aleut community had suffered severe blows, both physically and psychologically, from which it was unlikely they would completely recover.

Anfesia was born in Atka in 1900. When she was six years old, the family moved to Unalaska, then called Iliuliuk. Anfesia and her two brothers attended the Russian school there, where she learned to read Russian, as well as her own Aleut language. She also took classes at the government school, where she was taught English, along with such skills as cooking and sewing.

Anfesia was not a perfect student and told stories about having to kneel in front of an icon because she had not done her lessons. In later years she recalled that she had not been at all interested in learning to weave at school, as her mother, who was an expert Attu basket maker, wanted her to do. But her aunt was her teacher and would not let her say no, so she learned!

Anfesia's father died while she was a young teenager. When she was seventeen years old, Michael Tutiakoff, Anfesia's teacher in the Aleut language class, escorted her to choir practice in the winter, because her mother would not let her go out alone after dark. It was the next year, 1918, when Michael spoke to his father, telling him he would like to get married. He gave his father Anfesia's name, which his father gave to the Chief, Alexei Yatchmenoff, so that the marriage could be arranged. This was the native way, and the bride and groom usually did not know each other before the wedding.

As Anfesia slyly described it:

And so, when mother got word, she went and told my godmother and I had one step ahead of them, because I had already talked this over with Mike Tutiakoff before this all happened. He got my okay before he went and asked his father to marry me. The Chief and the rest of the people didn't know about that. So, I went one step ahead of them. Anyways, it was a good marriage.

Soon after wedding plans had begun, Anfesia's mother, her aunt, and Michael's father were among forty-four residents who died during the devastating flu epidemic that swept through Unalaska between May 26 and June 13 of 1919. Therefore, the Chief finished the arrangements for the marriage and the wedding took place soon thereafter.

Anfesia and Mike raised one daughter, Martha; three sons, Vincent, Tracy, and Philemon; and an adopted son, Timothy. Another daughter, Mayme, died in infancy.

The first year of their marriage, Mike worked at a whaling station on Akutan, then cooked for sulfur miners on Akun. After that they returned to Unalaska, where he worked for the church and received a small salary. The family lived a subsistence lifestyle, in the native way. Anfesia referred to it as "going out and hustling for food." Ducks and seals were plentiful, and from a boat they could drop a line anywhere, anytime, and catch fish from the numerous codfish grounds in Unalaska Bay. They gathered sea urchins and clams along the beach. In the summer and fall, berries were plentiful in the hills, and gardens produced vegetables. The family worked hard. Anfesia said, "If we didn't put up our winter supply, why, then the children went hungry."

Mike was becoming more of a leader, both in the Aleut community and the Russian Orthodox Church. He had been the church secretary for many years and had helped the priest and teachers at the Russian school.

In 1932, he became a deacon and he might have gone on to become a priest. But in January of 1933, he traveled with the bishop aboard the ship, the *Umnak Native*. The vessel broke apart during a violent storm, and Michael Tutiakoff drowned.

The next few years were difficult for Anfesia and the children. The Unalaska Sisterhood and Brotherhood helped them with food; friends also shared provisions. Anfesia fished from the beach and sometimes caught enough salmon to exchange with Pribilof Islanders for seal meat. And, of course, she picked berries for jams and pies, and grew potatoes. Help came when Chief Alexei Yatchmenoff once more arranged a marriage for her. In February of 1937, Anfesia married Sergie Shapsnikoff, a widower.

Sergie not only provided for Anfesia and her children, but he and she adopted two more children, Kathryn and Gregory. The children called him "Friend."

About that time, the bishop of Alaska, Bishop Alexei, visited the Aleutians. When he came to Unalaska, he blessed Anfesia as a reader in the Church of the Holy Ascension, a position that elevated her standing in the community. As a reader, she was called on to communicate with the many outsiders and officials who began to swarm the island as construction began on Dutch Harbor, the military facility on Amaknak Island. She had also become an expert weaver of baskets in the Attu tradition, as her mother had been before her.

Then came the war and evacuation.

After their return home from southeast Alaska, Anfesia's community came together and began reassembling the pieces of their disheveled lives. Anfesia's second husband had drowned while fishing to provide food for the family, only one of the numerous casualties of the evacuation.

Although her son, Vincent Tutiakoff, was officially the Chairman and Recording Secretary of the Church Committee, it fell to Anfesia to write letters for the committee. With her command of English, she wrote about missing church papers and other items, and about church property and repairs. Father Dionecious had not come back to Unalaska, so she was called on to conduct church services and to assist visiting priests.

In 1947, Vincent drowned at the age of twenty-five. He was an officer in the Orthodox Brotherhood and had been in line to become a church leader. Anfesia became quite ill with tuberculosis of the spine, but recovered, despite dire predictions from her doctors.

The last two decades brought the burgeoning king crab industry and another influx of people and commercial building to Unalaska. Although the companies did hire local help and brought money into the community, the aftereffects continued to destroy the Aleut native way of life. When Anfesia was a little girl growing up in Unalaska, she could drink clean water right from the creek, pick berries from the hills, and gather clams, mussels, and sea urchins on the beach. Because of pollution from the canneries and the ruins from the war, these simple pastimes were no longer easily accomplished.

Anfesia also recognized that the young people weren't interested in pursuing the subsistence lifestyle, even if it were still possible.

Many of them had turned their eyes Outside. They wanted jobs and the things that money could buy. She intensified her efforts to pass on the Aleut language and her skill of basket weaving to the next generation. By working with visiting linguists and anthropologists, she hoped to assure an accurate preservation of her people's language and traditions.

Anfesia's grandson, Vincent—known to his family as Buddy—eventually moved in with her. In 1956 she again became ill, and had to go to the hospital in Anchorage. Buddy stayed at the Baptist Mission in Kodiak until she was able to return three months later.

Anfesia had been communicating with the historical society in Kodiak, and after she recovered from her illness, she traveled there and gave the first of many basket-weaving classes. Her first class in 1957 consisted of nine students, and she returned to give classes there off and on for several years.

One summer she was giving a class in Kodiak during the historical society's outdoor theatre production of the *Cry of the Wild Ram*. The historical drama celebrated Alaska's Russian heritage, particularly the Russian colony on Kodiak. Anfesia was recruited to perform in the play.

"I'm the Aleut they found," she said, laughing.

She was supposed to squat down and weave a basket. Of course, to be authentic to the time, she couldn't wear her glasses, so decided to weave a fish basket because the weave was larger. As she still couldn't see well enough to weave, her class members would work on it some each day until they finished it for her.

"It was in display in Anchorage and it looked real nice and it was bought afterwards," she reported when telling the story.

In 1959, Alaska Governor William A. Egan put Anfesia in charge of the Alaska Booth at the Oregon Centennial in Portland. She took her "demonstration" basket, which she used in her classes, and was delighted when Senator John F. Kennedy held it in his hands and spoke with her. During the next few years, she traveled and gave talks and demonstrations in California and Arizona.

In the summer of 1967, Anfesia was invited to speak to the Resurrection Bay Historical Society in Seward as part of their Alaska Centennial Celebration. She told the group it was the first time she had given her presentation in Alaska. From Seward she traveled to Anchorage and Juneau, speaking, giving basket-weaving demonstrations, and, in Anchorage, even appearing on television.

From Anchorage she wrote to Margaret Hafemeister in Seward, "Busy, busy. I didn't know it would turn out this way, but I am wanted here and there. . . . Seems as if everyone knows me here, even the priest."

As part of the statewide Alaska Centennial Celebration in 1967, Anfesia was given the Governor's Award for perpetuating native arts and crafts through her basketry.

But even as the state was praising her, it was creating another tragedy in her community. That summer a social worker came to Unalaska bearing a list of about twenty children who were to be removed from their homes and raised in more "civilized" conditions. This was an affront to the Aleuts, and Anfesia took it personally.

She protested the policy and wrote to her friend, Ray Hudson, "I have written Juneau and told them what is happening. . . . I let them know Unalaska could keep neglected children too like elsewhere so they could know of their native ways, so Aleuts could be restored. . . ."

The welfare of Aleut children had always been one of Anfesia's primary concerns. She served several terms on the Unalaska City Council and was on the city's first Board of Health. In that capacity she contributed to the organization of the Iliuliuk Family and Health Services, incorporated in 1971 and still the primary health agency for the community.

Anfesia deeply lamented the declining interest of her people in speaking Aleut and maintaining their traditions. Hoping to preserve as much as possible, Anfesia went to the University of Alaska in Fairbanks, where she taught Aleut dancing as well as basket weaving, and recorded songs and stories. In fact, one of her last trips was to Fairbanks to work with the Alaska Native Languages Program, developing the Atka and Unalaska dialects.

Back in Unalaska, she gave basket-weaving classes from her home. She spoke to students about her childhood and native customs, and she sang to them and told them traditional stories. A booklet encompassing her childhood Christmas memories was distributed to Unalaska school children at Russian Christmas in January of 1972.

For several weeks, beginning in November of 1969, she inserted in *The Unalaskan* newspaper an item in Aleut. Underneath the first one it said in English, "If you don't understand this, learn it! And ask what it means." For the second and successive weeks, she included the translation for the previous week.

The item for the week of November 17 read:

Iig^akun tutalix aqaning waya malgakun ang^achin aqatalgaqangin–Ulux^waya galix tanax ama angachisin sulakyn. Malix miimiin tununalgilix. Tunuxtan.

Anfesia wrote Aleut in The Cyrillic script developed in the 1820s. This rendition is written in Roman letters. Each little cap goes above the letter preceding it. Here is the translation for the item:

Things I heard of long ago are happening. Unknown people are coming, taking over our land and the things we made our living with. So let's get together and prevent these, by speaking up.

Those long-ago predictions were certainly beginning to come true in 1970. The U.S. government planned to sell the land that it had claimed to build military facilities on Amaknak Island and surrounding the village. Anfesia blamed the military for much of the pollution of traditional fishing grounds. She would not stand by and let them take away the land, too. She had served on the Board of Equalization, and feared that the Aleuts would be forced to pay taxes on the land where they lived.

In January of 1971, the government sale was stopped by a civil lawsuit on behalf of Anfesia Shapsnikoff, Nick Peterson, and Henry Swanson, the eldest residents of Unalaska. In December President Richard Nixon signed the Alaska Native Claims Act. The land for sale on Amaknak and Unalaska Islands now belonged to the Aleut people.

In December of 1972, although ill and growing weaker, Anfesia supervised the cleaning of the interior of the Cathedral of the Holy Ascension in preparation for Christmas services. She had done this many times before as a member and officer of the Sisterhood. She recognized the importance of this church, both as a place of worship and as a building of great historic significance. The cathedral is on the National Register of Historic Places and is a National Historic Landmark.

The following January, Anfesia baptized her great-grandson, Vincent Michael Jr., although she was too weak to lift the baby the customary three times and had to perform the baptism in her home. She continued to weaken and died on the airplane taking her to the Native Hospital in Anchorage on January 15. She is buried in the church graveyard beside Alexei Yatchmenoff.

Anfesia's influence in the Aleut community endures after her death. Children she instructed in the teachings of her church have become important members of the congregation. Her passion for Aleut culture has infused various Aleut organizations, and her willingness to serve on civic boards has inspired others to follow her example. The basket-weaving classes continued to flourish in Kodiak, and in 2005 Hazel Jones, who was one of Anfesia's students in the early 1970s, taught the class. Anfesia received many awards and honors, including honorary lifetime memberships in the Resurrection Bay Historical Society and Kodiak Historical Society, and a special certificate from Bishop Theodosius for her long and outstanding service to the Orthodox faith.

Three weeks after her death, "Senate Concurrent Resolution No. 24 in the Legislature of the State of Alaska, Eighth Legislature—First Session: Honoring Anfesia Shapsnikoff" was read into the record on February 6, 1973. It concluded:

BE IT RESOLVED by the Alaska Legislature that it expresses its most profound sense of loss as a result of the death of this truly remarkable "Little Grandma" but affirms its belief that, because of her devotion to her people, her culture, her community, and her state, generations of Alaskans for years to come will be indebted to Anfesia Shapsnikoff and she will always be revered as a truly great Alaskan.

Lozen
183?–1889

"A Shield to Her People"

A few stars still glimmered and blinked as salmon-colored brushstrokes streaked across the eastern sky. The fall rains had brought a good spring to southern Arizona. The desert willows were bright with flowers, and the yucca blooms stood tall, like white waxed beacons among the mesquites. A coyote yipped and another answered.

The horses were clustered near camp. One stood apart, watching, listening, an equine sentinel, while the others dozed.

Only one human stirred. A slight young woman unwrapped herself from her blanket and walked silently to higher ground. She extended her arms, threw her head back, and sang, while turning slowly in a circle:

> *Upon this earth*
> *On which we live,*
> *Ussen has Power.*
> *This Power He grants me*
> *For locating the Enemy.*
> *I search for that Enemy*
> *Which only Ussen, Creator of Life,*
> *Can reveal to me.*

This morning, her palms were cool and remained the color of normal flesh. She was relieved. All too often lately, her hands had been hot, even purple—and always when she faced the approaching foe.

She didn't understand this ability of her body to locate the enemy, but it wasn't her role to understand or question. Her role was to protect her people.

The sun edged over the distant lavender mountains. Men and women stirred in the camp below. Lozen walked back down the hill to let them know they were safe.

For now.

Lozen, an Apache warrior, scout, and medicine woman, presents almost as much of a challenge to contemporary historians as she did to nineteenth-century soldiers. Not only did the Apaches leave no written record of her, but also the white men of the time were unable to imagine that any woman could have held as powerful and vital a role as she did—so they never mentioned her.

Some sources say the Apaches deliberately underplayed Lozen's importance as a way of protecting her. Most of the records that do exist are oral—historians' interviews of adult Apaches recalling their childhoods spent with the famous chiefs Geronimo, Cochise, Victorio, and others. Again and again, these eyewitnesses mention Lozen. One, James Kaywaykla, told an interviewer that the last free Apaches would have been captured years earlier than they were if not for Lozen's ability to locate the enemy. He remembers Chief Victorio saying, "Lozen is as my right hand. Strong as a man, braver than most, and cunning in strategy, Lozen is a shield to her people."

One historian has even said she can claim the title of "America's greatest guerilla fighter."

Lozen's story roams over more than just the Arizona Territory. The Apache tribe is usually divided into six groups: Western, Chiricahua (pronounced *cheer-ee-kah-wah*), Mescalero, Jicarilla, Lipan, and Kiowa.

The Western Apaches occupied eastern Arizona and western New Mexico and included the Warm Springs (also known as the Chihenne) and White Mountain bands. The Chiricahua lived in southwestern New Mexico, southeastern Arizona, and the adjacent Mexican states of Chihuahua and Sonora. The Mescalero still reside east of the Rio Grande in southern New Mexico.

The Apaches lived in the Southwest long before state and national boundaries. Topographical landmarks mattered far more to them than the arbitrary political lines drawn in the desert by white men. All the Indeh (the People) were nomadic, and they easily covered thousands of miles on horseback, often spending summers in the Arizona mountains and winters in central Mexico. The Chiricahua and Chihenne bands were closely related; they often intermarried and frequently traveled through each other's territories without acrimony.

Lozen was born into the Warm Springs band sometime in the early 1830s, probably in southern New Mexico. The band considered Ojo Caliente, between what are now Silver City and Socorro, to be its spiritual home—a place where they felt closest to Ussen, the Creator of Life. It's a beautiful area of high desert with islands of mountain ranges and a surprising number of volcanic hot springs.

Not much is known of Lozen's family except that she was the younger sister of Chief Victorio, who was born in 1825.

Although the women did most of the food gathering and cooking, Apache girls had the same training as boys: They learned to hunt, ride, and fight because the band might need every individual for defense. There was nothing squeamish about these women: If a family member was killed, the perpetrator was caught, brought back to camp, and turned loose among the angry women, who beat, stabbed, or stoned the assailant to death.

Lozen was small in stature but physically gifted; she soon proved to be a faster runner than most of the boys and a better marksman and equestrian as well. She was far more interested in warrior skills than cooking and quickly earned her name, which meant "Dexterous Horse Thief" in Apache.

A formative event in the childhoods of both Victorio and Lozen took place in the spring of 1837 and marked the beginning of animosity between the Apaches and white settlers. The Warm Springs band was lured to a fiesta by the residents of Santa Rita, located in the northern Mexico state of Sonora. The settlers, led by a Kentucky bounty hunter, John James Johnson, turned the "party" into a massacre, and among those killed was the leader of the band. As a result, Mangas Coloradas (Red Sleeves) became the new Warm Springs chief.

He soon realized Lozen had a talent even more valuable than stealing horses. Because the ceremony she performed allowed her to detect enemies, he invited her to participate in raids. On these raids Lozen's responsibilities were to protect the men and fight with them.

She never married. Legend has it that the chief of an unidentified Eastern band passed through, stopping off to visit the Warm Springs camp. According to James Kaywaykla's grandmother, "Lozen was too young for marriage, but she had seen this chief and no other man ever interested her. She put marriage from her mind and rode beside her brother as a warrior. She lives solely to aid him and her people. And she is sacred . . . ; she is respected above all living women."

By 1861 relations between the whites and the Apaches were deteriorating fast, but Mangas Coloradas still believed that surely the land could support both cultures. He arranged a meeting with the mining community in Pinos Altos, New Mexico, and planned to guide the miners to other gold-mining sites in exchange for their allowing his band to live on ancestral lands. But he quickly lost interest in the peace process when the miners captured him and tied him up and whipped him before his sons could come to his rescue. That same year, the peaceful Chiricahua chief Cochise, son-in-law of Mangas Coloradas, was falsely accused of kidnapping a white child. Soldiers reacted by killing Cochise's brother.

To the Chiricahua and the Chihenne, war was the only honorable response. Victorio, accompanied by another Warm Springs leader, Nana, along with Lozen, led many successful raids against white settlers. By now Lozen had proven herself on three apprenticeship raids and often advised Victorio about the most effective strategies. She was the only woman ever allowed in councils, though she was apparently shy and said little in public.

At first it seemed as if their raids had been effective. The soldiers marched away, and Lozen's ceremony was no longer needed. Little did the Apaches know that the soldiers were embroiled in a bigger battle and had been summoned east to fight in the Civil War.

The next summer white soldiers reappeared in even greater numbers, and this time they brought cannons. Lozen and her people realized what they were up against when they were forced to retreat at the Battle of Apache Pass, carrying a wounded Mangas Coloradas.

Although no written record exists, it's likely Lozen treated her chief's wound. Kaywaykla remembers Victorio extolling Lozen's ability as a healer, saying that she was "skillful in treating wounds; when I got a bullet in my shoulder, she burned the thorns from a leaf of nopal [prickly pear], split it and bound the fleshy side to the wound. The next day I rode."

Six months later Mangas Coloradas realized the People could not endure much longer and resolved to meet with the white men to talk peace. Too trusting once again, he went alone to the soldiers' camp under a flag of truce. The soldiers captured him, held red-hot bayonets to his feet, shot him, cut off his head, boiled it, and sent it to Washington, D.C.

Lozen, Victorio, Nana, and the rest of the band were devastated. They hid in their home mountains, only emerging for the occasional raid or supply trip. Because the soldiers were less inclined to shoot women, often Lozen was the one sent to Pinos Altos or Mesilla (now Las Cruces) to gather news.

The Apaches spent the next couple of years attending abortive peace conferences and waiting to see where the government would allow them to live. In 1870 the Chihenne reluctantly moved to Tularosa, an area they found too high, too cold, and too rocky for crops. In 1874 they were inexplicably allowed back to their ancestral land near Ojo Caliente, and all seemed calm for a year. But soon their allocations of stringy beef and moldy flour ran out, and the children were hungry.

In 1876 the Chiricahua were moved from their designated area in southeastern Arizona to the San Carlos Reservation farther north. When Geronimo was captured, he and his band were taken to San Carlos in chains, and the following year the Chihenne were marched there. Consolidating the reservations saved the U.S. government $25,000 for each closed reservation—but a price was paid in human lives. The camp was near Camp Goodwin in the marshes of the Gila River, and disease, which had already driven away the soldiers, killed many Apaches as well.

By September 1877 Lozen and Victorio could stand the camp no longer and broke out, leading 300 warriors, women, and children back to Ojo Caliente, where they lived quietly.

Once again, it seemed as if Lozen's skills as enemy locator and warrior wouldn't be needed.

But two years later the government again made them move, this time to the Mescalero Reservation. In June rumors flew that Victorio was to be arrested, and he and Lozen chose freedom over confinement.

For the next year they remained on the move all over New Mexico, western Texas, southeastern Arizona, and into Mexico. Geronimo, having escaped from San Carlos, joined them. When ammunition ran low, Lozen and Victorio decided that she should return to the Mescalero Reservation and come back with more warriors and supplies. Lozen, who always felt the women and children were her responsibility, also agreed to take a Mescalero woman and her infant back. Traveling was slow, and the two women arrived after many weeks, only to be faced with the worst possible news: Victorio had been killed in an ambush in Mexico.

Lozen was desolate—and angry. She rejoined the band, now led by Nana, in a retaliatory raid throughout the Southwest. Its sole goal was to kill as many settlers as possible. They covered 3,000 miles in two months, killed hundreds, won seven battles, stole 200 head of stock, and thanks to Lozen's skill in locating the enemy, never lost a warrior.

By 1881 many in the band were homesick for their families, and the group quietly slipped back to San Carlos. Once again, it seemed as if they'd be allowed to live in peace. But fighting broke out, this time at Cibecue. Although the Chihenne weren't blamed, Lozen and Nana feared repercussions and broke out from the reservation again, hoping to join Geronimo in his Mexican hideaway in the Sierra Madre.

Many other Apaches had the same idea, and 600 gathered in the mountain refuge: Chiricahua, Chihenne, Mescalero, and others. They all hid in Mexico uneventfully for a year, but the war leaders grew restless, and the need for ammunition for their American-made rifles and the desire to reunite their families grew strong. Geronimo, Nana, and Lozen decided to lead a group into Arizona and free their people from the San Carlos Reservation. The raid was successful, until U.S. soldiers followed them across the border into Mexico and killed a third of those rescued.

By May 1883 morale among the survivors was low, and most decided to surrender, including Geronimo, who told the white men he needed a month to round up the families.

By February 1884 the band was settled back at San Carlos, but the agent in charge was unable to maintain peace on the reservation among the different bands. In July 1885 Geronimo heard a rumor he was to be hanged, so he bolted—accompanied by Lozen, thirty-five warriors, and one hundred women and children.

Ironically, they stopped to rest in the Chiricahua Mountains at the now-abandoned Fort Bowie, site of the Battle of Apache Pass, where Mangas Coloradas had been wounded.

Again they headed for Mexico, where they hid in mountains accessible by only one narrow but easily defended trail.

By now the Americans had hired Apache scouts who knew the ways, trails, and hideaways of Lozen's group. Fights erupted and casualties began to mount. The band became more discouraged. The group had met with Gen. George Crook, known as Grey Fox, before and trusted him to make fair decisions. They sent Lozen and another woman, Dahteste, to talk to the commander to see if a surrender was still possible. Crook agreed to meet with the leaders in March 1886, in the Canyon de Los Embudos, 86 miles south of Fort Bowie.

Writer Peter Aleshire described Lozen's role in the historic meeting:

> Lozen remained in the back of the group, not talking but keeping her rifle ready. The White Eyes had never paid much attention to her and she did not want them to pay attention to her now. The leaders hid her importance when talking to the White Eyes, partly to protect her and partly so she could continue to be their messenger and go into the soldiers' camps, counting their guns. So Lozen did not speak and Grey Fox did not bother with her because the White Eyes did not think women important.

General Crook said the Apaches would have to be imprisoned for two years before being returned to their reservations. After many hours of talking, all the leaders, including Geronimo, decided to surrender.

During the night Geronimo changed his mind. With him went the last of the free Chihenne: Lozen, nineteen warriors, fourteen women, and six children.

They rode hard, rarely slept, relied heavily on Lozen's ceremony, and raided from Mexico north to Tucson and back. They stole horses, rode them into the ground, cut meals from the carcasses, and stole more. Geronimo himself told an interviewer: "We were reckless of our lives, because we felt every man's hand was against us. If we returned to the reservation we would be put in prison and killed; if we stayed in Mexico they would continue to send soldiers to fight us; so we gave no quarter to anyone and asked no favors."

But the soldiers kept coming. President Grover Cleveland, wanting Geronimo dead, was furious with what he saw as Crook's lenient surrender terms for the Chiricahua Apaches. The general, realizing he couldn't keep his promise to the Apaches, resigned. He was replaced by Gen. Nelson Miles, who sent 5,000 men—about a quarter of the U.S. Army—in search of the renegades.

Miles was clever, if unethical. In July 1886 he sent Lt. Charles Gatewood into Mexico with two of Geronimo's former colleagues to convince him to surrender. According to Gatewood's own account, he told Geronimo, "Surrender, and you will be sent to join the rest of your People in Florida, there to await the decision of the President as your final disposition. Accept these terms, or fight it out to the bitter end."

The talk went on for hours—until Gatewood broke the news that the Apaches' friends and families were already imprisoned in Florida. With that information the will to fight went out of the warriors, and all agreed to talk to General Miles.

It was a long, sad ride from Mexico's Sierra Madre to southern Arizona's Skeleton Canyon. On September 8, 1886, the last of the renegade Apaches, including the warrior Lozen, met with General Miles. He and Geronimo placed a stone on the blanket that lay between them and swore to do one another no harm.

Geronimo said, "Our treaty is made by this stone, and it will last until the stone should crumble to dust."

With those words the free Apaches were free no more. And with those words, Lozen disappeared from the record. One photograph of her has survived. It shows her with Geronimo and the other warriors when the train carrying the prisoners eastward paused in Texas.

Yet her name never appeared on the train's roster.

The train took the last Apaches to Fort Marion, Florida. There they joined all the other bands who'd been rounded up from the reservations, even though they'd been living peacefully.

James Kaywaykla told his biographer, Eve Ball: "Ours were a mountain people, and moreover, a dry land people. We were accustomed to dry heat, but in Florida the dampness and the mosquitoes took toll of us until it seemed that none would be left. Perhaps we were taken to Florida for that purpose; from our point of view, shooting would have been much less cruel."

After less than a year, the Apaches were shipped from Fort Marion to Mt. Vernon Barracks, north of Mobile, Alabama. Eugene Chihuahua, son of the Chiricahua Chief Chihuahua recalled: "We thought anything would be better than Fort Marion with its rain, mosquitoes, and malaria, but we were to find out that it was good in comparison with Mt. Vernon Barracks. We didn't know what misery was till they dumped us in those swamps. There was no place to climb or pray. If we wanted to see the sky, we had to climb a tall pine."

Half the prisoners were wiped out by hunger, disease, and heartbreak.

The woman whose power helped determine the course the Apaches took never again saw her beloved mountains, wide desert expanses, and vivid Southwestern skies.

Lozen caught the "coughing sickness," as tuberculosis was called, and died June 17, 1889, in Mt. Vernon, Alabama.

She lies buried in an unmarked grave.

Polingaysi Qöyawayma
1892–1990

❧

"Butterfly Sitting among the Flowers in the Breeze"

A bitter wind whipped through the brown, frost-burned Kansas cornstalks that morning in 1910. The air was brisk and cold enough that the two people entering the restaurant were glad of the establishment's warmth.

The woman, wrapped in a shawl and long cotton dress, was tiny, less than five feet tall and barely ninety pounds. Her dark eyes focused shyly on the floor, and her black hair was long, except for the bangs cut straight across her forehead. The man was tall, slender, dignified, and dressed in a dark suit. A Bible peeked out of his jacket pocket.

They stood near the doorway, an incongruous pair, before finding an empty table, and talked quietly about looking forward to something hot to drink.

The waitress, a surly, stout woman in a too-tight dress, walked past them, then paused to stare at the woman. She growled, "We don't serve colored."

The seated woman looked perplexed.

The man's mouth tightened, but his voice remained soft and polite. "My name is Reverend Jacob Frey. This is Elizabeth Ruth Qöyawayma, an American Indian visiting from Arizona. If you won't serve us, I'd like to speak to the manager."

The manager appeared, and the two men argued until the young woman suddenly rose from her seat, tears sliding down her face.

"Please, please, can we leave?" she begged the missionary. "I don't want to eat here. I couldn't swallow the food."

This incident was all too symbolic of Polingaysi Qöyawayma's life. No matter where she traveled, she seemed to fall between cultures. Many years later she would write: "What can one do about one's skin? We, who are clay blended by the Master Potter, come from the kiln of Creation in many hues. How can people say one skin is colored, when each has its own coloration? What should it matter that one bowl is dark and the other pale, if each is of good design and serves its purpose well?"

Eventually, she was able to accept and relish the traditions of her original culture and use them to help her people bridge the gap between their ways and those of the white man.

Polingaysi Qöyawayma was born in the Oraibi Pueblo on the Hopi Reservation in northeastern Arizona. Her name (pronounced *Poe-LING*-[slight pause]-*nigh-she*, *Ko-YAH*-[slight pause]-*why-mah*) translates to "Butterfly Sitting among the Flowers in the Breeze." The Hopis didn't keep track of dates, but she's said to have been born in the spring of 1892.

Spirituality is a vital part of Hopi life. As Polingaysi would later tell her biographer, their "religion was not a Sunday affair; it was a daily, hourly, constant communion with the Source, the Creator from whom came all things that were, large or small, animate or inanimate, the power behind Cloud People, Rain People, the Katsina, and all the other forces recognized and respected by the Hopi people."

Despite this deep faith, white missionaries considered all Native Americans to be sinful and in need of salvation. In the late 1880s, they began moving onto the reservations, determined to convert the "heathens."

Polingaysi's father, a member of the Badger Clan, worked for H. R. Voth, a Mennonite missionary who moved to Oraibi in 1893. "Qöyawayma" was too much of a tongue-tangler for English speakers, so the missionary simply called him Fred.

Reverend Voth was a kind man who recognized Fred's quick intelligence. He taught Fred carpentry and how to deliver babies and pull teeth. Fred also accompanied the minister on several trips to Kansas, an experience that would provide him with some perspective on why his daughter might someday want to follow the white man's way.

Polingaysi's mother, Sevenka, was a hard-working woman who had a beautiful singing voice. She was also deeply devout and, according to later accounts, lived by this philosophy: "We do not walk alone, Great Being walks beside us, Always know this, And be Grateful." She passed her musical ability on to her daughter, along with her connection to the Coyote Clan, descendants of the ancient Anasazi Pueblo of Sikyatki. Sevenka saw no reason to leave either the village or her adopted Hopi ways, and her conservative opinions would prove to be a source of friction between her and her daughter.

Records and artifacts show that the Hopi people and their predecessors have occupied the area since A.D. 500, longer than any other Native American tribe in the United States. Their homeland, or tutsqua, originally covered eighteen million acres, but now the Hopis have only 9 percent of their original holdings, and their land is surrounded by the Navajo reservation.

The Hopi leaders eventually established their villages on the mesas, which were named by early explorers—with a surprising lack of originality—First Mesa, Second Mesa, and Third Mesa. Oraibi was the first village on the Third Mesa, and because they were first to arrive, members of the Bear Clan were considered the leaders.

In the late 1890s government officials, along with the help of Navajo policemen, searched the houses of the Hopis, saying the children must go to school to learn the ways of the predominantly white culture—and unlearn their own. If the adults had enough warning, they hid the children. If not, the boys and girls were dragged off, screaming and crying, to the school building.

The Hopi families of Oraibi were intensely divided between the progressives, who believed the tribe should give in to the white man's way, and the conservatives, who said, "When a Hopi becomes a white man [takes on Caucasian ways], he no longer has a face. We want to be Hopis, not white men. We want our children to learn Hopi ways and live by them."

No matter which side the parents chose, soon most of the village children were in school—but not Polingaysi. Not only was she lonely, but she also noticed that her friends returned to the mesa at the end of each day apparently unharmed, and often they were even laughing.

If this development already interested her, the final enticement was when she learned the school day included lunch.

Even though Polingaysi knew her family would be angry and wounded, her curiosity drove her down off the mesa and into the school of her own free will. There she was given a bath, a new dress, and a meal consisting of a saucer of syrup and a piece of hardtack. The teacher handed her a pencil and she set to work, diligently reproducing the odd-looking marks she saw on the board.

That afternoon, when Sevenka realized that her daughter had willingly gone to school, she said, "You have taken a step in the wrong direction. A step away from your Hopi people. You have brought grief to us. To me, to your father, and to your grandparents. Now you must continue to go to school each day. You have brought this thing upon yourself, and there is no turning back."

Those words were prophetic of the intercultural war that Polingaysi would feel in her soul for many years to come. In fact, her biography, published six decades later, carried the title *No Turning Back: A Hopi Indian Woman's Struggle to Live in Two Worlds.*

It was a conflict that affected not just her, but all Hopis. The festering and simmering split between the progressives and the conservatives boiled over on September 6, 1906, when the Bear Clan forced out those in the conservative Spider Clan, which marked the establishment of Hotevilla and Bakavi. The dispute had a bitter ending for all, with no clear winners. Oraibi lost its heart, and year by year, more families left. The Qöyawaymas moved to a house in New Oraibi, now called Kykotsmovi, at the bottom of the mesa near the government school.

Polingaysi continued to attend school and soon found that academic work was easy, and that she was hungry for more learning. Later that same year, her own life became as fractured as that of her people. Many of her friends were attending the Sherman Institute in Riverside, California, an off-reservation boarding school for Indian children. After much begging on her part, her parents relented and let her go. Her years at Sherman were lonely ones, but she studied hard and continued the musical training she'd begun in the government school.

In 1910 Polingaysi returned to her village only to realize how far she'd drifted culturally. According to her biography: "Polingaysi looked at the little house and the windswept yard where chickens pecked at bits of grain. The poverty of the scene made her heartsick. This life was not for her. She would never again be happy in the old pattern. She had gone too far along the path of the white man."

After four years of schooling, she preferred eating from a table to sitting on the floor, and she wanted to sleep in a bed. She wanted to cook lavish pies and cakes instead of cornmeal, and, as one who'd recently adopted the Christian faith, she tried hard to persuade her family to abandon their native beliefs. No part of her attitude won her any fans in the community, and she became increasingly unhappy. But at the same time, she was still Hopi in her heart, and she loved her family and village and wanted some way to sink roots back into her community.

Fortunately, her father saw a potential solution and arranged for her to live with the new missionary, Rev. Jacob Frey, and his family in Moenkopi, about 40 miles from New Oraibi.

Before taking her there, however, he led her to a plot of land about half a mile from the family's house, where he'd planted a thriving young cottonwood tree. Here, Fred Qöyawayma told Polingaysi, was a place that was hers to build on. Like the cottonwood, she too would have a place to sink her roots. From that moment on she resolved to work hard and save money to build a house on that very spot.

The Freys made Polingaysi, whom they called Elizabeth Ruth, a part of their Mennonite family and provided opportunities for work, travel, and exposure to new experiences. A trip to Newton, Kansas, was particularly significant. It was there that she learned about discrimination when refused service at a restaurant. But it was also where Bethel Academy (now Bethel College) inspired her to continue her education as a Mennonite missionary.

The following year, 1911, she started school at Bethel, financing her tuition, room, and board by working in the kitchen and dining room.

By 1918 Polingaysi had finished college and started missionary work, but she realized that in spite of her accomplishments, she was restless and dissatisfied. The Hopis were happy with their own spiritual lives, and despite her missionary training, part of her agreed with them and saw no reason to influence them to change their faith.

In September she was asked to take a position of teaching assistant in the Kayenta Indian boarding school, near the Utah state line and Monument Valley. Oddly enough, because she never had a chance to start the job, the opportunity would change the course of her life.

She traveled to Kayenta, but the day she was due to start her new position, the influenza epidemic sweeping the world hit the nearby town of Tuba City, and she was needed to help care for the sick. She too came down with the disease and was hospitalized. She survived, unlike 600,000 Americans, including hundreds of Hopis and Navajos.

After her recovery she was offered a position at the Tuba City boarding school and worked there as a substitute teacher for one term.

Still thinking that her doubts about being a missionary meant she needed more education, she moved to California to attend the Los Angeles Bible Institute. After two years she returned to the reservation to at last begin building the house of her dreams under the cottonwood tree.

In 1924 the government day school at Hotevilla offered her a position as housekeeper. She was torn: The job would bring a steady paycheck that would help pay for her house—and it was an alternative to mission work. Despite her concern that the Freys and her other Mennonite friends would be shocked and hurt, she nonetheless accepted the offer with relief. She also worried that the Hopis of Hotevilla would not accept her. She had, after all, urged them to give up their culture. Besides, they were descendants of those who had been ejected from the original village in 1906, and she feared they might resent her Oraibi origins.

Thanks to Polingaysi's solid work ethic and cheerful disposition, she was not only accepted by the other Hopis, but soon school officials asked her to teach the beginning and first-grade children. She'd never taken the government service examination, nor had she any formal teaching credentials, and school policy prohibited the use of the Hopi language. Yet, she found a way to connect with the children while teaching them English. Hopi stories and legends became the bridge between cultures and a basis for a vocabulary built of simple familiar things from home. Within a few months her students could spell simple words, count, and even speak whole sentences in English.

With that success Polingaysi began to feel as if she'd found her place between the two cultures she'd been straddling and to understand the vital role education played in the process.

I tell the young people this: "Your foundation is in your parents and your home, as well as in your Hopi culture pattern. Evaluate the best there is in your own culture and hang onto it, for it will always be foremost in your life; but do not fail to take also the best from the other cultures to blend with what you already have. We are not a boastful people, so do not allow your educational advantages to make you feel contempt for the older ones of no education who have made your progress possible. Give them credit for the good that is in them and for the love they have in their hearts for you. Don't boast, but on the other hand, don't set limitations on yourself. If you want more and still more education, reach out for it without fear. You have in you the qualities of persistence and endurance. Use them."

Within a year she passed the U.S. Indian Service test to become a full-time government employee. Still determined to further her undergraduate education, she spent the summer taking classes at the teaching college in Flagstaff, side by side with white schoolteachers.

After several years of teaching, she was transferred to New Mexico, first to Chinle, then Toadlena, to teach Navajo children.

By this time Polingaysi was approaching forty and longed for children of her own. She had become friends with a part-Cherokee man, and, in the spring of 1931, she and Lloyd White were married at the Bloomfield Trading Post in Toadlena. She also received the good news that she'd been transferred back to Hopiland and would be teaching in the Hopi village of Polacca in the fall.

The couple spent the summer in Oraibi, where they received a warm welcome from Polingaysi's parents, although many others in the community disapproved of her marrying outside the Hopi tribe. Soon, deep disagreements divided the newlyweds, and the marriage ended—without children—within a couple of years.

In the meantime Polingaysi had been adding rooms to her house. Music and singing had always provided a soul-satisfying emotional refuge for her, and at last she had a home for her piano. She also had sufficient room to take in paying guests during summer vacations. There was nowhere else to stay in Hopiland, and many politicians, anthropologists, and writers enjoyed her hospitality for the next three or four decades. Theodore Roosevelt and Ernest Hemingway were but two of her guests.

After two terms of teaching at Polacca, she was again transferred, at last to her home ground of Kykotsmovi, the former New Oraibi. It was a mixed blessing—she was home, close to her family and friends, but she still had to face resentment and rejection by some in her community.

She became silent, introspective, brooding. Once more she was trapped in a spider-web structure of suspicion, based on her own fears. The more she tried to push it away, the more entangled she became. The sense of rejection which had haunted her all her life bowed her spirit down with grief. Because of her Hopi heritage, she told herself, she would never be fully accepted by the white world, and her own Hopi people resented her interest in the world and her ability to work in it. Which way could she turn?

Ironically, relying on that very combination of cultures—the Hopi tradition of nonresistance and the comfort of her Christian faith—helped ease her out of the depression. In addition, her teaching methods had gained national attention and honors. In 1941 she was chosen from all the U.S. Indian Service teachers to demonstrate to school officials from around the continent her way of teaching Indian children, using their own traditions.

She also wrote a children's book, *The Sun Girl*, about a young Hopi girl who has to make a difficult choice between her grandparents. The book earned her the Arizona Author Award from the Arizona State Library Association and the Libraries Limited Group.

In the late 1940s Fred Qöyawayma developed diabetes and moved into Polingaysi's home, where she could provide the nursing care he needed. He, of all people, understood her best, and she missed him terribly when he died. Soon, Sevenka's health failed as well, and she died in 1951.

By 1954 Polingaysi was more than sixty years old and ready to retire from teaching. To her surprise her retirement celebration drew hundreds of friends and former students—as well as a bronze medal of commendation and the Distinguished Service Award from the U.S. Department of the Interior.

Never one to lapse into inactivity, Polingaysi launched herself into a new life of music, art, and writing, while continuing to help her Hopi people. She set up a scholarship fund for Hopi students that continues today at Northern Arizona University. She began working with clay and created beautiful pots in a style all her own, with raised symbols on a soft pink clay, reminiscent of her native mesas. Some of her pots are in a permanent collection at Phoenix's prestigious Heard Museum.

Her artistic and educational legacies live on through the work of the nephew she mentored, Al Qöyawayma. Like his aunt, he too is a bridge between worlds, although in his case he straddles art and science, as well as tribal traditions and contemporary high-tech environments. He is both a gifted ceramicist, whose work has been featured internationally, and an engineer with patents in high-tech guidance systems for commercial and military aircraft and airborne star trackers. But what might please Polingaysi the most is that her nephew cofounded the American Indian Science and Engineering Society, which funds scholarships for indigenous peoples. As of 2002 the society had 300 student and professional chapters worldwide.

The early 1970s were difficult for Polingaysi. Not only was she almost killed in 1972 when hit by a pickup truck, but the house that meant so much to her was destroyed by fire in 1974, along with everything in it, including her beloved piano. Two years later, thanks to family and friends, the house was rebuilt, and she was able to go back to pottery and her other activities.

Recognition for her accomplishments continued to flow in, and in 1976 the Museum of Northern Arizona asked the famed sculptor Una Hanbury to do a bronze sculpture of Polingaysi. Bethel College recognized her as 1979's Outstanding Alumna, and during the next few years, she also was awarded the Arizona Indian Living Treasure tribute, the Heard Museum's Gold Medal, and Bullock's national "Be Beautiful" Award.

Polingaysi was fortunate to remain healthy into her eighties, but in 1981 she suffered a stroke and soon needed home health care. In 1989 she grew so frail that she had to move from New Oraibi to a Phoenix nursing home. She died there on December 6, 1990.

In 1991 she was included in the Arizona Women's Hall of Fame.

In a recent interview, Al Qöyawayma said of his aunt:

There are people who transcend their culture. It doesn't matter if she'd been born in Russia, in China, or here. She would have been something different, but she would have still been a force. There are two kinds of forces. One comes up against a mountain, yells, screams, and brings in the earth movers. The other comes up against a mountain, puts a hand on it—and the mountain begins to move. That was her.

Gladys Tantaquidgeon
1899–2005

&

Mohegan Medicine Woman

Gladys Tantaquidgeon remembers exactly the day in 1904 when she began her training as a medicine woman of the Mohegan tribe. She was barely five years old and had been invited by three elder women of her tribe to accompany them on one of their walks through the fields and woods. The women often made these treks to gather herbs and plants to use as medicines in their healing practices.

Gladys called the women "Nanu," or grandmother, and all three held positions of importance in her life. Her great-aunt Emma Fielding Baker was the chief medicine woman of the tribe, a position she had inherited from her grandmother. It was she who kept the written tribal records and preserved the tribal history. Lydia Fielding and Mercy Ann Nonesuch Mathews were both experts at preparing curative medicines and developing healing practices. The three were a familiar sight, roaming the forests and fields throughout the Mohegan tribal lands, gathering such plants as bloodroot, motherwort, and ginseng to treat the tribe's ills. Gladys herself had watched them depart to work in the fields and return with their herbs many times.

But this time it would be different. This time Gladys was invited to join them, not as a tagalong granddaughter, but as a respected member of the tribe who was being groomed for an important position. The women were growing older. They had already discussed which little girl would be best suited to replace them in time, and they all agreed that small, soft-spoken Gladys showed the most promise. Though she was still very young, they could tell that she was bright enough to learn their skills and honorable enough to be entrusted with their secrets. The grandmothers took her by the hand and began to show her how to choose the best plants to be gathered, dried, and used for medicine and food.

Gladys knew that something special was happening that day. There was magic in the air—the magic of the Nanus. Children love magic and Gladys was no exception. She listened to the Nanus because she had been taught to respect her elders. She helped them choose various plants and herbs. As she grew she would follow the Nanus' teachings and learn their medicine. She would travel far to study the white man's way and the Indian's way, and she would form a bridge between the two cultures that would ultimately help to restore the tribal status of her nation.

Gladys Tantaquidgeon was born on June 15, 1899, near Montville in southeastern Connecticut, the third of the seven living children of Harriet and John Tantaquidgeon. Three other children had died in infancy. Gladys's mother was skilled at the crafts of beading, sewing, and quilting. Although her father was primarily a farmer, he, too, was skilled at native crafts and excelled at wood carving, basket weaving, and stone masonry. The family lived in a rambling farmhouse across the road from an ancient hill that had been a stronghold in the defense of Mohegan lands from intrusion by the Narragansett tribe from the east in the seventeenth century.

Gladys Tantaquidgeon (pronounced *Tant-a-QUID'geon*, and which means "going along fast on the land or in the water") is a member of the Mohegan, an Algonquin tribe, distantly related to but different from the Mohican tribe of New York State. Around the time of the arrival of English settlers the tribe migrated from New York State to the southeastern part of Connecticut and was originally associated with the neighboring Pequot tribe. Around 1635 a conflict in tribal leadership between the Pequot sachem (chief) Sassacus and his brother-in-law Uncas caused the people to separate into two tribes. Uncas moved with his followers to the west bank of the Thames River and claimed for his people the name Mohegan, meaning "wolf people." In 1637 the Mohegan fought with the English and the Narragansett tribe against the Pequot, and in 1640 and 1675 fought with the English against the Narragansett. Chief Uncas was Gladys Tantaquidgeon's ninth-generation grandfather.

Since 1638 the Mohegan tribe has enjoyed cordial diplomatic relations with first the Crown Colony and later with the State of Connecticut, but over the years they watched their reservation shrink as the white man encroached more and more upon their lands. In 1790 the tribe held about 2,700 acres of property. By 1872 the only property left was the church and the tribal burying grounds.

In 1830 the United States government passed the Indian Removal Act, which attempted to force tribes living east of the Mississippi to relinquish their land in exchange for western prairie land. Only those tribes who attended church and provided schooling for their children could avoid such displacement. Thus the Mohegans built a church on their land that also served as a school, named the Indian Congregational Church of Montville, a church that stands to this day. In 1978 the tribe sought formal recognition from the United States government, and it was finally granted in 1994.

Gladys's parents raised her and her siblings in accordance with traditional Indian beliefs. Her mother trimmed her hair only by the waning moon to insure its thickness and health. Her father planted a cedar tree when she was born and taught her to divine for water under ground with forked sticks made of forest woods. Both parents taught their children to respect their Indian heritage, to love the land, and to appreciate the value of hard work. At the same time they were very much aware of the white culture of the twentieth century that was swirling around them just down the road from Mohegan Hill in Uncasville.

Gladys attended the non-Indian local school, and after school she was free to roam with her brothers and sisters through the woods surrounding their house searching for arrowheads—concrete evidence of the presence of their ancestors. In winter the children enjoyed skating parties on the Thames River and raced on homemade sleds. As a youngster Gladys was taught to sew and cook and learned to make quilts and pincushions. She helped her tribe celebrate the Wigwam, or corn festival, in the fall. The Wigwam (which means, "come into my home") featured delicious Indian foods and offered Indian crafts for sale—beaded purses made by the women and carved bowls, spoons, and baskets made by the men. The Wigwam celebration brought the tribal members together and offered Gladys and her family a chance to feel "one with the spirit of all Mohegans."

When Gladys was about eight years old, her parents moved to New London, where she attended Nathan Hale Grammar School for about seven years before the family moved back to Mohegan Hill. Although Gladys never attended high school, she was far from uneducated. She continued to be instructed by the grandmothers in the traditional tribal beliefs. The Nanus taught her that cedar and quartz, sweet grass and corn could evoke good spirits and could protect against bad spirits. She learned the meanings of Mohegan symbols like The Trail of Life symbol, whose arrow points east to west, signifying the passage of spirits and the path of the sun. The Trail begins in the east with birth, goes on to death and entrance into the spirit world in the west, and circles back again to rebirth in the east; the four-domed medallion represents the four directions. Gladys learned never to gather more herbs than she needed and which plants were poisonous. But her education was further enhanced by her close relationship with a young anthropologist named Frank Speck.

Frank Speck had come as a student to study the tribal language spoken by Gladys's great aunt, Fidelia Fielding, who was a friend of the Speck family. Fidelia welcomed Frank into her home in the Connecticut woods, introduced him to the ways of the Indian, and filled him with a lasting love and respect for the knowledge, traditions, and languages of Native American tribes. Since Fidelia was the last to speak the language of the Mohegan tribe, Frank's close relationship with her offered him a unique opportunity to study that dying language and imbued him with a commitment to preserve and record dying languages and cultures throughout the Native American world.

Frank Speck would go on to become a professor of anthropology at the University of Pennsylvania. He returned often to his friends on Mohegan Hill and eventually translated four of Fidelia's diaries. He also enjoyed a lasting friendship with Gladys's older brother Harold, who later became chief of the tribe. On his visits to the tribe Frank also struck up a friendship with young Gladys, and she in turn showed an interest in his work. He and his wife began to include Gladys on their summer vacations and invited Gladys and Harold to visit them at their home in New Hampshire. There the Tantaquidgeons met members of other tribes—the Penobscot and the Micmac. Through Frank Gladys learned of a world far beyond the comfortable family compound on Mohegan Hill. So in 1919, at the age of twenty, Gladys began the study of anthropology at the University of Pennsylvania, with Frank Speck as her mentor. In addition to her formal studies, she acted as his assistant and was often sent to visit and research other eastern tribes.

In 1928 Gladys lived with and studied the Gay Head and Mashpee Indians of Massachusetts. Like the Mohegan, the Gay Head and Mashpee believed in the existence of the mythical Granny Squannit, leader of the Makiawisug, or Little People, of the forest who, if she wished, could help the tribal medicine man or woman select the right plant to secure a cure for his or her patient. Legend advised that small offerings of food or wine must be left for Granny Squannit in the forest in tiny baskets. The next day the gifts would be gone, and in their place would be the correct herb or plant that would effect the cure the medicine man or woman was seeking. Granny Squannit's husband, Moshup, was also a respected folk hero. Moshup's strength was legend; it was believed he was strong enough to capture whales. Some Indians reported seeing Granny Squannit and Moshup, while others asserted they were invisible.

In 1930 Gladys began studying the Delaware Indians of Oklahoma, specifically their medical practices and folk beliefs. She was aided in this study by a member of the tribe, Wi-tapanóxwe (pronounced Wee-tah-pah-NOKH-way), whose name means "walks with daylight," and whose visit to Philadelphia was sponsored in part by the Pennsylvania Historical Commission. Wi-tapanóxwe—a medicine man himself—reminded Gladys that the Indians had lived healthy lives before the coming of the white settlers and that such health depended on "pure, natural" food which modern-day Indians found difficult to obtain. The Delaware Indian still depended on corn or maize as a staple crop and, like the Mohegan, believed it held nourishment for both the body and spirit. Gladys was always very respectful of the information that Wi-tapanóxwe shared with her, as it was believed that the theories, practices, and beliefs of a medicine man or woman were the personal property of the practitioner, who had been blessed with those skills by the Creator.

Gladys later published her findings on the Delaware in a monograph, *Folk Medicine of the Delaware and Related Algonkian Indians.* Included in the book is valuable information from older members of the community about the Mohegan tribe as well, including a detailed list of plants and herbs used as remedies for various maladies. In her work Gladys advises that tea made from dried yarrow leaves might be used to treat liver and kidney problems and tells us that the fresh leaves of the plantain could be used to draw out snake poison. She goes on to report that yokeag (dried, pulverized corn kernels) is a favorite food of the Mohegans,

Gladys Tantaquidgeon

and its uses are many, including a dependable and totable source of nourishment on long trips.

In 1934 Congress passed the Wheeler-Howard Act, also known as the Indian Reorganization Act, which was an attempt by the federal government to correct years of abuse of the Native Americans, including the practice regarded as "forced assimilation." At the closing of the nineteenth century Indian culture was still considered by the majority of the population to be inferior to that of white, European settlers. Thus, Indians were strongly encouraged by the federal government to turn away from their ancestry, forego their language, and embrace a strictly "American" culture. Indian tribal governments and religions were eradicated. Children were removed from the reservations and sent to distant boarding schools where strict discipline was often imposed and where the ability of their parents to influence their education and upbringing was severely restricted.

Fidelia Fielding had been forbidden to speak her native Mohegan language in such a school and so had been afraid to teach it to Gladys. Indians were discouraged from doing beadwork, weaving, and using religious and ceremonial icons such as dolls and sacred images. They were afraid to teach their children the sacred dances and tribal celebrations.

By 1929 it was acknowledged that the policy of forced assimilation had been a dismal failure, and the Wheeler-Howard Act of 1934 was passed in an attempt to reverse some of that damage. The act encouraged tribes to return to self-government and to re-establish tribal councils and identity. It encouraged the restoration of cultural practices, including knowledge of native languages. Funds were made available to tribes for the establishment of cooperative business enterprises. Schools were re-established on the reservations, and in 1946 a special Indian Claims Commission was established for the express purpose of allowing tribes to make claims for lands taken from them in the past.

In 1934 Gladys was hired by the federal government to assist in administering the benefits of the Wheeler-Howard Act. One of her duties as an employee of the Bureau of Indian Affairs was to determine which young Indians might be eligible to receive educational scholarships under the act, and to this end she traveled throughout New England visiting other tribes.

She was then sent west to South Dakota to work among the Lakota Sioux in an effort to acquaint those tribes with the benefits available to them under the new act. There on a sprinkling of reservations throughout the state Gladys discovered fellow Indians living in abject poverty, confined to lands ill-suited to agriculture, with their individual tribal identities in ruins. She and her co-workers lived among the tribes and shared both their isolation and their deprivations. Winters were harsh, food was scarce, and death often visited even the youngest tribal members. One of Gladys's jobs was to travel the reservations, advising parents that their children would no longer attend boarding schools but would be educated on the reservation. This change created anxiety among the parents, who feared they would be responsible for providing food and clothing for their children all winter. Gladys tried to allay their fears and assure them that the government would provide for their needs. She found her job was a bit easier because she herself was an Indian. "Some of the Sioux were not too keen on having a government agent present," she told an interviewer in later years, "but because of my Indian descent I was accepted."

But she was not always accepted everywhere, and at times she was forced to face the unpleasant realities of racial discrimination. Indians, like blacks, were often asked to sit in the back of a bus and were frequently denied service in restaurants and shops.

After three years of working with the Sioux, Gladys accepted another federal position with the Indian Arts and Crafts Board, which represented an attempt by the government to restore respect for traditional Indian artwork and ceremonies. This job was more suited to Gladys's talents and heritage. Both of her parents were gifted native artists. In addition to her skills in the medical arts, Gladys herself had been taught as a child the traditional arts of basket weaving, beadwork, and sewing. Now she traveled throughout the Dakotas, Montana, and Wyoming, encouraging Indians to again create native crafts and to revive native dances and ceremonies. She assisted them in marketing their crafts and encouraged them to place their work in museums. Respect for Indian art grew and was encouraged by such public figures as First Lady Eleanor Roosevelt.

In 1947, after years of travel and work, Gladys retired from government employment and returned to her home on Mohegan Hill. Her three Nanus had died. Now it was time for her to assume the role of Nanu, to counsel younger tribal members, to continue her work as a medicine woman, and to protect the identity of the Mohegan tribe. In 1931 her father and brother had built the Tantaquidgeon Indian Museum in Uncasville as a home for the artifacts of their tribe. Gladys would now use the experience and knowledge she had learned in her government job to help her brother further develop the Mohegan museum.

After a brief stint as a social worker in a nearby prison, she retired to work exclusively in the museum. Gladys had collected Indian art during her work in the west, and these she also displayed in the family museum. In addition to these artifacts from other tribes, the Tantaquidgeon Indian Museum exhibits items that specifically demonstrate the history of the Mohegan tribe, from the tiny baskets used to offer gifts to the Makiawisug to the larger, more elaborate baskets woven by tribal members. There are arrowheads and tomahawks, mortars and pestles that had been used to grind corn, and birch bark canoes that were used as transportation. As its collections and reputation grew, two more rooms were added, and the museum welcomed visitors from around the world. Today the Tantaquidgeon Indian Museum is open to the public from Memorial Day to Labor Day and is said to be the oldest museum run by Indians in the United States.

For centuries the Mohegan had suffered the indignity of having their burial grounds desecrated, looted of the sacred objects that had been buried with their ancestors. Ancient jewelry, stone pipes, bowls, and arrowheads have found their way over the years into the collections of various museums and historical societies. Gladys and her fellow Mohegans have tried for years to reclaim these items and were encouraged by the passage in 1990 of the Native American Graves Protection and Repatriation Act. The tribe continues to work with museums and historical societies to reclaim those sacred objects that are vital to the history of their tribe.

In addition to working in the museum Gladys assumed responsibility for a cache of tribal papers bequeathed to her care from Nanu Emma Baker—birth certificates, marriage papers, death certificates, and postcards from Mohegans who had traveled around the world. In 1978, when the tribe applied to the federal government for formal recognition of their status as a tribe, the papers that Gladys and Emma Baker collected and preserved offered just the crucial evidence the tribe needed. In an interview in the *New York Times* on June 4, 1997, a historian for the Bureau of Indian Affairs reported that Gladys's tribal archives provided the key to tribal identity. "We needed those pieces of papers," historian Virginia DeMarre declared. "They left no questions whatsoever." Tribal recognition of the Mohegans led to the building of the Mohegan Sun Casino in Uncasville, Connecticut, one of a string of gambling casinos built by Native American tribes over the last few years.

Kudos for Gladys have been many. In 1986 she was honored by the University of Connecticut with an award named for her, in recognition of her role in "diminishing the dual invisibility of women of minority cultures in the United States." In 1992 the

Mohegan tribe bestowed upon Gladys official status as medicine woman; in 1993 she was awarded an honorary doctoral degree by the University of Pennsylvania; and on June 15, 1999, a day declared by the State of Connecticut as Gladys Tantaquidgeon Day, she celebrated her one hundredth birthday with a gala celebration replete with honors from many quarters, including representatives of other tribes. She never married and, at press time, still lives at her home with her family in Uncasville.

Gladys Tantaquidgeon was born at a time when respect for the Native American was almost nonexistent. Indians were often vilified and stereotyped by whites as violent, naked savages. She has fought against this prejudice her entire life. She left her comfortable family home to travel and work with both cultures in an attempt to administer the white man's laws to her people. It has not always been an easy task. The Indian has traditionally been wary of the white man's promises, with the memory of hundreds of years of abuse still fresh in their minds.

Gladys's life has touched three centuries, and throughout she has labored to keep the spirit of her tribe alive and to instill respect for tribal history in the young Mohegans of today. She has treasured the arts, crafts, and medicinal remedies of her people and has encouraged other tribes to do the same. Where there were no written records, she collected the stories and wrote them down for future generations to learn from and enjoy. And like her brother, Chief Harold Tantaquidgeon, when she told those stories she admonished her fellow Mohegans to, "Listen, and never forget."

She has worked ceaselessly to promote greater understanding of the Mohegans, to preserve her tribe's identity, and to establish its sovereignty for future generations. While she travels her life's trail, she embodies beautifully the Mohegan belief that future generations can be guided by the wisdom of their past.

Mary Musgrove Bosomworth
ca. 1700–1765

ℳ

Pocahontas of Georgia

From adolescence until the end of her life, Mary Musgrove Bosomworth, as she is remembered in history, straddled two worlds: her Indian heritage and her white way of life. She lived like the English with regard to home, clothing, marriage, and political activity, but she remained strongly connected to the Native American peoples. Both cultures respected and misunderstood her.

The circumstances that thrust Mary into the spotlight of history actually started in England in 1729. General James Oglethorpe, a soldier, statesman, and humanitarian, secured a commission from King George II to establish the Colony of Georgia in the New World. Oglethorpe hoped it would serve as a haven for Europe's oppressed, especially debtors and religious refugees. The king signed the charter for the colony that would be named for him on June 9, 1732.

In November 1732 Oglethorpe—the only member of the trustees of the colony charter to actually travel to Georgia—left England with about 120 colonists. The ship stopped in South Carolina, then Oglethorpe and a few others paddled boats up the Savannah River. He spotted a bluff that would provide a good location for a settlement.

The Yamacraws, a split-off group of Creek Indians, lived about 3 miles from the bluff, so the spot was called Yamacraw Bluff. Tomochichi, their mico, or chief, greeted the English.

Oglethorpe wished to ask permission for his band to settle on the bluff, yet neither man spoke the other's language. The chief sent for

Mary Musgrove, the daughter of his sister, the old matriarch. The chief also had a brother, Old Brim, called "Emperor of the Creeks," so the Indians had given Mary the title of princess. Mary spoke English well and translated between the two leaders. In addition she helped placate the Indians' objections to the English settling there; and over the years she monitored transactions between the Indians and colonists.

Oglethorpe hired Mary, agreeing to pay her one hundred English pounds—some say two hundred, while some say he promised her nothing—per year. The general treated her with "great Esteem" and made her his emissary to the Creeks.

Tiny Mary, standing five feet tall and weighing one hundred pounds, was thirty-three years old at that time. Her black hair hung in two long braids and she stuck a feather into a band of beads she wore across her forehead. One colonist wrote that she was "an Indian woman in mean and lowe circumstances, being only Cloathed with a Red Stroud Petticoat and an Osnabrig shift." Mary later disputed that report, saying that she and her husband were "on the verge of great riches."

Mary's story has roots in the settling of South Carolina. When the English settled Charlestown (later Charleston), South Carolina, in 1670, the Creek Indians welcomed them to get protection from other Indians and the Spanish friars who were establishing missions and converting Indians. Henry Woodward, responding to this welcome, established a trading center at Coweta, a major Creek town on the Ockmulgee River.

However, the Creeks' loyalty to the English did not last long. In 1715 they joined forces with their relatives—the Yemassees—to attack Charlestown, starting the devastating Yemassee War. From the Creek point of view, the attack was a failure. The Creeks then sought Cherokee help to pursue another attack, but the Cherokee aligned with the Carolinians against the Creeks. After the Creeks sought protection from the French and the Spanish, they signed a peace treaty with the Carolinians that ended the war. The Creeks and the Carolinians began to trade again in 1718.

Mary was born around 1700 in Coweta. Her Creek name has different spellings: Cousaponakeesa, Cooszaponakeesa, Coosaponakessa, or Consaponakeeso. Although the identity of her father is not certain, John Bee, the leading Indian trader in this period, has been considered a possibility. More recent scholarship, however, proposes that Mary's father was more likely Edward Griffin, a licensed trader, or possibly Henry Woodward.

When she was between the ages of seven and ten, Mary's father took her to Pomponne—now Pon Pon—in Colleton County, South Carolina. There the girl was baptized and educated as a Christian, learned to speak English, and was given the Christian name Mary. Mary stayed there for the war's duration.

In 1716 the government of South Carolina sent Colonel John Musgrove to negotiate the treaty that would end the Yemassee War. His son, John Musgrove Jr., accompanied his father and fell in love with the Indian "princess" and asked her to marry him. The bridegroom, an Indian trader and government agent, probably had a Native American mother. Colonel Musgrove may have arranged the marriage, which took place in 1717. Although Mary married two more times, she is best known today by the name Mary Musgrove.

The newlyweds lived among the Cherokee in Georgia for several years. They then returned to South Carolina about 1723 and lived there for more than seven years. They had two sons, Edward and James. They relocated in June 1732 to Yamacraw Bluff, the site of present-day Savannah, a year before General James Oglethorpe founded the Georgia colony.

At the request of the Creek Nation and by the consent of South Carolina Governor Robert Johnson, the couple opened a trading post. Mary, an extremely talented woman, showed her skills in business, and the trading post grew significantly. One-sixth of Charlestown's annual export—twelve thousand pounds of deerskins—passed through the Musgroves' hands. They also owned cattle and three Native American slaves.

When Oglethorpe settled the new colony of Georgia, he gave Mary gifts to secure her friendship. Georgia had few leaders among its small number of early settlers and, in order to survive, those settlers had to establish relations with the local Indians and those in South Carolina. Oglethorpe often called on Mary to interpret and negotiate between his government and Indians. In one instance Mary used her influence to convince the Yamacraw Indians to cede a portion of their land to the colonists. Oglethorpe admired and trusted her so much that he began to regularly seek her advice, which did not set well with some of the other Englishmen.

Both Georgia and South Carolina vied to have the upper hand in trade with the local Native Americans and in the rum trade. Mary helped Georgia win in that rivalry when she negotiated travel agreements between the British in Georgia and the Chocktaw. In 1734 Mary again used her influence when she interpreted at the meeting between Chocktaw Chief Redshoes and Georgia's leaders.

Two years later, when tensions arose, Oglethorpe again asked Mary to serve as interpreter at a meeting with Chigilly, leader of the Lower Creeks, and Malchi—Brim's son and Mary's cousin—who would succeed Chigilly.

Two or three years after the Musgroves moved to Georgia, John Musgrove died. Different sources list his death as 1734, 1735, and 1739. At the time of his death, Mary had a home in Savannah and 1,400 acres of land. She also held an important position in the colony because of her relationship with Oglethorpe and her ability to provide supplies to the early settlers.

Mary received a condolence letter from Oglethorpe. She did not remain widowed for long; she soon married Jacob Matthews.

At the time, Matthews, who came to Georgia as an indentured servant—and possibly had been Mary's servant—commanded twenty rangers stationed near the new trading post. "His marriage to Mary completely changed him," E. Merton Coulter wrote in his article, "Mary Musgrove, Queen of the Creeks: A Chapter of Early Georgia Troubles." "He was now a 'lusty . . . Fellow' . . . who became . . . 'blown up with Pride.'" Quarrelsome and given to drink, he gathered about him the colony malcontents. Coulter continued:

> *A man of this disposition would not fail to make full use of the Indians and to employ all the means in his power to secure the aid of Mary . . . in his plans. He and Mary were soon complaining that the Indians were not being given their full quota of presents, and to better play on their sensibilities he frequently made them drunk. . . . During the period of her alliance with Jacob, Mary had begun to show signs of being weaned away from the best interest of the colony and the fact that she did not drift further away was, perhaps, due to the presence of Oglethorpe.*

Mary's influence in the colony continued during her five-year marriage to Jacob Matthews. Oglethorpe asked Mary to start a second trading post on the south side of the forks of the Altamaha River at Mount Venture to help protect Georgia against Spanish invasion. Mary would look out for any suspicious Spanish movements and try to warn the colonists.

She aided in concluding treaties and in securing Creek warriors to fight with the British against Spain in the War of Jenkins' Ear, 1739–44. Mary influenced the Indians to side with Oglethorpe, and she even sent her own traders into battle. Creek warriors went with Oglethorpe when he attacked the fort at St. Augustine, unsuccessfully, in 1740. Mary's brother, Edward Griffin, who had acted as Georgia's emissary to the Creeks, died in the battle, along with other family members.

Around 1738 a group of Creeks gave Mary title to three offshore Georgia islands, Sapelo, Osaabaw, and St. Catherines, plus a tract of land that Oglethorpe had ceded to the Creeks in earlier treaties.

Jacob Matthews became ill in 1742 and, although Mary took him to Savannah for medical care, he died on May 8. Yamasee or Spanish Indians demolished Mary's unprotected trading post at Mount Venture, taking away her cattle and raiding the Yamacraw post.

Mary continued to barter with traders at Yamacraw. She also sold colonists meat, bread, and other foods that were sorely needed in those early years before the colonists began to produce these items themselves. Many of the colonists never paid their bills, so she virtually gave away a lot of produce, losing about 826 English pounds due to bad debts.

In 1743 Oglethorpe left Savannah, giving Mary a going-away present of one of his own diamond rings, taken from his finger, valued at two hundred pounds. To demonstrate his esteem and appreciation for her services, he promised her one hundred pounds a year to continue as interpreter and promised two thousand more pounds to sweeten the pot.

Again, Mary did not remain widowed for long. Coulter wrote, "When it came to marrying, Mary was either designing or gullible; it seemed she could have no rest unless she was married to somebody." She married Englishman Thomas Bosomworth on July 8, 1744.

When Oglethorpe left, he recommended that William Stephens be made president of the colony and consequently leader of the governing council. Thomas Bosomworth worked as a clerk for Stephens, who later appointed him as secretary of Indian affairs. He had volunteered to fight alongside Oglethorpe at St. Augustine before traveling to England to take holy orders, after which he was appointed the Church of England's minister to Georgia, serving at one time as chaplain to Oglethorpe's regiment. He later abandoned his religious calling and became an adventurer, described as a man of "sprightly Temper" with a "Little Share of classical Learning." The Bosomworths opened a new trading post on a spot called "the Forks," where the Ockmulgee and Oconee Rivers met.

Although her benefactor, Oglethorpe, was gone, Mary continued to help the colony. During the War of the Austrian Succession, she worked successfully to convince the Creeks not to respond to the French appeal for help. During the Creek-Cherokee war in 1747–48, she persuaded the Creeks to remain loyal to the English after the Spanish courted them.

Although Coulter wrote that it was during Mary's marriage to Jacob Matthews that her attitude toward the colony changed, it wasn't until after Oglethorpe left that relations between Mary and the colonists turned hostile. First, the colonists no longer treated Mary with her former respect, which insulted her. Mary also felt angry about the lack of payment for the goods and services she had provided colonists. She had continued to interpret for colonial leaders, according to her agreement with Oglethorpe, and it was when Mary asked for the payment that Oglethorpe had promised her that relations between herself and the whites became strained.

A major conflict occurred when Mary and Thomas Bosomworth attempted to lay claim to the property Mary had received earlier from the Creeks. Georgia leaders denied Mary's claim to ownership of the islands, and she would spend much of the rest of her life fighting to secure British recognition of her claim. Most historians believe that Thomas Bosomworth influenced—and misled—his wife, convincing her that the colonists had wronged her. When referring to Thomas Bosomworth, historians use words and phrases such as "foment a scheme," "take advantage both of the Creeks and of the colony government," "ambitious," "an unscrupulous fortune seeker," "adventurer," "carpet-bagger," "a troublemaker," and "fortune hunter."

In *A History of Georgia,* William Bacon Stevens took an especially cynical view of Bosomworth. He wrote:

> *Hitherto the career of Mary had been one of generous self-denial, and of unmerited labors for the good of the colony. She had not indeed received the full reward of her services; but she rested in security on the faith of the government, and was, until her marriage with Bosomworth, quiet in her conduct, and moderate in her demands. But, from 1744 [the date of her marriage], her whole was changed; and the colony . . . was now, through her misdirected influence, to feel the dreadful horrors of expected massacre and extermination.*

Up until 1743 Mary had received only about one thousand dollars, so she had a justified claim, but Stevens wrote, ". . . her avaricious husband . . . stepped in with an exorbitant demand for nearly twenty-five thousand dollars."

However it came about, Mary's attitude toward the colony shifted from friendly to adversarial. After the couple had been married one year, Thomas Bosomworth went to England, writing the trustees of the colony that he would not return. After he had been in England for two years, though, he came back to Georgia. For the next two years, he stirred up the colony with his attempts to get compensation for Mary's services and to get the property. In addition he gave up all ecclesiastical duties and defied the colony trustees' ban against slavery by bringing six black slaves in from South Carolina for his and Mary's use. The trustees sent the slaves back, which doubtless angered Thomas Bosomworth.

Bosomworth secured the support of Major William Horton, Oglethorpe's commander of the regiment from the town of Frederica, Georgia, and other officers. When Colonel Alexander Heron arrived in 1747 to replace Horton, he supported the Bosomworths. Thomas gathered a group of Indians, led by Malatchee, Mary's brother, to confer with Horton. Malatchee summarized Mary's services and asked that Thomas's brother, Abraham, be sent to England to plead Mary's cause to the king. Thomas Bosomworth proposed that the Indians crown Malatchee king, and it was done. The Indians deeded to Mary all their hunting lands "from the fourth day of the wintry moon and so long as the waters run down to the ocean forever." By 1750 Mary had secured the signatures of seven Creek Nation chieftains who supported her demands for payment of past services and her demands that certain lands be deeded to herself and Thomas.

The Creeks supported Mary in her claims and threatened to block any further colonial settlement in areas agreed upon under the Creek-Colonial treaty of 1739. The situation became so combative that Mary, presenting herself as queen of the Creeks, led about two hundred Creeks into Savannah on August 7, 1749. Thomas Bosomworth walked beside her in his canonical robes. The Indians fired guns as they walked, indicating their support of Mary, and William Stephens and the council members became understandably alarmed.

The council entertained the Indians at a banquet where rum flowed freely, and they convinced them that Bosomworth was trying to take lands that belonged to all the Indians. Mary, also intoxicated, rushed into the meeting and threatened the colonists, who arrested her and her husband.

Upon her release she continued her battle.

Abraham Bosomworth took documentation to England, hoping the king would recognize the legitimacy of Mary's property ownership. Thomas, optimistic about a positive response, bought a herd of cattle from South Carolina merchants on credit. Mary, Thomas, and the cattle settled on St. Catherines Island.

The Board of Trade in London, in turn, received strong documentation from the Georgia colony stating that Creek leaders disputed Mary's claims. Feeling that their cause could be pursued more favorably in person, Mary and Thomas sold some of their property to raise cash to pay for a trip to England.

When the couple arrived in Charlestown in 1752 to begin their trip, they were caught up in the aftermath of a Lower Creek Indian uprising. Near there, a Creek, Acorn Whistler, had killed four Cherokees and taken another prisoner. Horses had also been stolen from the Indian traders. Prior to the attack, both Indian groups had pledged friendship before the colony's governor, James Glen, and the South Carolina Council. Thus Glen, who felt that his authority had been challenged, requested that the Council appoint Mary as agent to resolve the dispute.

The Council resisted the governor's request. They agreed to Mary acting as interpreter but appointed Thomas Bosomworth as agent. Thomas would be paid seven hundred pounds for the negotiations. The Bosomworths spent five months among the Creeks and successfully negotiated terms agreeable to both sides.

Mary remained with the Creeks until the spring of 1753, and Thomas returned to Charlestown in January to take care of their fragile financial situation. Creditors in the city were hounding them, and they had exhausted their trip funds to pay for the Creek treaty mission. It was only through Governor Glen's intervention with writs of protection that the couple stayed out of jail.

The matter became more tense when the Commons House of Assembly defied Glen and dismissed the couple's requests for payment. Thomas appealed to the General Assembly and Glen for nearly a year. Relief came in May 1754 when the Commons House authorized 2,266 pounds for Thomas. The issue was not resolved, however, because the public treasurer refused to release the total amount. Thomas responded by filing a lawsuit, but he left the state before the matter came to trial.

The dispute took a new turn in June 1753 when the trustees of Georgia gave ownership of the colony over to the King of England. In 1754 the Bosomworths made their trip to England. To their disappointment the Board of Trade rendered a decision in 1759 that disallowed their claims. When they returned to Georgia, Mary accepted a compromise in 1760 from Henry Ellis, who had been recently been appointed governor of the state. William Bacon Stevens wrote, "Thus after long years of litigation, after the most threatening disturbances, after scenes of turmoil and chicanery that embroiled the colony almost in civil war, and put in serious jeopardy its best interests, was this troublous claim adjusted to the satisfaction of all parties, and up on terms honourable and beneficial to each."

The colony council and governor resolved the issue by giving Mary title to St. Catherines Island and cash from the sale of Ossabaw and Sapelo Islands. The acquisition of St. Catherines plus her earlier properties made her the largest landowner in Georgia. The Bosomworths relinquished all claims against the government in June 1760. They had enough money to build a grand home on St. Catherines, where they lived until Mary's death in 1765.

Mary Musgrove Matthews Bosomworth is buried on St. Catherines Island.

In *Unsung Heroines of the Carolina Frontier,* Alexia Jones Helsley wrote: "Mary . . . was a remarkable woman. At a time when the 'troika . . . wife, mother, and household mistress,' defined the lives of most women, she exercised extraordinary influence not only in Creek–Georgia relations but also as an emissary of South Carolina. Few women in her time approached her level of importance."

"Mary Musgrove Matthews Bosomworth rose to become an outstanding leader," wrote Linda K. Kerber in *Women of the Republic: Intellect and Ideology in Revolutionary America.* "She was a woman without equal on the Carolina–Georgia frontier and one who contributed profoundly not only to the success of the Colony of Georgia but to the success of the Carolina venture as well."

Historians hold differing viewpoints about Mary's value to Oglethorpe and thus to the colony of Georgia and her status in history. Some consider her one of the most important figures in Georgia's colonial history and an outstanding woman. Some take a more cynical view. However, she undoubtedly provided an invaluable service to Oglethorpe. Surely the development of Georgia would have gone quite differently without her aid.

Frances Slocum

1773–1847

Little Bear Woman

Frances Slocum huddled alone and scared under the stairway of her family's large farmhouse. She had just seen her mother snatch up the baby of the family and hurry outside, along with two of the other children, to take cover in some bushes. Five-year-old Frances had been told to hide indoors, but now she wanted the comfort of her mother's strong but surprisingly gentle hands. And what would happen to her father, who was out working in the fields?

A few moments earlier, a gunshot had sounded across the farmlands of Pennsylvania's Wyoming Valley. Though the Revolutionary War was still being fought between American colonists and British soldiers, Frances was experiencing an Indian raid, not a military battle. Indian attacks were common in the area near Wilkes-Barre where Quakers Jonathan and Ruth Slocum had settled to farm and raise their ten children.

Most of the 200-plus residents of the valley had already been killed or had abandoned their homes out of fear for their lives. But Jonathan Slocum wasn't afraid of the native Delaware people. Like his fellow Quaker, the illustrious leader William Penn (who had established good relations with Indian groups in Pennsylvania, and who, like Slocum, wore a black, broad-brimmed hat), Jonathan wanted to build trust with his native neighbors. But his eldest son, nineteen-year-old Giles, felt differently and had covertly joined with other settlers to fight the Indians.

The Delawares thought that the Slocums had turned against them and decided to strike. A group stormed the farm, and several

Indians came into the house looking for food and useful items. They found little auburn-haired Frances instead, having seen her toes poking out beneath the stairs.

The raiders carried off Frances and her twelve-year-old brother Ebeneezer. Also taken was Wareham Kingsley, a neighbor boy who was in the Slocum's yard at the time. Seeing this, Ruth Slocum and one of her older daughters emerged from their hiding place to plead for their family members. Desperate, they pointed out that Ebeneezer's foot was crippled; the Delaware raiders could see this was true and let him go. The Slocums urged the Indians to release Frances as well, but could only watch as the barefoot child screamed for her mother as she was taken away. This was the last time Ruth would see her daughter, though she never gave up hope that Frances would return.

The day was November 2, 1778. It would be sixty years before Frances Slocum would see any member of her birth family again. She didn't know that Indians returned to the farm six weeks later and killed her father, Jonathan Slocum, and maternal grandfather, Isaac Tripp, also wounding her brother William. Remaining members of the family and their neighbors searched for Frances in the weeks and years to come but found no sign of her.

Six years after the kidnapping incident, as the American colonists continued to create an independent nation, Wareham Kingsley found his way back to the Wyoming Valley after being released from captivity. Unfortunately, he didn't know what had happened to Frances because the two had been separated soon after their capture. Wareham provided some relief to the Slocums by telling them that Frances had been treated kindly: Her captors had given her food, carried her when she was tired, and given her moccasins to wear.

Ruth Slocum sent sons Giles and William to Niagara Falls in 1784, and then to Ohio in 1788. In both places, white people who had been taken as children by Indians were searching for their families. The Slocums didn't find Frances either time. How would they know her after so many years in a different culture, surrounded by an unfamiliar language and way of life? The brothers looked for a girl with a missing fingertip—Frances had been involved in a farm accident as a young child. The family offered a reward for information. Members of the Slocum family continued to travel to New York and Ohio to talk to children who had survived capture by Indians, but none had any information about Frances.

Twelve years after the kidnapping, Giles Slocum met a man named Colonel Thomas Proctor, who had been sent by the secretary of war early in 1791 to visit Native-American settlements around Lake Erie. Giles begged him to help his family by negotiating with the Indians who had taken Frances. A note in Proctor's travel journal dated a month later noted that he encountered Frances somewhere during his travels. However, he did nothing to inform the Slocum family.

Before Ruth Slocum died, twenty-eight years after the disappearance of Frances, she asked her children to continue to look for their lost sister after her death. Several of the Slocum boys who had become businessmen made inquiries about Frances when they traded with indigenous groups—but to no avail.

Half a century and several hundred miles from the time and place of Frances's kidnapping, on the banks of the Mississinewa River near where it spills into the waters of the Wabash, a trader and interpreter named James T. Miller suggested to his companion, Indian agent and merchant Colonel George Washington Ewing, that they seek lodging for the night at the home of a white woman living among the Miami Indians. Ewing had not previously met her. That night two women served dinner, and Ewing talked with one of their husbands; however, it was an elderly woman also at the table who most interested him. He made polite conversation with her in the language of the Miami and was surprised when she signaled that she wished to speak with him after the others fell asleep.

The story that Ewing heard was remarkable. The old woman told him that she was a white woman who had been taken from her family by Indians. Her memories were distant and few, but in six decades she had not forgotten her name, or the image of her father in his broad-brimmed hat, or the family's big house by the Susquehanna River. She also remembered small details about her siblings. Her Miami name was Maconaquah, the old woman revealed, but she had been born to a white family as Frances Slocum.

Frances, her face rough and creased from years of living and working outdoors, was not unhappy about her life. An older Indian couple whose own child had died had adopted her when she'd arrived at their camp with Indian raiders. She'd had a happy childhood, moving often with her new family and community to Pennsylvania, Ohio, and Michigan, near the Niagara in Canada, and to Fort Wayne, Indiana. Her Miami husband, Shepoconah, had become war chief at the Osage Village, but when he later lost his hearing, he gave up his position and moved his family 4 miles up the river to a site then known as "the Deaf Man's Village." Her marriage had produced four children, though two sons had died, and she now had three grandchildren.

Frances asked Ewing not to tell anyone about her identity until after her death, because she feared being taken away again—this time from her Miami family. But she wanted to share her story with someone before she died.

The tale was too extraordinary for Ewing to keep secret; he told his mother, who advised him to try to contact the old woman's relatives. The story almost ends there. Ewing wrote down what Slocum had told him and mailed it to Lancaster, Pennsylvania, asking that the letter be delivered to anyone with the surname of Slocum. Postmaster Mary Dickinson thought it was a strange piece of mail and put it away. The story was rediscovered two years later when a new postmaster found the lost message and took it to the local newspaper, the *Lancaster Intelligencer.*

The letter was published, and a friend sent a copy of the article to Joseph Slocum, a younger brother of Frances. Though it had been almost sixty years since the kidnapping, the incident had certainly not been forgotten. Jonathan Slocum, Joseph's son, wrote to George Washington Ewing and received a reply in three weeks. Ewing was still in touch with the woman known as Maconaquah. He informed the Slocums that the old woman was healthier than when he had first met her but was uncertain how much longer she would live.

Joseph Slocum contacted his other living siblings who were elsewhere in Ohio—brother Isaac and sister Mary Towne. Could Maconaquah be the sibling they had missed all these years? Joseph traveled to Ohio and the three, all in their sixties, set out for the Miami Indian village near present-day Peru, Indiana.

Upon their arrival, Mary rested while the brothers explored the town and contacted merchant James Miller, who left two Miami women tending his store while he met the Slocums at their hotel. When Miller met Joseph and Isaac Slocum, he immediately connected them to Frances, seeing a strong family resemblance. According to Miller, the two Indians he had entrusted with the store were the daughters of Frances Slocum, whom he of course knew as Maconaquah. Miller told Frances's daughters the identity of the town visitors, and the women were immediately afraid. Would these men take their mother? Miller assured them that the Slocums wanted only to be reunited with their lost sister. Miller took the Slocum brothers to the village to see Frances. After sixty years, Frances no longer spoke English and was skeptical that the men were her brothers; other white people had previously tried to claim they were her long-lost family. But Joseph and Isaac told Frances that they recognized her by her missing fingertip. Soon Frances warmed to the men, inviting them into her home. The evening hours found them sitting on a bench in the comfortable log cabin, communicating as best they could; Miller found them still there in the morning.

Through an interpreter, most likely James Miller, Frances described her life among the Delaware and the Miami people. She had distant memories of her abduction, though she did not like to talk about the incident. She remembered other children who were taken from neighboring farms in Pennsylvania; two of them, she recalled with sadness, had been killed because they had cried constantly. Eventually, Frances learned the language of her captors and was given the Delaware name Weletawash.

The Slocums wanted their sister to return east with them for a visit with extended family, but Frances was reluctant. She had told her husband before he died that she would not leave her Indian family and friends. She wouldn't know how to behave, she told her brothers, if she wasn't among the Miami:

I am an old tree. I cannot move about; I was a young sapling when they took me away. It is all gone past. I am afraid I should die and never come back. I am happy here. I shall die here and lie in that graveyard, and they will raise the pole at my grave, with the white flag on it, and the Great Spirit will know where to find me.

Frances did travel to the hotel in Peru, Indiana, where her sister Mary waited. Her daughters and son-in-law accompanied Frances, bringing deer meat as a gift for the Slocums. The first visit was brief; Mary was emotional and Frances was cool toward the Slocums. But the next day, Frances and her children returned, and they stayed for three days—talking, walking, and eating together. Frances did not want to talk very much about her capture, but the Slocums related their long search for her. After the reunion, they all returned to their homes.

Two years later, Joseph Slocum and his daughters Hannah and Harriet returned to the Peru area—a twenty-three day trip from

Pennsylvania—and the woman they knew as Aunt Frances, along with her daughters, gladly welcomed them. Frances hosted them in her log cabin, which stood on 640 acres of land granted to her daughters as part of a government agreement. The family had hogs, cattle, geese, and chickens.

One of Joseph's daughters kept a diary of the trip, writing about Frances:

> She is of small stature, not very much bent, had her hair clubbed behind in calico, tied with worsted ferret; her hair is somewhat gray; her eyes a bright chestnut, clear and sprightly for one of her age; her face is very much wrinkled and weatherbeaten. She has a scar on her left cheek received at an Indian dance; her skin is not as dark as you would expect from her age and constant exposure; her teeth are remarkably good. Her dress was a blue calico short gown, a white Mackinaw blanket, somewhat soiled by constant wear; a fold of blue broadcloth lapped around her; red cloth leggins and buckskin moccasins. The interior of her hut seemed well supplied with all the necessaries, if not with luxuries.

Apparently, Frances had taught her daughters something of the way in which white families prepared dinner. Her niece wrote in her journal:

> They spread the table with a white cotton cloth, and wiped the dishes, as they took them from the cupboard, with a clean cloth. They prepared an excellent dinner of fried venison, potatoes, shortcake, and coffee. Their cups and saucers were small, and they put three or four tablespoonfuls of maple sugar in a cup. The eldest daughter waited on the table, while her mother sat at the table and ate with her white relations. After dinner they washed the dishes, and replaced them upon the shelves, and then swept the floor.

One daughter's name was Kekenokeshwa, meaning "cut finger," because she was the eldest daughter of Maconaquah (who was known to have part of her finger missing); her English name was Nancy Brouillette. At the time of the reunion, she was thirty-six years old.

The younger daughter's name was Ozahshinquah, meaning "yellow leaf," and her English name was Jane. She was then around twenty-four years old and had been married three times, to Indians who were not good husbands. She had three daughters, whose names in English meant "Corn Tassel," "Blue Corn," and "Young Panther." They were later known as Eliza, Frances, and Elizabeth.

George Slocum, the son of Frances's brother Isaac, visited Frances and her daughters in 1845. They all got along so well that Frances asked him to come and live with them; she had asked the same of Joseph Slocum five years before, but he had felt he was too old to move from Pennsylvania. The following year, George brought his wife and two young daughters from Bellevue, Ohio, to live near Frances and her Miami family. He would come to hear much more about her life, including information about her marriages. She told him:

My father was a Delaware and thought I should marry a Delaware. This Indian came and wanted me to be his wife. He looked all right, but my father was not sure that he would do. So he said, "Do you love this squaw?" "Yes I do," said he. "Then take her and be good to her," my father said. So I went with him back to his wigwam and tried to be a good wife, but he was mean to me. So I went back to my father, for I had a good home there. Then my Delaware husband came and promised me he would be very good to me and I went with him again. But he was still mean and I would not stay with him any longer. I went back to my Indian parents and stayed. He came once more but my father drove him away. I never saw him again. He must have gone into battle and been killed.

Tensions between white settlers and native groups in the region had been escalating as Frances, known as Weletawash by the Delaware, was growing into womanhood. She felt the tension of being a white woman among the Indians, but they continued to accept her. After a particularly difficult conflict between Indian groups and an army general, Frances's adopted family stayed near Kekionga, which the white people called Fort Wayne, Indiana. Then they were on the move again, back east to Ohio. It was there that she met Shepoconah, a Miami Indian chief.

One day when my parents and I were going down the river we came upon a place where there had been much fighting and many were dead. We saw one young man who was dressed like a chief. He was wounded badly. We wanted to help him and did what we could to heal his wounds. He stayed with us until he was well. During this time he and I spent many hours together. He was of the Miamis and my Indian parents were of the Delawares. I learned much about his people. He told me how great they had been. I came to love him but was slow to tell my parents. They, too, thought much of him. He had brought us much food from Fort Wayne in the winter time. When he felt he must return to his people my Indian father told him that he would give me to him for his wife. This pleased Shepoconah very much, for that was his name. And so we were married according to Indian fashion. Not much was said or done about it. This agreement was made between Shepoconah and my parents and we were married.

Frances and Shepoconah went back to Fort Wayne to live. When her parents died, the Miami Indians became her people. Though the Delawares had called her Weletawash, the Miamis named her Maconaquah, because she was a "strong little bear woman" who went hunting with her husband and tamed ponies no one else could handle.

Shepoconah and Maconaquah moved with their first-born daughter to the other side of the Mississinewa River, having found a place to live that offered a strong-running spring. Their home became a stopping place for many travelers. Two sons were born, though their lives were short, and another daughter joined the family as well. The family grew corn, squash, and fruits, and raised ponies; they still went hunting, though less frequently, as Shepoconah was growing older and had become deaf. Maconaquah had lived a peaceful, if hardworking, life.

Frances told the Slocums, "The Indians knew I was a white woman. Some of the traders knew that I was, but they did not know where I came from. I was not the only white woman among the Indians, and most of them did not pay much attention to me."

Frances did cross back into the white world—on behalf of her Indian family. In 1840 the Miamis were made to give up their land in northern Indiana and move west; the U.S. government gave the Indian group five years to comply. Frances did not want to move and asked her white brothers for advice. They encouraged her to appeal to Congress as a white woman, not as an Indian. In January 1845 Frances asked the U.S. government for special consideration so she did not have to relocate like the other Miamis, arguing that she and her offspring should be allowed to continue to live on a section of land granted to them in an 1838 treaty. Congressmen from both Indiana and Pennsylvania, the state from which she had been abducted, supported her petition, and the U.S. Congress granted her request.

George Slocum, the nephew who had brought his family to live with Frances near Logansport, Indiana, tried to talk with Frances about Christianity. He would later recall that Frances "believed in a Great Spirit who had given them blessings while they lived and would reward them" in the afterlife. "It was this Good Spirit that caused the maple trees to give sweet water to the Indian for making syrup and sugar. The same spirit caused the corn to grow and bring forth good ears."

In 1847, around six months after George moved to Indiana from Ohio, Frances participated in an all-night dance as part of a thanksgiving celebration. She was seventy-six years old. Afterward, she became ill. She died on March 9, 1847, at her home on the Mississinewa River. Following a Christian burial directed by George, she was buried with a brass kettle and a cream pitcher next to her husband and sons in the Indian cemetery near her home. A pole with a white flag was raised over her grave so "the Great Spirit would know where she was."

Nampeyo

1860–1942

※

Hopi Master Potter

"My daughter, be sure you have your hands. Train your hand so that it feels the pottery. The wall, the thickness of molding, where you are, and especially when you are rubbing your pottery. Make sure your hands are good enough so that you know just how thick your potteries are, where it is thick and where it is thin. And with molding, when you get blind, it is going to show you how you are molding; when you are blind you can still go around it with your feeling. So it won't be too bad, if you can't design. You will be able to just mold it and to rub it. Because you have a feeling of it. You know how the pottery feels."

Nampeyo, which means "snake that does not bite," is one of the most celebrated Native American potters in the world. She is credited for both the revival of ancient Hopi pottery techniques and the resurgence of contemporary Hopi pottery, but she spent the second half of her creative life blind. She lost her eyesight to trachoma, a disease that was brought to the Southwest by white Europeans. Thus, ironically, the same group of people that brought her worldwide acclaim also brought her blindness.

Nampeyo is given credit for the so-called "Sikyatki Revival," which resurrected the ancient Hopi techniques for fashioning pottery. She was influenced by designs from her own Hopi past but also by cultures other than the Hopi, some ancient and some contemporary. In this sense Nampeyo is credited with the birth of contemporary Hopi pottery, now called Hano Polychrome. Without Nampeyo, Hopi pottery may have remained a lost art, buried in the dust of antiquity.

In order to put Nampeyo's contribution into the proper perspective, it's helpful to understand a little bit about what life was like for the Hopis while Nampeyo was creating her pots. Anglo society had decided that they were going to "civilize" the Hopi and other tribal nations. They began a widespread campaign to Anglicize the Pueblo Indians by imposing white culture upon them, against their will. The goal was to turn all Native Americans into English-speaking, tax-paying Christians, without any understanding of or concern for the Hopi's culture, history, or humanity.

When adults proved too resistant, the campaign turned its attention to the children. Pueblo children over the age of six were kidnapped from tribal lands throughout New Mexico and placed into "Indian Schools," sometimes in states as far away as California. They were forced to cut their hair and wear the white man's clothing, which was a disgrace in Hopi culture. And to make matters worse, the increase in American visitors to Pueblo lands brought diseases such as influenza, smallpox, tuberculosis, and the trachoma that caused Nampeyo's blindness. This decimated Pueblo populations. So Nampeyo's commitment to expressing the ancient techniques and traditions of her Hopi heritage was not only a creative statement but a way to keep the heart and soul of her beleaguered culture alive in an environment that was predisposed to its ultimate destruction.

It's also important, when considering the Nampeyo phenomenon, to understand something about the history of Hopi pottery. The heart of Hopi country is located on the tops of three mesas that the European explorers, for the sake of convenience, named First Mesa, Second Mesa, and Third Mesa. Three small villages that still exist occupied the top of First Mesa. The oldest is Walpi on the west, then Sichimovi in the middle, and Hano on the east. The prehistoric Anasazi culture first introduced the art of pottery making to these villages around A.D. 700. The art progressed from a crude gray-ware pinch-pot to more elaborate decorative work around A.D. 1000. The use of colors evolved between the eleventh and the fourteenth centuries.

The fourteenth century was a very important period for ancient Hopi pottery. New clays and firing techniques were discovered, which radically changed the texture of the early pottery, which was originally rough and soft. Suddenly the finish on the pots became much smoother and harder, due to a new kind of slip clay the Hopis had discovered on their land. This resulted in a far superior surface, and elaborate designs painted directly onto the surface of a pot.

Entering the fifteenth century with this new and more refined pottery, the Hopis began experimenting with sophisticated symmetry and design, including the depiction of life forms and stories on the pots. This movement culminated in the development of Sikyatki Polychrome, which was one of the most significant leaps forward in pottery making of that time.

Sityatki Polychrome uses paint made from a mixture of boiled herbs, ground minerals, or colored clays painted directly onto the pot itself. This mixture resulted in more colorful pottery. Now, rather than just black and white and gray pottery, ancient Hopi potters were producing startling palettes of reds, oranges, yellows, and browns. This style lasted until the early 1700s, at which time the quality of Hopi pottery began suddenly to deteriorate. Before long Hopi pottery and thousands of years of design preeminence had all but disappeared, until the emergence of Nampeyo, who revived the ancient Sikyatki artistry of her ancestors.

Nampeyo was of Hopi-Tewa descent. Her birth date is placed at somewhere around 1860. She was born in Hano, a small Hopi-Tewa village on First Mesa. Her mother was a Tewa woman of

the Corn Clan from Hano, called White Corn, and her father was
a Hopi man from the Snake Clan from nearby Walpi. The Hopi
nation is divided into clans such as the Bear Clan, the Snow Clan,
and the Snake Clan, and each clan is guided by the attributes of
their hallmark, which is rather like a family crest, and the names
of clan members usually reflect their clan. Clan affiliation is also
reflected in the designs used in each clan's pottery and jewelry.
For example, the hallmark of the Snow Clan is a snow cloud,
and the hallmark of the Corn Clan is an ear of corn. These clan
hallmarks are also found in ancient hieroglyphs marking sacred
Hopi territory.

Nampeyo grew up with her mother's Corn Clan family in
Hano. She came from a family of potters, so, as was the Hopi way,
she became a potter herself, learning the traditional designs and
techniques from her mother. Nampeyo was a capable potter and
a fully contributing member of her village by the time she was
fifteen. By the time Nampeyo was nineteen, she was already a
well-recognized potter, and her reputation had reached far beyond
the confines of her village.

The Hopis are a deeply religious people, and Nampeyo's early
life was filled with the richly textured ceremonies and rituals
of Hopi tradition, including colorful kachina dances. Kachina
dancers wore masks that represented the spirit guides and retold,
in movement, the ancient Hopi legends about creation, hunting,
the changing of the seasons, and other fundamental mysteries of
life and nature.

So from the beginning Nampeyo's cultural and physical
landscapes were colorful, and her entire life was profoundly
attached to the contemporary expression of ancient traditions. It's
not surprising, therefore, that Nampeyo was drawn to the Hopi
and Zuni ruins near her home in Hano. There, with her mother,
she made a startling discovery that was to change the course of
her life, as well as the creative lives of generations of potters to

come after her. She rediscovered the fine slip clay that had allowed her ancient Hopi ancestors to create the unique Sityatki pots. Nampeyo also found artifacts and pottery shards from which she relearned the ancient designs and symmetry and gave them new life in the pottery of contemporary Hopi culture.

Nampeyo was described as a small woman who was kind and gracious. She was also very beautiful, so beautiful, in fact, that her first husband left her because he feared that her beauty would make her an unfaithful wife. In 1878, when Nampeyo was twenty, she married the man who was to become her lifelong husband and creative partner. Lesso was the son of a Walpi elder, and after they married, as is Hopi tradition, Lesso came to live with Nampeyo near her mother's home in Hano. There, they had five children: Annie, 1884; William, 1887; Nellie, 1896; Wesley, 1899; and Fannie, 1900. They were together until Lesso died in 1932, more than fifty years later.

Nampeyo worked on her pots both for use in village life and for sale at the trading post that was opened by Thomas Keam on Hopi land in 1875. Nampeyo lived a quiet life with her family in her village of Hano without much national acclaim until the 1880s, when she began to flower as a nationally recognized artist. As is usually the case, her recognition was the result of a combination of her great skill and a little luck. Public attention had suddenly turned with a great deal of enthusiasm toward the art and culture of the Pueblo Indians during this period. Creatively, philosophically, and spiritually, turn-of-the-century Americans looked to the Southwest for healing truths and a simpler life.

In addition, during the winter of 1888, Richard Wetherill discovered the Cliff Palace and other Anasazi dwellings on Mesa Verde, Colorado. Americans received this discovery with a great deal of hoopla. The national curiosity and preoccupation with the Southwest culminated in the 1892 World's Fair, which featured exhibits showcasing ancient and contemporary southwestern

Indian handcrafts, complete with real live Native Americans performing their crafts before the eyes of an amazed public.

While the public spotlight might have been a bit uncomfortable, it did increase the demand for artifacts from the Hopi mesas, including contemporary Hopi pottery, especially pots made by Nampeyo. As a result of this national exposure, the standout quality of Nampeyo's work became the paradigm against which all others were measured.

The new fascination with the Southwest that gripped America also brought many exploratory expeditions to the region. Jesse W. Fewkes, director of the Hemenway Archaeological Expedition, made an expedition to First Mesa in 1891 to explore the abandoned ruins of Sikyatki, the site where Nampeyo collected her shards and learned her craft from the vestiges left by her ancestors. During this first exploratory mission, Fewkes met Nampeyo for the first time.

Fewkes returned in 1895 and spent two months excavating the Sikyatki ruins. He used local Hopi men to do the excavating and uncovered a vast number of Sikyatki pots, many in remarkably good condition. Some historians say that Nampeyo's husband, Lesso, was employed by the Fewkes expedition and that it was as a consequence of his involvement with this excavation that Nampeyo was led to the shards that inspired her work. Other historians are careful to point out, however, that it is hardly likely that it would take an expedition of white men, new to the region, to point out something on Hopi land to a Hopi. Besides, Nampeyo was already a well-established potter working in the Sikyatki tradition a good ten years prior to Fewkes arrival.

In 1884 the U.S. Army conquered Geronimo and ended once and for all the open warfare with southwestern Indian tribes. Buffalo Bill started his Wild West Show in 1880, and even the great outdoorsman Teddy Roosevelt came west in 1884, which made the Southwest even more popular with American tourists than it already had been. This led to a great literary outpouring about the Southwest in pamphlets, books, and brochures. In addition, socialite Mabel Dodge Luhan had begun attracting to New Mexico a great number of notable artists, who spread the fame of the Southwest worldwide. The 1881 completion of the Santa Fe Railroad through Arizona and the eventual opening of Grand Canyon National Park brought even more activity to Hopi land. Most important for tourism, it brought the Fred Harvey Company.

At the turn of the century, the Southwest was becoming popular as a tourist destination, but getting there was far from the comfortable pleasure trip that would draw the numbers of people that the railroad was hoping for. Accommodations along the railway were scarce, and the food was horrible, making the experience a decidedly less-than-luxurious experience. Trains stopped for only a brief half hour in station towns that were not equipped to handle this new influx of visitors, and often people were left hungry or, worse yet, sick from tainted food that they'd either brought along with them or eaten in haste in a local beanery.

To solve this problem, the Santa Fe Railroad hired a man named Fred Harvey to provide first-class food and lodging to Santa Fe Railroad travelers and to make vacations west a pleasant, rather than a punishing, experience. Fred Harvey delivered fine food in a civilized setting for a reasonable price, all within the half-hour window that train stopovers mandated. He also built large and luxurious "Harvey Houses" all along the Santa Fe line, which snaked its way through the Southwest. Once merely wayhouses where passengers could put up for the evening, these houses eventually became destinations in and of themselves, thanks to the unique charm of Harvey hotels.

Fred Harvey was also a very good businessman and an expert at reading trends. He noticed the new American preoccupation with Native American handcrafts, so he took a tip from the World's Fair and featured Native American art and culture in most of his hotels. With the help of architect Mary Colter, Harvey Houses provided a unique window into Native American culture and featured a generous display of Pueblo Indian arts and crafts, complete with demonstrations of these crafts by the artists themselves. Because of her notoriety, Nampeyo and her family were invited to give demonstrations at Fred Harvey's Hopi House at its opening in 1905. In 1910 the Nampeyo family gave demonstrations at the Chicago Exposition in the Coliseum.

No one is exactly sure when Nampeyo stopped making her unique Sityatki-inspired style of pottery. By 1915 this era had clearly come to a close, and some people believe that her failing eyesight prevented her from carrying on in this highly detailed design style. By 1920 Nampeyo was almost completely blind, and her daughters were painting the designs on most of her pottery. Even Lesso became part of the painting team and was apparently quite talented at it. As Nampeyo's granddaughter tells it: "I learned from Nampeyo, and so did my mother, Annie. Everybody painted for her—Nellie, Fannie, and my mother helped her a lot, painted those little fine lines. Her husband, Lesso, he helped, he sure could paint, that old man."

Although many people believed that Nampeyo stopped creating the highly detailed designs of the Sityatki style because her vision declined, Nampeyo's family insists that it wasn't blindness but creative curiosity that inspired Nampeyo to begin experimenting with more tactile and less design-oriented forms.

Nampeyo passed away in 1942, ending an era in Hopi pottery and leaving behind a legacy of craftsmanship and ancient authenticity that prevails to this day. Nampeyo's commitment to resurrecting the ancient techniques of her people was not only a creative vision but one that had a very important social result for the Hopi people and, indeed, all Pueblo Indians. It brought Native American and, in particular, Hopi culture and ancient traditions into Anglo consciousness and forced white society to recognize, for perhaps the first time, the beauty and value of what they were attempting to destroy. In so doing Nampeyo ensured that some aspect of her culture would survive and opened the door to greater understanding and appreciation between Anglo and Native American people.

Neither injustice nor the loss of her eyesight stopped Nampeyo from continuing her craft, nor did it stop her daughters or her granddaughters, who all became potters and many of whom also became blind from the same disease that had taken Nampeyo's vision. But thanks to the skills and innate understanding of the craft, handed down from mother to daughter, the Nampeyo tradition lived on, despite enormous obstacles.

The matriarch of the Nampeyo family would be proud of the fine lineage of potters who have succeeded her, starting with her three daughters—Fannie, Nellie, and Annie—and now extending to her great-grandchildren. The Nampeyo name has become a watermark of excellence in the world of Native American art.

Kick-Is-Om-Lo
1811–1896

Princess Angeline – Seattle's Last Royalty

Coins collected by Seattle schoolchildren paid for this princess's headstone. When she died on May 31, 1896, her friends carved her a casket in the shape of a canoe. The funeral service was held at Our Lady of Good Help Cathedral, which was packed to capacity with an audience of Seattle citizens. A black hearse, drawn by matching dark horses, carried the unique coffin. The noblewoman was buried in the canoe-shaped coffin with a paddle laid across the stern. During the burial, a sprig of cedar was dropped into the grave, and local children tossed flowers atop the mound. Seattle's prominent pioneer families buried the princess in their cemetery, Lakeview Cemetery, on Capital Hill. Her grave is marked with a simple granite boulder bearing the inscription, "Princess Angeline."

Few cities in the late nineteenth century could claim an Indian princess among its citizens. A frequent sight on the streets of Seattle, this princess's crown was a red bandanna tied over wiry gray locks; the staff she carried, a bent, fire-charred, walking stick; her robe, a tattered shawl; her gowns, well-worn, calico skirts topping mismatched water-soaked shoes, if she wore any at all. The royal palace in which she lived and died was a tiny, ramshackle, wood hut on Seattle's waterfront.

Princess Angeline, or "Kick-Is-Om-Lo" in the language of her tribe, is believed to have been born in 1811. She was the daughter of Chief Seattle,[1] chief of the Suquamish, Duwamish, and six allied

---

[1] According to Chief Seattle's son-in-law, William DeShaw, and friend, Doc Maynard, the pronunciation of the chief's name was closest to "Seattle." "Sealth" is a later interpretation.

tribes, and namesake of the city of Seattle. The daughter of Chief Seattle's first wife, Princess Angeline told a newspaper reporter in 1891 that her father was twenty-five when she was born. She outlived three brothers and two sisters born to the chief and his second wife.

The name Angeline was bestowed upon her by her friend, Catherine Maynard, the wife of one of Seattle's more colorful pioneers, David "Doc" Maynard. When the princess was introduced to Mrs. Maynard by her married name, Kick-Is-Om-Lo Dokub Cud, Catherine Maynard replied, "Why you are much too good looking a woman to carry around such a name. I now christen you, Angeline." In her later years, she was commonly referred to as "Old Angeline," or "Princess Angeline," by the people of Seattle.

The Suquamish were one of several coastal tribes living on Puget Sound. Angeline's father, Chief Seattle, was the hereditary chief of the Suquamish Tribe who was later made chief of six allied coastal tribes for his acts of wartime bravery and skill. The people of the tribe, including young Kick-Is-Om-Lo, lived in rectangular houses made from poles, bark, and boards of cedar, with woven mats covering the doorways. The cedar roofs were each constructed with a hole to allow smoke to escape from the fires within the homes. They made clothing from deer and other animal skins which they sometimes adorned with shells and feathers. Capes and hats woven of cedar and reeds repelled the moisture from the area's frequent rain storms.

The Northwest rains nurtured a great variety of plants, wildlife, and sea creatures, giving Chief Seattle's people a wealth of choice in food. The Suquamish and Duwamish found deer, bear, cougar, and small game plentiful in the woods, an abundance of waterfowl and fish in the many freshwater lakes, and salmon and shellfish in and around Puget Sound's salty shores. Women dug for clams from the beaches and roots in the meadows and picked several types of berries. The men of these coastal tribes were known for their skill in carving cedar canoes, and the women for their weaving skills in creating baskets and clothing.

Kick-Is-Om-Lo witnessed the coming of the first white settlers to the area, beginning with the Hudson's Bay Company and settlers at Fort Nisqually near Tacoma. She and her father befriended and aided the first settlers to land on Elliott Bay. By some accounts, it was Chief Seattle who recommended to the Denny party, the first white settlers to the area, that they would have better shelter if they resided at the site of the present-day Seattle, rather than on Alki Point where they first landed. Both Chief Seattle and Princess Angeline were converted to Christianity by the early settlers.

The princess and her people showed the pioneers the bounties of the environment. On such an occasion, Angeline and her daughters took several pioneer women with them in their canoe to find the succulent blackberries growing at the water's edge. The party left the canoe tied to a rock on the shore during a low tide and ventured inland in search of berries. The women, engrossed in their harvesting of blackberries, did not notice that the tide was coming in rapidly. When they tried to return to their boat, they found it to be high tide, and their canoe was now quite a distance from the shoreline. Not only was the canoe beyond their reach, but the rock tied to the canoe was now an anchor under several feet of water.

Without saying a word, one of Angeline's daughters dashed onto the beach, removed her clothing and moccasins, and dove into the frigid waters of Puget Sound. She swam to the canoe, dove down, and retrieved the line anchoring the craft. Once the line was above water, Princess Angeline's daughter climbed into the canoe and paddled to shore to retrieve her mother and the other women.

According to legend, Princess Angeline had heard from other Indians that an attack was planned on the early pioneers' village, but she did not know exactly when this was to occur. When she heard the warriors in the woods surrounding the town signal to each other using "hooting" type sounds, Angeline knew the attackers were near and hastened to tell her settler friends. Other accounts say she paddled her canoe across Puget Sound in a raging storm to warn her friend Henry Yesler and the other settlers that the Northwest's inland and coastal tribes would soon attack. The 1856 Battle of Seattle followed.

The warship *Decatur* sailed into Elliott Bay to protect the city. Its captain, having been informed of the plan for attack, fired *Decatur*'s guns into the forest at the edge of Seattle. The shot was answered by yells and gunfire from the warriors. Settlers who heard the guns rushed to the blockade at the foot of Cherry Street. The fighting ensued. Two settlers were killed, yet the number of Indian casualties was never known. According to the legend, Angeline regretted warning the settlers of the attack after her Indian lover was killed during the shelling. Two houses within the city were burned, one after looting by the warriors, the other ignited when fired upon by the ship's guns. When the fighting slowed, women and children were moved from the blockade to the ship. By morning, the warring party had gone.

Whether or not Angeline paddled her canoe across the sound to warn the settlers is disputed, but the legend contributed to her celebrity status. Yesler later denied that Angeline was responsible for warning of the attack, instead giving credit to a native man who was nicknamed Salmon Bay Curley. Mrs. Maynard maintained the legend was true.

It is, however, undisputed that in March of 1892, Angeline marched into the Seattle Police headquarters to warn the citizens of Seattle that the world would end in June of that year. Wah-Kee-Wee-Kum, the spirit of a great medicine man, had visited her to impart this knowledge and Angeline, in her typical magnanimous spirit, decided to share this information with her white neighbors. City officials, to whom she reported her prophesy, made light of the warning by asking her if she could predict which city employee their cantankerous mayor would fire next.

As a young woman, Princess Angeline was married to Dokub Cud, a half-Cowichan chief of the Skagit Tribe. By midcentury, Dokub Cud died, leaving Angeline a widow. Angeline gave birth to two daughters, Betsy and Mary, both of whom married white settlers. Mary wed William De Shaw, a respected, local merchant. De Shaw accumulated wealth through a variety of enterprises, including smoking salmon for market. No doubt, Mary enjoyed a better life than that of her sister.

Daughter Betsy suffered much abuse from her mean-spirited, alcoholic husband. As a way of escaping this abuse, Betsy hanged herself with a red bandanna tied to a beam in a shed on Commercial Street. Angeline discovered the body of her daughter hanging from the rafters of her cabin, her baby boy wailing in a basket at her feet. Betsy's infant son, Joe Foster, went to live with his grandmother. Angeline raised the child with love, but he took after his father. He was always in trouble, frequently in jail, and he caused her much grief.

It was a common sight to see Angeline sitting on city sidewalks, hawking her wares. Angeline sold clams and baskets on the streets of Seattle and moccasins to people arriving in ships at the waterfront piers. She also did wash for many of Seattle's founding families. These tasks would have afforded her a comfortable living had she not spent most of her earnings posting bail and paying fines for her wayward grandson, Joe Foster.

A favorite subject for visiting journalists and photographers, her fame spread, and Angeline was invited to tour the world with George Francis Train in his quest to promote the Northwest. After a purse of several thousand dollars was raised for her fare, a delegation of local citizens visited her to propose the promotional trip. The delegates were dumbfounded when the princess flatly refused their offer. She explained that her revered father (whom she called "Hy-as Ty-ee," or "Great Father") would be so angry at her for running off with a crazy man that he would turn in his grave.

Carnival operators and dime museum owners also offered
Angeline money to travel with them as she became known
nationwide. Aiding in the spread of her fame were souvenir
spoons and dishes bearing her likeness which were sold to tourists.
Though she would not hear of leaving her home, and she refused
to be displayed in such a manner, Angeline did enjoy being shown
off as a local celebrity and became the most photographed face in
the city, although no photos of her as a young woman exist. Never
wishing to leave Seattle, she expressed a desire to be buried with
her pioneer friends, or "tillicums."

The farthest Angeline ever traveled from home was on a trip
to Olympia with her famous father to protest the naming of the
city after the great chief. The law among the Duwamish and
Suquamish tribes was that when a person died, his name was not
to be spoken aloud for five years. If the deceased was a chief, the
silence was observed for ten years. When the name was passed on to
a son, this law became moot. Should the tradition not be observed,
the dead chief would roll over in his grave every time his name
was spoken. Chief Seattle was horrified when the founding fathers
proposed naming the city after him. Wishing to avoid a terrible
fate, he took his entire family to Olympia to ask the governor to
intercede. The governor was eventually able to convince Seattle
that his last sleep would be peaceful. Reportedly, the chief was
ultimately pleased with the honor.

On May 6, 1891, President Benjamin Harrison arrived for an
official visit to Seattle, and the people of Seattle did their best
to honor the occasion despite a torrential rainstorm. Angeline
was presented to the President as the daughter of Chief Seattle
and the head of her nation. Although she understood English,
she always spoke in the Chinook jargon (the common language
of traders and the various Northwest tribes). The princess
shook President Harrison's hand, curtsied, and greeted him,
"Kla-how-ya."

"Hello, how are you?" the usually staid head of state responded politely in turn.

As she aged, Angeline became quick tempered and sensitive to insult. Often teased by the local boys, she carried rocks in her skirt pockets which she tossed with great accuracy to ward off such attacks.

One pioneer woman recounted her experience with the wrath of Angeline. After moving to Seattle in 1880, she and Angeline had become friends. Angeline frequently visited her home, always bringing freshly dug clams with her. On one occasion, the young mother was strolling the city streets with her small daughter and pushing her baby in a buggy. Not seeing Angeline sitting on the sidewalk, she rolled the wheels of the stroller over Angeline's toes. Angeline leapt to her feet and began to curse profusely at the startled woman. No apology would do, and from that day on whenever the woman encountered Angeline on the streets of Seattle, Angeline would point to her foot and proceed to swear at the embarrassed lady. The most hurtful thing for the pioneer woman was that Angeline never again returned to her home for a friendly visit.

The early Seattleites owed their lives to Chief Seattle and his people. Perhaps they looked after Angeline in her later years because they felt responsible for her fate. Although this woman of noble birth lived her later years emersed in the white man's world, she always seemed out of place in the bustling "modern" city.

Angeline's needs were simple; she never took anything she did not need. If she had extras, she "potlatched" the item, or gave it away in the Indian manner. After she could no longer dig clams, gather firewood, or work for a living, the charity of the early settlers kept her going. When she needed shelter, Henry Yesler donated lumber from his mill to build the princess a waterfront cabin.

At the onset of her illness, her well-meaning, pioneer friends placed her in Seattle General Hospital. Angeline railed against being taken from her simple home and placed in what she deemed a jail. After much wailing and thrashing about, she was returned to her cabin, where she died on May 31, 1896. A black crêpe drape was hung across her doorway on the day of her death.

When she died at the estimated age of eighty-five, the population of Seattle was more than 60,000. Angeline had witnessed the growth of her small Indian village into a log-cabin settlement; and, by the end of her life, the land over which her father once reigned had become a thriving metropolis.

Isabel Friedlander Arcasa
1889–1992

❦

Custodian of Colville Heritage

Hunting deep in the forests of the Cascade Mountains, the band of natives froze in their tracks and stared in amazement. There in the clearing, standing just where they had last seen him exactly one year ago, was their fellow Wenatchee tribesman. He stood with his arms folded over his chest, staring straight ahead as if in a trance. A strange dog was by his side. The dog barked once at the approaching hunters, then sat silently next to his master.

Eventually, they were able to rouse the man from his trance-like state. He told of being captured and held prisoner by a band of Sasquatches—the mammoth, hair-covered creature, also known as Bigfoot. For one year he had lived in their cedar bark shelters and shared their food as an equal. The Sasquatches were great hunters who were able to scamper up steep inclines and shoulder heavy loads of game. They hunted by night, leaving their crude bark houses and returning early in the morning with game. The Indian learned the signals with which the band communicated. Their sounds were much like the hooting of owls. After he lived with them for one year, the Sasquatches brought the man back to the exact spot where they found him. They hypnotized him and left a dog with him for protection.

That Wenatchee tribesman was Isabel Friedlander Arcasa's great-great-great grandfather. "The reports of the big foot prints are nothing new. We Indian people know all about those dark people even if we have never seen them." This story has been passed down through Isabel's family for generations, and is regarded not as legend, but as family heritage.

Isabel Friedlander Arcasa was well known and respected for her great storytelling ability. Through Isabel, tribal lore and traditions going back thousands of years were kept and passed on to today's generations. For all of her 102 years, Isabel remained sharp witted and maintained a wonderful sense of humor. She loved to share her tales with everyone around her.

In the Indian way, Isabel had many names throughout her long life. The first girl born after five boys, her mother called her "Kee-arna," meaning "little girl." When her brother Bill could not pronounce the word, the family shortened her name to "Wana." As she grew older her mother gave her the name of her Skokomish great-grandmother, "Ti-men-wy."

Then while visiting her grandmother, she met an old woman of the San Poil Tribe to whom her grandmother had given shelter. One day the feeble old woman called young Isabel to her bedside and whispered to her, "I do not have long to live. When I die, I want you to carry on my name, 'K-new-teet-kw.' I want you to have my things and keep my name alive." The old woman then handed Isabel a long string of copper, Hudson's Bay beads, a necklace of blue and white glass beads, and two ceremonial pipes. Finally, most Indians at this time had English names as well as Indian names. She was baptized "Isabel" by a Catholic priest.

The Wenatchee, Chelan, and Entiat tribes accepted Catholicism around 1870 when Father Urban Grassi founded his mission in the area. Isabel's grandfather, Chief Tsil-hoo-sas-ket of the "En-tee-etkw," or Entiat Tribe, was baptized Catholic but balked when Father Grassi told him he must give up one of his two wives. Chief Tsil-hoo-sas-ket was married to Isabel's grandmother Sts-kul-nas-ket, as well as to her younger sister, La-mee-iy. Being a good Catholic, Sts-kul-nas-ket, christened Suzanne, told her husband that she would leave him so that he could marry La-mee-iy, or

Rosalie, in the Catholic Church. Suzanne's children were grown, but Rosalie still had a small baby. Suzanne left her husband and returned to the camp of her father. Rosalie and Chief Tsil-hoo-sas-ket were then married in the church. Not satisfied with this arrangement, the chief rode into Suzanne's camp one day and asked her to return with him. She refused, but he would not leave. That night, saying she was going to the river to take a bath, Suzanne left camp. She escaped by paddling her canoe and swimming her horse across the Columbia River. Suzanne hid from Tsil-hoo-sas-ket until, after several days waiting, he gave up and returned to his village of Entiat. Chief Tsil-hoo-sas-ket and his brother, Wapato John, became staunch Catholics, building churches for their people in Entiat and Manson, near Lake Chelan.

Isabel Friedlander was born on the banks of the Columbia River on November 22, 1889, the year Washington became a state. She was the daughter of an Entiat Indian mother and white Jewish father. Though the mixing of white men and Indian women was not uncommon in the American West, the story Isabel tells of how she became a Friedlander is truly unique and fascinating.

Isabel's mother was Skn-wheulks, later christened Elizabeth. Elizabeth's father was Tsil-hoo-sas-ket, chief of the Entiat Tribe. His father and grandfather, also named Tsil-hoo-sas-ket, had all been chiefs of the Entiat Tribe. His mother was a member of the Skokomish Tribe from western Washington. Elizabaeth's mother, Sts-kul-nas-ket, or Suzanne, was descended from the Wenatchee and San Poil Tribes.[1]

When Elizabeth grew older, Chief Tsil-hoo-sas-ket made arrangements with the Moses Band of the Columbia Tribe for his

[1] In 1872, the U.S. Government established the Colville Reservation, eventually combining eleven separate tribes: the Colville, Arrow Lake, Columbia, Chelan, Entiat, Wenatchee, Okanogan, San Poil, Methow, Nespelem, and Joseph Band of Nez Perce.

daughter to be married to Chief Moses's younger brother, Tser-men-tsoot. In those days, the Indians arranged trades to find brides for their young men. The Moses people gave Elizabeth's father horses and possessions for his daughter.

Tser-men-tsoot was already married to a woman by the name of In-ha-noomt, who later left her husband. Elizabeth had three children by Tser-men-tsoot; only one, a baby named Mary, lived. One fall, when Mary was two years old, all of the Moses Band camped near Vantage, on the Columbia River, for their horse races. During the races, Elizabeth's husband, Tser-men-tsoot, was killed. It was the custom of these tribes that when a woman was widowed, the deceased husband's brother would become her husband. It was then the brother's obligation to provide for and watch out for the widow and her children.

All of the band went into mourning, and they buried Tser-men-tsoot. Chief Moses, Tser-men-tsoot's older brother, attended the funeral, but after it was over, he told his people it was time to move on. Chief Moses took all of Tser-men-tsoot's many racehorses and valuable belongings away with him. He even took with him a small pony belonging to the baby, Mary. In his wake, Elizabeth was left stranded with her baby and a few in-laws. Without possessions, Elizabeth stayed at the Vantage camp throughout the harsh winter.

In the spring, an old woman asked Elizabeth if she wanted to return to her people. The desperate Elizabeth eagerly accepted the invitation. The elder woman gave the young widow a riding horse and a pack horse so she could return with baby Mary to her father's camp.

Elizabeth wasted no time traveling to her family's village in Entiat. Later that fall, Elizabeth went with her aunt and Uncle Louie to a little trading post across from the mouth of Lake Chelan. A soldier from Camp Chelan was running the trading post. His name was Herman Friedlander, but the Indian people called him "Peranik."

Elizabeth was a handsome woman, and Herman Friedlander could not take his eyes off her. Peranik questioned Uncle Louie about Elizabeth. "Gee, that's sure a beautiful woman! I sure would like to have her for my wife." Uncle Louie replied, "Oh, you can't have anything to do with her; she is just a widow." The soldier was undaunted, "Well, you tell her if she ever wants to get married, that I'd sure like to marry her!" Uncle Louie told Elizabeth of the conversation during the trip home.

While Elizabeth and her aunt and uncle were in Chelan, Chief Moses arrived at the camp of Elizabeth's father, Chief Tsil-hoo-sas-ket. Moses exclaimed, "I am going to come and get my little niece and my brother's wife to marry now. I will bring you some horses, saddles, blankets and valuables." Tsil-hoo-sas-ket agreed, following the Indian custom that a man could marry his deceased brother's wife and eager to obtain horses, saddles, and blankets from the other chief.

Upon returning from the trip to the trading post in Chelan, Elizabeth's father told her of Moses's visit. Elizabeth was furious, when she heard of Moses's intentions. She was angry at the way Chief Moses had left her all alone with no horses in Vantage. Elizabeth declared, "I would never marry Moses, even if he was the last man on earth! Does he not realize what he has done to us? What he did to his little niece, when he took everything away from us and left us stranded? If it had not been for some good people, we would have been lost."

Elizabeth told her Uncle Louie, "You just take me back to the Chelan Trading Post tomorrow. I will marry that white man!"

The next day Elizabeth and her Uncle Louie traveled to the trading post in Chelan. Elizabeth spoke no English, so her Uncle Louie explained to Herman Friedlander the situation with Chief Moses. "She says she doesn't want him. She says she'll marry you." Herman Friedlander found the nearest justice of the peace and they were married that day!

A few weeks later, Chief Moses rode into Entiat with his string of horses for Chief Tsil-hoo-sas-ket. Elizabeth's father had to decline the horses, telling Moses, "I'm sorry, but your sister-in-law went to Chelan and got married to that white man, Peranik." With that, Moses became enraged. "I am going over there, and I'm going to kill him for taking my wife." So he left his string of horses right there and rode to the trading post.

In Chelan, Elizabeth and Herman were living in a square, canvas soldier's tent. The couple heard a rider approaching at a frantic pace. Herman took his gun outside to greet the rider. As he rode up, Moses hollered, "You took my wife! I am going to kill you! She is my wife!"

"No!" exclaimed Herman, "She is my wife. We were married by a justice of the peace."

Moses insisted, "She was my brother's wife, so now she is my wife. I am going to kill you!"

"Well, go ahead and shoot," said Herman as he leveled his rifle directly at the chief.

When Moses saw the rifle pointing at him, he became silent. He turned his horse around and rode off, never to return.

For the first few years of their marriage, Herman and Elizabeth lived in Chelan where he ran a small store and saloon. Herman Friedlander had been born into a wealthy East Coast family, but his father disowned him for marrying a full-blooded Indian woman. Herman's two brothers, Frank and Sam, also came west and founded jewelry stores bearing their name in Seattle and Portland.

From Chelan, Elizabeth, Herman, and Mary moved up the Columbia River to Lincoln, across from the San Poil Tribes's Village of White Stone, where Elizabeth's family lived. Herman bought a farm with an orchard and ran a store in the nearby town of Wilbur. The Friedlanders lived happily and had seven children together: Louie, Sam, Herman, Bill, Isabel, Millie, and Ed. Elizabeth and Herman never spoke the same language, though they probably both spoke some Chinook jargon. The children spoke the languages of both their parents and they grew up paddling canoes back and forth across the river between their farm and the San Poil village of cabins and tepees, where their grandparents lived.

Herman Friedlander died of a heart ailment when Isabel was only eight years old. Elizabeth eventually sold the farm and store and moved to the White Stone Village with her parents. In those days, many generations lived under one roof so houses were full with beds covering every inch of the floor at night. Elizabeth later married an Indian man, Charlie Comedale, who died within a year of their marriage.

At the age of six, Isabel and her brothers were sent to the Indian boarding school in Tonasket. When the school burned, Isabel was transferred to the mission schools in Omak and Ward. At just seven years old, Isabel took her five-year-old sister, Millie, and ran away from school. Her older brother found the sisters and returned them to the school.

The nuns at the mission schools punished the students when they spoke their native Indian languages. After three years of such treatment, the children could barely understand their aunt when she came to take them home. Once home, they regained fluency in their language quickly. Isabel was then sent to school at Fort Spokane where she remained until she was fifteen.

Arranged marriages were still common among Indian people when Isabel was a young girl. Trading horses and cattle with Isabel's stepfather, a man arranged a marriage between fourteen-year-old Isabel and his son. In spite of her mother and aunt's objections and Isabel's cries, the two youngsters were married by a priest. Upon leaving the church, other children teased Isabel and in anger, she threw her wedding ring into the dirt and ran off. The two never lived together as husband and wife.

When she was eighteen, a man from the Umatilla Tribe named Julius LaCourse asked for her hand. Worried about the validity of her first marriage, Isabel consulted a priest who told her he would have to write a letter to the Pope. A month later, the papal letter arrived and dictated, "This woman is not an animal that can be sold. Her parents cannot accept presents and sell her like an animal. Her first marriage is annulled."

Isabel married Julius LaCourse and they moved to Pendleton, Oregon. Five children were born to them: Herman, Melvin, Maybelle, and two babies that died in infancy. The family moved where there was work—living in Pendleton, Nespelem, Quincy, Taholah, and Seattle. All of the family worked as migrants, following the crops during the summer, then settling in so the children could attend school in the fall. When her daughter, Maybelle, became sick with tuberculosis, Isabel took a job at Cushman Hospital in Tacoma to be near her.

Julius was a talented musician. He played violin, with Isabel who played piano, in a dance band that played for grange hall dances on weekends. With their children lying beside them on a mattress they brought from home, Isabel and Julius played late into the night.

After twenty-three years of marriage, Isabel gave Julius an ultimatum—he had to quit drinking or she would leave him. When he refused to give up the bottle, she left, divorcing him, although she remained a practicing Catholic. She met her next husband, Marcel Arcasa, while she was working at a youth camp on the Colville Reservation.

Isabel knew a lifetime of hard labor, working as both a cook and waitress. She plowed fields, worked farms, nursed the sick, and acted as a midwife. As a midwife she brought twenty-eight babies into the world and saved the lives of two of their mothers.

Besides raising her own three children, she raised five orphans. In her eighties, she took in her three-year-old great-grandson when his parents were killed.

For her tireless work on behalf of the church and community, Isabel received a papal blessing and Pro Ecclesia Et Pontifice award from the Catholic Church. Always looking after those in need, she canned fruits and vegetables to give hungry families to tide them over through the winters. Young priests were taken under her wing as soon as they moved to her town of Nespelem.

In 1989, Isabel celebrated her 100th birthday, the same year the state of Washington celebrated its centennial. The Eastern Washington Historical Society awarded her the honor of "Pioneer of the Year." Along with other centenarians, Isabel was invited to an honorary dinner at the State Capitol. Seated next to Governor Booth Gardner, she entertained him with stories of capturing and racing wild horses in her youth. She was not afraid of the wild ones, she explained, it was the tame horses that always bucked her off!

Though most of her prized possessions (including woven baskets, beaded bags, moccasins, dresses, and two tepees) burned in a house fire, Isabel was rich in family and friends. She had grandchildren, great-grandchildren, and even great-great-grandchildren at the time of her death, not to mention her countless nieces and nephews. Many accomplished women can be counted among Isabel's descendants, including her niece Lucy Friedlander Covington, who was a Colville tribal councilwoman of great renown. A tireless champion of Indian rights, it has been said that without Lucy's efforts, the Colville Reservation might have been lost to the Termination Bills of the 1960s. Isabel's granddaughter, Anita Dupris, is an attorney, who has worked for years as a judge in the Colville tribal court system.

Isabel passed away on April 24, 1992, at the age of 102. As a legacy to her people, Isabel left behind many stories and legends in the form of manuscripts and tapes of interviews she gave in her twilight years. Always happy to be interviewed, she told her friend, Father Tom Connolly, as he prepared audiotapes of her histories, "I don't care if anyone hears my voice after I'm gone. That's the only way I can haunt you folks!"

Helen P. Clarke

?–1923

❧

Indian Advocate

Malcolm Clarke and his twenty-four-year-old daughter, Helen, were engrossed in a game of backgammon when they heard their dogs announce a visitor. They glanced up, startled. Who would call at their ranch north of Helena, Montana Territory, at nine o'clock in the evening? It must be a Blackfeet Indian, the pair decided. The neighboring Blackfeet, unfettered by the customs of white society, sometimes knocked on the Clarkes' door in the middle of the night.

Father and daughter returned their attention to the game. The arrival of Blackfeet didn't worry them. After all, Malcolm's wife Coth-co-co-na was a Pikuni Blackfeet herself; one of her relatives had probably come to call. But the sounds of hurrying feet and strange voices finally broke Helen's concentration. She put down her dice and bustled to the back of the house to find out who was there.

In the kitchen, Helen's mother and two sisters were greeting a handful of Blackfeet braves, including Ne-tus-che-o, Coth-co-co-na's cousin. The smiling warrior pumped Malcolm's hand and embraced Helen's twenty-year-old brother, Horace. Malcolm showed his hospitality by filling his pipe and passing it to one of the visitors. The men sat in a circle, puffing in turn, while Coth-co-co-na and her aunt, Black Bear, prepared a meal for them.

The Clarkes had no reason to fear their Blackfeet kin, even though relations between the tribe and white settlers had soured in the past month. The trouble had started earlier that summer of 1869 when some residents of Fort Benton had murdered two Blackfeet—an old man and a boy—in retaliation for the deaths of two white cattle herders who, it turned out, had been killed by Crows. The incident had spawned a rash of horse thefts and murderous attacks on isolated ranches.

Two years earlier, some of Ne-tus-che-o's horses had been stolen by white men while he was a guest at the Clarke ranch. Horses were among the most prized possessions of the nomadic Blackfeet, and the outraged warrior responded by abducting some of the Clarkes' herd. When Malcolm and Horace went to the Blackfeet village to retrieve their animals, they found Ne-tus-che-o seated on the younger Clarke's favorite mount. Horace lost his temper, called the warrior a dog, and lashed him across the face with his riding whip. Fortunately, Malcolm and some of the tribal elders intervened and kept the confrontation from ending in bloodshed.

Certainly Ne-tus-che-o's behavior on this balmy August evening implied that he'd put the quarrel behind him. In fact, the Blackfeet announced that they had come to return some horses taken from the Clarkes three years earlier by members of a Canadian tribe of Blackfeet, the Bloods. They also wanted to tell Malcolm—or Four Bears, as they called him—that he was welcome to come and trade with their village.

As Horace prepared to go identify the horses the visitors had brought with them, Helen noticed that the warriors seemed agitated. One of them paced the room, fingering the family's belongings. But the behavior didn't trouble her. When Horace couldn't find his gun belt to take with him, she told him "What is the use of a firearm? You are with a friend." Horace left the house unarmed in the company of one of the Blackfeet men.

Meanwhile, Malcolm and the others continued to chat. Helen noticed that Ne-tus-che-o kept his hands hidden in his blanket, and she wondered briefly if he were cold. Then he and her father rose to go outside for a private conversation. The door had scarcely closed behind them when a gunshot cracked the peace. Helen later described the pandemonium that followed.

*I was seized with a sudden faintness. . . . I went to [the door];
and imagine my terror at the confusion that passed before my
vision. Horses and Indians running backwards and forwards
with aimless purpose. Not one, not two, but hundreds it seemed to
me, and for a moment I thought the demons in hell had broken
loose. . . .*

*Just then I heard my brother's voice. He was about a
hundred yards away. Clear and distinct his words fell on my
ears: "Father, I am shot." [But] father had already received his
final blow. The shot that was fired at the moment Horace's words
came to me was the fatal one. . . . [M]y heart's premonitions had
already told me that he had passed into the shadowy river, and
was far on his way into the unknown land. I ran out to assist
Horace; even then I could not, would not, believe it was Blackfeet
who had done this deed. . . . I said to Horace: "It was not that
Indian who went with you that shot you . . . ! It was a Pend
d'Oreille, was it not?" "No, Nellie, it was that one," he replied. . . .
It was so hard to believe that they, the Pi-kan-ies, our blood, had
proved so unworthy of the trust we had reposed in them.*

Horace had been shot in the face and left for dead. Although he
was bleeding heavily, he had managed to crawl close enough to
the house to call for help. Along with her great aunt, Black Bear,
Helen lugged him inside and laid him in a rude bed she made on
the floor of her father's room. He was faint with the loss of blood,
and she wondered how she could ever staunch the flow. Then
she thought of an old Blackfeet remedy. Frantically, she grabbed
her father's tobacco pouch, wet the contents, and applied them to
Horace's gaping wound.

Meanwhile, Helen's eleven-year-old sister, Isabel, had discovered
their father. He lay within a few feet of the house with a bullet
through his heart and the gash of an ax across his brow. Helen, her
mother, and Black Bear managed to haul him into the house and lay

him in the middle of the main room. Then, Black Bear went looking for the attackers, to try to talk them out of more bloody vengeance.

Helen knew the Blackfeet warriors would likely be back. The front door had no lock, so Coth-co-co-na dragged a heavy bedstead in front of it. As she passed a window, a bullet whizzed by her head. The family decided to barricade itself in Helen's room, which was toward the back of the house. Though they knew it was pointless, they nailed the door shut. Then they huddled together, listening for sounds of the men's return. For an hour, all was quiet.

Finally, the terrorized family heard the tramping of horses. Through the bedroom door, they could hear the intruders enter the house and begin ransacking the family's belongings. They cringed at the sounds of shattering glass and splintering wood. Then came the most frightening sounds of all. The familiar Blackfeet voices began to argue over what to do with the family. Helen later recalled their horrifying debate.

We kept so still—so still. Death seemed awaiting us. One or two of them were in favor of taking us prisoners; others in favor of killing us. My mother was to die any way. Ne-tus-che-o then said: "Horace is alive, he is somewhere in the house, and he is in that room," pointing to mine. He had his hand on the door, about to enter. The door creaked and groaned. My brother, weak as he was, rose to his feet with hatchet raised, determined to make a resolute struggle for his mother and his sisters.

But fate—in the form of Helen's great aunt, Black Bear—intervened just in time. The old woman tried to reason with the warriors, claiming that Horace was dead and begging them to take pity. "The man murdered tonight was your best friend," she scolded. "You have committed a deed so dark, so terrible that the trees will whisper it, and before the sun reddens these mountains a hundred horsemen will be here to avenge his death."

The Blackfeet braves faltered. "That which the old woman utters is true," Helen heard one of them say. "Enough blood has been shed. I came not here to make war on women and children."

It was about midnight when the warriors galloped away, driving the Clarkes' cattle before them and venting their rage and frustration by shooting into the herd. The family huddled in the dark until five in the morning, when a hint of daylight revealed no one lurking in the yard. Helen and Isabel hiked three-quarters of a mile to the nearest ranch for help, all the while fearing the warriors would leap at them from the underbrush like hungry wolves. But they made it safely.

That afternoon, a doctor arrived from Helena, twenty-five miles south, and was able to give them encouraging news. Horace would recover fully from his wound. Two days later, on August 19, 1869, the Clarkes buried their patriarch—one of the most prominent men in the region—at the mouth of Little Prickly Pear Canyon.

Unfortunately, the clash between whites and Blackfeet didn't end with Clarke's tragic murder. In response to settlers' demands for reprisal, Major Eugene M. Baker set out from Fort Ellis in January 1870 with orders to find Ne-tus-che-o's band and "strike them hard." On a bitter cold morning, he and his troops attacked an unsuspecting Blackfeet village and slaughtered 173 of its occupants, including fifty-three women and children. But it was the wrong village. This was not Ne-tus-che-o's band. It was that of a peaceable Blackfeet chief. Easterners were outraged, but the Baker Massacre, as the incident became known, largely ended Blackfeet resistance to white invasion of their homeland.

The murder of Malcolm Clarke had a lasting effect on Helen's life. Soon after, she was sent to live with an aunt in Cincinnati, Ohio, but she didn't succumb to bitterness and reject her mother's people. She wisely realized that Malcolm's murder was the act of a few vengeful individuals, not the desire of the Blackfeet nation. Twenty years later, she would return to Montana to help the tribe adjust to the new ways of life imposed on them by the U.S. government.

Helen Clarke was born on October 11 at a fur-trading post at the mouth of the Judith River in what would one day be Fergus County, Montana. In those days, no one bothered to record the birth of a child in the wilderness, so the year in which Helen was born is uncertain. Her death certificate, for which her sister Isabel supplied much of the information, puts it at 1845. Her obituary says 1848, and her tombstone says 1846.

Helen's father, Egbert Malcolm Clarke, was a graduate of West Point, who came to the Northern Rockies in 1841 to work as a clerk for the American Fur Company. A few years later, he married Coth-co-co-na, the daughter of a Pikuni chief. Helen—or Nellie, as her friends and family called her—was the oldest of the couple's four children. Her Blackfeet name, Pio-to-po-waka, has been translated as Bird That Comes Home.

At the age of three, Helen went to live with an aunt in Minneapolis, Minnesota, and attended convent schools there. She returned to Montana to live with her parents sometime in the 1860s, when Malcolm left the fur-trading business and established a horse and cattle ranch on Prickly Pear Creek. After his tragic death, she went back East again, this time to live with another aunt in Cincinnati. She continued her education there and went on to attend a school of drama in New York City.

Helen's striking appearance and deep, vibrant voice helped to launch a brief but impressive theatrical career. She performed in New York, London, Paris, and Berlin, at least once sharing the stage with the famous French actress Sarah Bernhardt. The German Kaiser once commended her portrayal of Shakespeare's Lady Macbeth.

But Helen soon grew disillusioned with acting and was unconvinced of her talent. "I was too much . . . [my]self to become great," she once wrote. "I could not forget that I was Helen Clarke and become the new being of imagination."

So in 1875, Helen returned to Montana and taught school in Fort Benton and Helena. Seven years later, she was elected Lewis and Clark County superintendent of schools, apparently making her the first woman ever to hold elective office in Montana.

Helen never married, although she had plenty of suitors. According to some accounts, she didn't think she could find a man who would neither pity nor patronize her for having mixed blood, and she didn't want a relationship in which she was not an equal.

Yet she never denied her heritage. Once, in fact, she made a point of responding to a newspaper article that claimed she was ashamed of her Blackfeet blood. Indignant, she told the *Montana Daily Record* in Helena,

> *Now, as a matter of fact, I am far from being ashamed of my origin, but, on the other hand am proud of both my father and mother. My father was one of the first settlers of the Northwest. . . . He was one of the old-timers of Fort Benton, and, like many pioneers, married an Indian girl. She was a good woman, a good wife and a loving mother, and why anyone should be ashamed of her is more than I can comprehend.*

Helen got a chance to serve her mother's people in 1891, when the federal Office of Indian Affairs asked her to act as an interpreter and mediator on the Blackfeet reservation in northern Montana. Her job was to help the Blackfeet understand and accept a new law that required each family to choose a plot of land on which to settle and farm. Officials wanted Native Americans to assimilate into white culture, and the Interior Department considered land allotments the best solution to the problem of "civilizing" these native people.

Helen was one of only a few women to help manage the federal allotment program. Because of her success on the Blackfeet reservation, she was transferred to Oklahoma to work with the

Ponca, Oto, Pawnee, and Missouri tribes. She returned to Montana
in 1895 to help the Blackfeet negotiate the sale of the mountainous
western section of their reservation, which would become part of
Glacier National Park.

In 1900 Helen moved to San Francisco, where she taught public-
speaking classes and took French lessons. But the glamour of city
life soon paled, and in 1902, she applied for and got permission to
live on the Blackfeet reservation and become an official member of
the tribe. She went to live with her brother Horace on a cattle ranch
near Midvale (now East Glacier), where she kept a large library and
entertained writers, artists, and musicians from across the nation.
Her door was always open to those who needed her help.

Helen died of pneumonia on March 5, 1923, and is buried in the
shadow of the spectacular, snow-capped peaks of Glacier National
Park. At her burial, a Catholic priest expressed the love and respect
with which she would be remembered.

*Her life was an open book and on its every golden page are
inscribed the good deeds of one who loved her God, her Church,
her people, her country and was faithful to them. . . . She led a life
of unbending integrity, a life of simple virtue, a life of unsullied
honor. She ever carried with her a smiling cheerfulness, an
unswerving devotion, a gentle courtesy. To those whose privilege
it was to know her intimately, she was the friend the soul is ever
seeking, the friend that understands, the friend that sympathizes,
the friend that knows our weakness and still loves us, the friend
that sees only the best in us.*

Chipeta
1843–1924

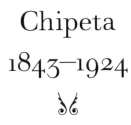

Indian Peacemaker

Ouray, the charismatic chief of the Ute Indians, did not realize the danger he faced as he traveled to the Los Pinos Indian Agency in 1872. The federal government had officially recognized him as the leader of the Utes, but some tribal members resented his authority and blamed him when the government broke its treaty promises. Five Utes had hatched a plot to murder Ouray when he reached the agency in southwestern Colorado.

At the last minute, the conspirators had a change of heart—except for a warrior named Sapovanero, who happened to be the stepbrother of Ouray's wife, Chipeta. As Ouray hitched his horse to a post at the agency, Sapovanero lunged from a hiding spot, brandishing an axe. Ouray sensed that something was wrong and jumped aside just as his brother-in-law swung the axe at his head.

Ouray tackled Sapovanero and grabbed him by the throat, but before he could take his revenge, Chipeta snatched Ouray's knife from its scabbard and out of his reach. Her quick reflexes saved her stepbrother's life. More importantly, she averted a calamitous split among the Ute leaders. The incident was one of many in her lifetime that demonstrated her courage and commitment to peace.

"Chipeta was well thought of by her own people and was always allowed and often especially invited to take part in the council meetings—no other Ute woman . . . was ever so allowed," wrote Albert B. Reagan and Wallace Stark, government agents who worked with the Utes in the early 1900s.

Chipeta was born June 10, 1843, to Kiowa Apache parents who were killed by Indian raiders when she was still a baby. A band of Tabeguache Utes found her crawling around her parents' ransacked camp. They raised her and named her Chipeta, which has been translated both as "White Singing Bird" and "The Charitable One."

Ouray was one of the Utes' most respected hunters and warriors. When his first wife died in 1859, Chipeta began caring for his son, Paron. She quickly impressed Ouray with her intelligence and beauty. Ouray, who was twenty-six, asked Chipeta, then sixteen, to marry him. According to historian P. David Smith:

She was a typical Ute wife of the time: hard-working, shy, quiet, and the person who did almost all of the day-to-day household tasks, which would have included tanning Ouray's deerskins and elkskins to use for sewing his clothes and moccasins; cooking, including preparing dried meats; hauling wood; and carrying water. Chipeta helped raise Paron and loved him as her own child.

Chipeta was as devastated as Ouray when Sioux warriors raided their hunting camp north of Denver in 1863 and kidnapped Paron. The Sioux later gave the boy to a group of Arapahoes, traditional enemies of the Utes. Chipeta and Ouray spent years fruitlessly searching for him. Federal officials once tried to exploit Ouray's concern for Paron by promising to find and return him if Ouray complied with their treaty demands, but father and son were never reunited.

Although Ouray and Chipeta had no children of their own, they adopted three young Utes. By tribal custom, Ouray could have married another woman who could bear him children, but he refused to do so out of love for Chipeta.

When gold was discovered near Pikes Peak in 1859, white prospectors and settlers flooded Colorado. Confrontations between them and the native tribes escalated. When Indians were shot without provocation, some Utes wanted to retaliate.

Ouray had already distinguished himself as a skilled hunter and ferocious warrior, but he realized that the Utes could never drive off the settlers. There were simply too many of them. He advised his people to try to live alongside the whites and negotiate treaties that would preserve their way of life. As a result, he became known as the Peace Chief.

One early settler in northwestern Colorado, David S. Gray, remembered an occasion during his childhood when he met Ouray face to face. A group of Indians had surrounded the Gray family's new home one day in the late 1870s, and Gray and his siblings panicked and fled. One of the Indians raced after them on horseback and assured the children that they were in no danger.

"He spoke excellent English and seemed much disturbed at having caused so much excitement," Gray later recalled. "That party was Chief Ouray and his family. We saw many Indians in the years that followed. They were always friendly and very hungry."

Ouray had no close male friends. He preferred to spend time with Chipeta, despite the commonly held Ute belief that women were inferior to men and should be ignored as much as possible. Chipeta had the respect of other Utes, too, because of her beauty, intelligence, and bearing. Some of the Indian agents referred to her as the "Queen of the Utes."

Chipeta actively supported her husband's peace policies. She lobbied other tribal leaders and joined Ouray on trips to Washington, D.C., to discuss treaties with federal officials. On one such trip in 1880, "Chipeta, with her native charm and dignity, became the darling of Washington society," according to author Jeanne Varnell. "She was dressed in Victorian finery and was given valuable gifts of silk dresses, millinery, gloves, and silver pieces for her home."

Colorado newspaper editor Caroline N. Churchill reported at the time that Chipeta's "appearance was so picturesque as to teach a national lesson, that beauty or style need not be confined exclusively to any one portion of the race."

When frontier explorer Ernest Ingersoll met Chipeta in 1874, he found her "about the most prepossessing Indian woman" he ever saw. "Ouray was immensely proud of her."

Chipeta and Ouray eventually settled on a productive 300-acre farm on the western slopes of the Colorado Rockies. Federal agents deeded the farm to Ouray and agreed to pay him one thousand dollars in return for his willingness to work with them as chief of the Utes. Over the years, Ouray, who spoke several languages, negotiated treaties that guaranteed specific lands for Utes in return for other land and government aid.

To encourage assimilation, Ouray and Chipeta donned whites' clothing, adopted their customs, and entertained white friends at their sixteen-room adobe house. Chipeta served meals on fine china and entertained by playing guitar and singing.

But the couple's comfortable lives were shattered in 1879 when White River Utes rebelled against Nathan Meeker, a misguided Indian agent who was trying to force them to cease their nomadic ways and become farmers and ranchers. The angry Utes slaughtered Meeker and twenty-nine other men. They also kidnapped three white women, including Meeker's wife and daughter. When Ouray intervened, the warriors agreed to release the women. Nonetheless, whites around the country were outraged when they learned that the Meeker women had been raped. They paid scant attention to the Meeker women's statements that Ouray and Chipeta had treated them with kindness.

"We were given the whole house, and found carpets on the floor, lamps on the tables and a stove with a fire brightly burning," Meeker's daughter, Josephine, later wrote. "Mrs. Ouray shed tears over us."

In the wake of the Meeker Massacre, white settlers demanded that the federal government remove the Utes from Colorado. Despite Ouray's efforts to reestablish peace, in 1880 officials canceled the Utes' treaty rights to their 12-million-acre homeland on Colorado's western slopes and prepared to move them to a new reservation on a barren tract of land in eastern Utah.

Ouray continued to urge the Utes to live peacefully with whites. In 1880, at the age of forty-seven, he died while on a treaty mission near Durango. With his death Chipeta lost her influence. When a white settler wanted her farm in 1881, she was forced to leave it. She joined 1,400 other Utes on a forced march to a reservation on Bitter Creek in Utah. Officials promised her a new home as nice as her old one, but she was given an unfurnished two-room place with unplastered walls. Outside, there was no water to irrigate crops.

A Denver newspaper reported that Chipeta married a sheepherder named "Toomuchagut." But given the unlikeliness of the name, some people suspected that the story was concocted to belittle the Utes.

What historians do know is that Chipeta, disillusioned by the government's treatment of her people, eventually abandoned any vestige of white culture and reverted to the nomadic Indian life she had known as a child. Her days in Utah were filled with indignities. Once, in 1887, armed white men rode into her camp while she was gathering food with other Ute women. The men threatened to rape them, then burned the camp to the ground when Chipeta helped the women escape.

As Chipeta got older, she reverted to living in a tepee. She was nearly blind with cataracts and suffered from rheumatism. In 1916, when she was seventy-three, a sympathetic Indian Affairs official visited her at Bitter Creek to see if he could do anything for her. She replied, "I desire nothing; what is good enough for my people is good enough for me. And I expect to die very soon."

But Chipeta lived on for eight more years. She died on August 17, 1924, and was buried in a ravine near Utah's Book Cliffs. The following year, when friends worried that her remains might wash away in a flash flood, they reburied her near her old farm a couple of miles south of Montrose. More than five thousand people formed a procession a mile long as they came to pay tribute to her memory. The honor contrasted starkly with the last days of her life, when she had lived in near anonymity. Finally, Coloradans had recognized the important role she played in western history.

Today, the nine-acre historic site where Chipeta is buried— Ouray Memorial Park—features the Ute Indian Museum, Chipeta's large granite tomb, and a tall stone monument to Ouray.

"It is somehow fitting that Colorado's largest and finest tribute to any Indian or Indian tribe is located at this spot—a spot first given to Ouray and Chipeta, then taken away from them, and finally dedicated to their memory," said historian Smith.

In a more poetic tribute, Colorado writer Eugene Field wrote almost a century ago:

But give her a page in history, too,
Tho' she be rotting in humble shrouds,
And write on the whitest of God's white clouds
Chipeta's name in eternal blue.

Malee Francis
1803–1848

❧

Florida's Pocahontas

It was on or about August 27, 1818, and the still Florida air almost dripped its humidity. A group of 188 bedraggled Indians, mostly women and children in starving condition, shuffled silently into Fort Gadsden near the mouth of the Apalachicola River on Florida's Gulf Coast. They surrendered themselves to the fort's commander, Colonel Matthew Arbuckle. Among them were the recent widow and two daughters of the Prophet Francis. The younger daughter, fifteen-year-old Malee, or Milly, as she was known to the Americans, was strikingly beautiful and was well known to the whites for having saved the life of one of their soldiers.

Nearly overwhelmed by their numbers and their sorry condition, Colonel Arbuckle did all in his power to tend to their immediate needs, providing food, water, medicines, and a place for them to rest. He also sent word to the soldier Malee had saved, Private Duncan McKrimmon, who had been returned to his home in Milledgeville, Georgia.

While Malee and the group rested, regaining their strength, the young soldier made his way to Fort Gadsden, carrying donations from Milledgeville citizens, who were eager to show their appreciation for Malee's efforts on McKrimmon's behalf. Remembering how she had interceded for him at the risk of her own life, Private McKrimmon presented her with the gifts and asked her to be his wife.

Malee gratefully accepted the donations, which she shared with the other Indians, but she gracefully declined his offer of matrimony. "I did not save you for that," she said. "I do not want any man." Colonel Arbuckle reported that Malee said she saved McKrimmon's life "from feelings of humanity alone, and that she would have rendered the same service to any other white man similarly circumstanced." She was therefore "not disposed to accept of his offer of matrimony."

The nobility of her sentiments is extraordinary when one considers that already in her young life she had been witness to countless perfidious acts by white invaders and untold numbers of cruelties on both sides. Perhaps the beautiful fifteen-year-old girl had decided, "Enough." If so, Private Duncan McKrimmon was the beneficiary of her mature decision.

Malee was born about 1803, the youngest daughter of Hillis Hadjo, known in English as the Prophet Francis or Josiah Francis, a prominent Creek chief who was the offspring of an Englishman and a Creek woman. Malee's older sister's name is unrecorded, and there was also a boy named Earle, about whom some mystery persists. Earle was said to have become a silversmith and a prophet like his father, and like his father, he died at the hands of whites, but in a Montgomery jail.

Malee's mother was the only family member who did not speak any English. Since most Indian girls received little education except from their mothers, Francis must have taken it upon himself to instruct his children in English, at least.

Confusion abounded among whites with regard to Indian names. Girls usually kept the same name they were given at birth, but not so with boys. At birth a boy was given his baby name, such as "Little Cub," then another name when he reached warrior age and completed a dangerous deed, and sometimes a third one later, after he completed another daring act. Further, as males achieved other goals, still more names were added. Hillis hayas were medicine men; whites frequently called them prophets. Warriors often had second names—Hadjo, Francis's name, meant "furious battle." Whites muddled things even further by phonetically writing Indian names, which they heard through ears accustomed to white names, such as Milly for Malee.

In the early 1800s, Spain, Britain, and America battled each other and the Indians for control of Florida, rendering it a scene of never-ending maneuverings. With the outbreak of the War of 1812, Francis, who then lived with his family near the Chattahoochee River in what is now Alabama, was enlisted by a friend to join the English cause. He was known to have assisted the British against Andrew Jackson and the Americans. When Jackson initiated his brutal raids against the Creeks in 1813 and 1814, Francis took his family south, establishing a new Seminole village in Spanish Florida, south of Tallahassee, near Fort St. Marks.

In 1816, Francis, accompanied by a British officer, embarked on a trip to England where, in recognition of his assistance, he was received with great ceremony by Prince Regent George IV. He was commissioned a brigadier general in the British army, presented with a diamond snuff box, an elaborate uniform of red and gold, 325 British pounds, and a tomahawk mounted in gold. An elegant ball was held in his honor aboard a Russian frigate anchored nearby, where trumpets heralded his arrival, according to London newspapers. But interestingly, Francis never tried to help England after that. He sailed home, determined to live at peace with the white man.

Upon her father's return from England in June 1817, Malee received many presents of "dresses, shoes and bonnets and much unaccustomed finery and learned to make graceful use of them."

At that time, hostilities were escalating among the Americans, the Spaniards, the British, and the Indians, resulting in another invasion by Andrew Jackson's army in early 1818. Entering Florida near the mouth of the Chattahoochee River, Jackson continued along the Apalachicola River to a defunct fort, where he built another garrison, naming it Fort Gadsden.

While his army was at rest, Private Duncan McKrimmon, Second Regiment of the Georgia militia attached to General Jackson's army, went fishing early one morning, became confused trying to return to camp, and was lost for several days. He was wandering about, trying to find his way, when he was spotted by a party of unfriendly Indians who overpowered him and took him to the town of the Prophet Francis.

Francis, appearing in his splendid uniform with a brace of pistols on his belt, proudly displayed his British commission to the prisoner. He then allowed the captors to interrogate McKrimmon, who eventually gave them the information they wanted regarding the strength and location of the American forces. That done, they prepared him for sacrifice.

McKrimmon was stripped naked and his face was blackened with soot before he was tied to a stake. Bone-chilling war cries commenced, magnifying the young man's terror.

Malee and her sister, who were playing on the riverbank near their home, immediately understood the significance of what they heard and hurried in the direction of the sounds. Seeing the terrified youth who was not much older than they were, they stopped. He was tied to a tree and helpless while two warriors danced menacingly around him with rifles ready to shoot, and onlookers stood by with approving expressions on their faces. Malee, overcome with sadness, remained silent, unable to participate in the merriment surrounding her.

It was their right, she knew, for it was accepted that if an Indian caught a white person, he had that life in his power and could not be interfered with, not even by a chief. Seeing the terror on the young prisoner's face, Malee ran to her father, imploring him to do something, but, as she knew he would, he said he was helpless, that she should speak to the captors. It was her only chance to affect the outcome.

Racing back to the warriors, she begged them to stop, saying McKrimmon was just a boy. One of the warriors became enraged, telling her he had lost two sisters in the war with the white men. Unwilling to give up, Malee kept on pleading, reminding him that killing the prisoner wouldn't bring his sisters back. The warriors were unmoved.

When it seemed all was lost, when the captors were ready "to terminate forever the mortal existence of the unfortunate McKrimmon," as reported by the *Georgia Journal*, Malee placed herself between the captive and death, telling the "astonished executioner, if he thirsted for blood, to shed hers."

Challenged by the brave daughter of their chief, the two warriors finally relented. They agreed to let McKrimmon live if he would consent to have his head shaved and not try to escape.

Without hesitation, McKrimmon agreed. His head was shaved, except for a scalp lock, which the Indians adorned with feathers. After they painted him and dressed him in their style, they considered him adopted.

Malee showed McKrimmon much kindness for the next several days, before he was taken away to Fort St. Marks, where his ransom was negotiated with a sympathetic Spanish commander named Luengo. He was released for seven and a half gallons of rum and permitted to rejoin his army.

Preceding Jackson's army into Fort St. Marks in April were two schooners sent there to act as reinforcements. They made their way up the Appalachee River, where they anchored, flying British flags to conceal their identity. The newly freed McKrimmon, having been informed of the schooners' mission, rowed out and boarded one ship, the *Thomas Shields*. Since British flags were displayed, Francis and another chief rowed out to visit what they thought was a friendly ship. The captain welcomed them onboard, inviting them to his cabin for refreshments. As they followed him, several Americans emerged from hiding, rushed toward the two

Indians, and captured them. Inside the ship, American flags were prominently exhibited.

When McKrimmon appeared, Francis scornfully reminded him of how his life had been spared such a short time before.

"You did not save my life," the private replied. "It was your daughter. I will do all I can to save you."

That afternoon, Malee was seen paddling around the schooner, apparently searching for her father. Suddenly, shots were fired on her from the ship. She grabbed a rifle she had concealed in the bottom of her canoe and returned fire before disappearing.

McKrimmon's efforts at saving the lives of the two chiefs were fruitless when Andrew Jackson arrived the next morning and received a report on the previous day's events. Jackson had previously written to Washington, "The Prophet Francis . . . is exciting the Seminoles to hostility. . . . It is important that these men should be captured and made an example of." Now, Francis was in Jackson's power and, still clad in his opulent British uniform, was hanged along with his friend.

Within days, Jackson ordered the execution of two more men—British traders engaged in legitimate trade, but of whom Jackson was suspicious. One of them, a man named Armbrister, was much smitten with Malee and had proposed marriage to her, but she declined. It was said by some that after Armbrister's death, Malee could be found lying "upon his grave every moon, weeping."

After Francis's death, conditions in his village continued to decline, and shortly after the mass surrender at Fort Gadsden, his family joined other Seminoles on the long, difficult journey to Oklahoma Territory for resettlement.

Years passed, during which there is no recorded account of Malee's exact whereabouts or activities. We only know that she survived the journey of hundreds of miles from her familiar, verdant home to a strange, new country.

On their way to and in the Oklahoma Territory, Malee's tribe had to compete with other tribes for scarce resources. Indian agents and contractors hired by the government to guarantee provisions for the migrating tribes along the way and for one year after they were resettled, grafted supplies, depriving the Indians. In 1842, under intense political pressure, President John Tyler chose Colonel Ethan Allen Hitchcock, grandson of Ethan Allen, the Revolutionary War legend, to conduct an inquiry into the activities of Indian agents.

Hitchcock was a man of unimpeachable honor and unassailable credentials. While on his mission, he heard about Malee's saving of McKrimmon's life and that she was living nearby, near the Arkansas River, close to where the present-day town of Muscogee is located. Hitchcock sent for her and when she arrived, he saw that, after a difficult life, she was "still attractive." She verified the facts of the story as he had heard them, adding that following relocation, she had married an Indian man who had since died. Although she had had eight children, just three were living, two boys and a girl. Times were very hard, she said, and she and her children lived in poverty.

When Hitchcock returned to Washington, he made no attempt to soften his opinion of Jackson's conduct in Florida, nor did his damaging report spare others. Because of it, reforms were instituted and he immediately set out to procure a small government pension for Malee. After delaying considerably, Congress passed a bill to provide Malee with ninety-six dollars a year for the rest of her life "as a testimonial of the gratitude and bounty of the United States, for the humanity displayed by her." Further, it was enacted that a "medal with appropriate devices impressed thereon" be given to her as an additional testimonial of the gratitude of the United States.

Congress passed the bill two years later, and then took another three years before getting the proclamation to Malee. By the time Indian agent James Logan reached her with the news, she was very ill with tuberculosis and "in dying circumstances." Agent Logan reported to his superiors in June 1848 that he immediately procured medical aid for her and "did all that was possible to alleviate her sufferings" while reading the proclamation to her. "She was so highly elated," he wrote, "that I flattered myself she was recovering."

She did not recover. Florida's Pocahontas died on May 19, 1848, and was buried somewhere between the city of Muscogee and the banks of the Arkansas River.

Malee did not live long enough to receive a cent of her pension or her medal, the only one in United States history ever specially awarded to a woman.

Magdelaine LaFramboise
1780–1846

⁕

A Bridge between Cultures

In the early years of the nineteenth century, fur was international currency in the "western" wilds of the new United States. This "frontier," of course, barely reached the Mississippi River. In Michigan and other Great Lakes states, French and French-Canadian voyageurs had been involved in the fur trade business for nearly two hundred years.

French trappers, voyageurs, and traders settled in the Midwest, particularly in fur-rich forest areas near the Great Lakes and nearby rivers. While some spent a few years in America, seeking adventure and wild times before returning to traditional life in France, many men married native women and made the Midwest their home. The community and people that emerged from this blending of cultures were called "Métis," from the French word meaning "mixed."

In 1780 a daughter was born to Jean Baptiste Marcot, a French fur trader well known in the Great Lakes region, and Misigan "Marie" Neskech, daughter of Chief Kewinaquot of the Ottawa tribe. The child, baptized in her father's Catholic religion as Magdelaine, would become a community leader, successful businesswoman, and dedicated supporter of Catholic ministry and missions.

Magdelaine Marcot spent her early years with her widowed mother. After Jean Baptiste's death, Marie returned to the safety of the Ottawa lands along the Grand River near present-day Grand Haven, Michigan. Magdelaine was raised among her mother's people in traditional ways. However, she was bilingual and her life shows strong influence from her father's Catholic religious heritage.

It is probable that Marie and her extended family received income from fur trapping and trading. Evidence for this comes from church records documenting Magdelaine's baptism, at about age six, at the Catholic mission church on Mackinac Island.

Mackinac was a traditional site for the fur traders' rendezvous, an annual gathering at which voyageurs and local trappers sold their furs. For Ottawa Indians to make the long trek from their Grand River lands in southern Michigan to Mackinac Island strongly suggests they were transporting furs for sale. Perhaps, during one such trading trip, Marie sought out the island's Catholic priest to baptize her daughter.

At about age fourteen, Magdelaine married Joseph LaFramboise, a French-Canadian fur trader. Although this marriage was, at first, *a la façon du pays* (literally, in the manner or custom of the country), the couple formalized their union about ten years later before a priest named Fr. Jean Dilhet on Mackinac Island. They also brought their children to St. Anne's Church on Mackinac Island for baptism—Josette, born in 1799 when Magdelaine was only fifteen years old, and Joseph, born in 1806.

It was common for Métis couples to first formalize their relationship within the Indian community and then to ask a priest, when available, to witness their vows and marry them within the legal structure of the Catholic Church. This practice reflected the melding of cultures in the Métis community.

Today Joseph would be described as a middleman in the fur trade. He bought furs from Ottawa trappers and sold them at Mackinac Island. At first furs were purchased from middlemen or directly from trappers by investor-backed groups from Europe. One of the best known of these groups was the Hudson's Bay Company, which was established in the 1600s. In 1822 American entrepreneur John Jacob Astor undercut the European competition by establishing trade between U.S. business interests and local fur traders.

Joseph and Magdelaine followed the fur trade in a semi-nomadic life. They wintered in Ada, Michigan, near present-day Grand Haven. There they built a trading post, the first mercantile establishment in Ada. They traded with area Indians, purchasing animal pelts with such trade goods as blankets, axes, iron or brass cooking pots, knives, household goods, and guns. All winter they accumulated furs.

In spring they loaded the furs onto bateaux—flat-bottomed, low boats. They hired local Ottawa men as boatmen and made the long journey up the coast of Lake Michigan to Mackinac Island. They relied on income from the furs to purchase more trade goods and other necessities during the rest of the year.

In the fall of 1806, with an infant in tow, Magdelaine and Joseph returned from Mackinac Island. About a day's journey from Grand Haven, they stopped for the night on a beach. At some point, a native man asked Joseph for alcohol. Joseph refused, and the man returned that evening and shot him.

In an instant Magdelaine was left widowed with two young children. She ordered the boatmen to load Joseph's body into a bateau and she took him to Grand Haven to be buried. Then she did what was necessary to support herself and her children.

Before Joseph's sudden and shocking death, Magdelaine had been an active participant in their fur-trading business. She used her language skills to negotiate with area Indian trappers by speaking Ottawa, Ojibwe or Chippewa, French, and English. But, with her husband dead, she could either return to her Ottawa family or take over the fur-trading business herself. She chose to continue the business.

Women were rare, although not unknown, in the fur trade. Some Métis women had achieved some success in this largely male-controlled business. For the next six years, until the War of 1812 disturbed relationships between French, English, Indian, and U.S. communities, Madame LaFramboise ran her business much as she and her husband had done. Yearly trips to Mackinac Island cemented relationships with fellow Métis traders and the Catholic mission church. History records that she was a shrewd businesswoman. Under her leadership the business grew.

Therese Marcot Schindler, Magdelaine's older sister, was one of the Métis women living on Mackinac Island. Therese had married a Protestant fur trader from the island in 1804. After poor health forced her husband to retire, the couple started a school for boys. Therese followed in her sister's footsteps and continued to make a living in the fur trade. The two women remained close.

During the first quarter of the nineteenth century, John Jacob Astor, an American businessman, entered and began to change the fur trade. His American Fur Company gained a foothold in the Great Lakes Area. However, the War of 1812 hurt Astor and other trading companies. Some trading posts were lost to the British.

So one by one, Astor forced his competitors out of business. He pressured Canadian traders to sell their enterprises in U.S. territory. While many of her counterparts became bankrupt, unable to compete with Astor's growing operation, Magdelaine remained independent and successful.

Then, in 1817, the American Congress passed a law expelling all foreign fur traders from U.S. lands. This placed almost the entire American fur trade directly under John Jacob Astor's control. Suddenly Magdelaine had to deal with a monopoly run by an Oregon-based business known for cutthroat tactics and the crushing of all opposition. Flexibility was the key.

In the years following Magdelaine sometimes worked independently and sometimes worked directly for Astor's American Fur Company. In 1818 her name appears on a list of employees, listing her as "employed at Grand River." In 1922 records indicate she was again trading independently with local trappers.

Independent trading was risky. Traders were required to obtain a federal license to trade each year. Indian and Métis traders were sometimes the victims of racism on the part of government officials. Large companies sometimes bribed officials to deny licenses to competitors.

One of Astor's methods of extending his control of the market was to refuse to buy furs from independent middlemen. Because Magdelaine had many contacts and relationships within the Indian communities in the region, she had ready and abundant sources for furs. She knew the best trappers and the most successful families or tribal clans. However, when she bought those furs, she always risked the possibility that Astor would refuse to purchase them or that his growing business had swallowed up all other potential buyers.

Still, Magdelaine was successful. She used her language skills and relationships within the native communities to build sound trading relationships. Perhaps local trappers preferred trading with the daughter of an Ottawa chief to strangers from the American Fur Company.

During these years Magdelaine straddled the French and Indian worlds. She sent her daughter, Josette, to Montreal to be educated, and Josette became more European than Indian. In 1815, at about age sixteen, Josette met and fell in love with Capt. Benjamin K. Pierce during a winter stay at Mackinac Island. Pierce was stationed at Fort Mackinac during the unstable years after the War of 1812.

Josette and Benjamin Pierce married in a small ceremony, perhaps conducted by a military officer, at Mackinac Island on April 2, 1816. Evidently, Magdelaine was away, probably still collecting furs in Grand Haven in preparation for the spring selling.

When Magdelaine returned to the island, she held a second wedding for the couple at a friend's large home. Captain Pierce's fellow officers, their families, and two leading Métis families from the island community were welcomed by Madame LaFramboise herself and her sister, Therese, both formally dressed in traditional Ottawa clothing.

In 1819 Madame LaFramboise accompanied her son, Joseph, to school in Montreal. This journey, which took weeks, was made by canoe. Magdelaine was nearly forty years old. Joseph remained in Montreal with his father's relative, a nephew named Alexis LaFramboise. Magdelaine paid for Joseph's education herself.

Records seem to indicate that during the next decade, Madame LaFramboise sold the trading post she and Joseph had established to a Grand Haven fur trader. For some time she worked as an agent for John Jacob Astor's American Fur Company. Then Astor purchased the LaFramboise company outright. Magdelaine LaFramboise became a very wealthy woman.

The LaFramboise trading operation was a lucrative one. When Astor bought the business, history records her "retiring" to her beloved Mackinac Island, where she invested herself and her considerable fortune in the people and matters she valued most.

Madame LaFramboise believed education was crucial to success. At significant cost, she ensured that Josette and Joseph received the best education Montreal could offer at that time. After Josette and her infant son died in 1821, Benjamin Pierce left their daughter, Josette Harriet, with Magdelaine. Then, it appears, he abandoned the family. Magdelaine took responsibility for raising and educating Josette Harriet.

Magdelaine's support of education extended beyond educating her own family. In 1823, Rev. William Ferry, a Presbyterian missionary, requested her help in establishing a school on the island. Madame LaFramboise first offered part of her own home to be used by the school, the Reverend Ferry, and twelve boarding students.

With a school operating in her home, Magdelaine took the opportunity to learn to read and write. Documents show that in 1821 she could speak four languages but was unable to write even

her name in any of the four. By 1830 she had learned to read and
write both French and English. She used those skills to teach the
Roman Catholic catechism to children.

Madame LaFramboise became increasingly important in the
Mackinac Island community. When the Reverend Ferry found a
permanent location for his school, Magdelaine opened her home
to other visitors and guests. She often acted as hostess to island
visitors while wearing traditional Ottawa dress.

Indian Agent Henry Schoolcraft, for whom the Michigan
community of Schoolcraft is named, was a guest in her home and
wrote about her in his journal.

John and Juliette Kinzie visited Madame LaFramboise during
their journey from Detroit to the emerging Lake Michigan
harbor city of Chicago. Juliette wrote *Wau-Bon*, one of the early
eyewitness histories of the settlement of the "northwest." In it she
called Mackinac Island "that gem of the Lake." About Madame
LaFramboise she wrote, "It was her custom to receive a class of
young pupils daily at her house, that she might give them lessons.
. . . She was a woman of a vast deal of energy and enterprise—of a
tall and commanding figure and most dignified deportment."

In 1831 French aristocrat and writer Alexis de Tocqueville
visited Mackinac Island during his extensive travels in America.
De Tocqueville was delighted to meet an articulate, multilingual
native woman. Because the two could converse in French, he
interviewed Madame LaFramboise at length about her Ottawa
ancestry and culture.

Margaret Fuller, a writer, critic, and international reporter for
the *New York Tribune*, visited the island in 1843. Fuller wrote about
Magdelaine, describing her as "wearing the dress of her country.
She spoke French fluently . . . They were all the time coming to
pay her homage or get her aid and advice, for she is, I am told, a
shrewd woman of business." Mackinac Island so impressed Fuller
that she wrote about it in her memoir *Summer on the Lakes*.

Fuller's perception of Magdelaine's role and position within the island community was accurate. Madame LaFramboise was a bridge between the Métis and both the French- and English-speaking communities. While it is possible that some visitors were curious or even amused by the sight of an English-speaking, wealthy woman in traditional Ottawa dress, history records the deep respect by which she was held by those who knew her.

Magdelaine knew times were changing and that her people, the French and Métis, would have to change with them. The culture of French, Indian, and Métis fur traders would soon be swallowed up by American culture, business, and government. She knew education in English and French would be critical to the survival of the next generation. To that end she educated both her children and granddaughter in Montreal. Then she invested considerable money in schooling for Métis and Indian children on the island.

Within fifty years Métis culture would largely disappear. By 1850 fur had fallen out of fashion in Europe. The market collapsed and John Jacob Astor transformed fur storage buildings on the island to transfer sites for fish.

Even in relatively undeveloped regions such as northern Michigan, the once comfortable blending of French and Indian cultures was forever altered by the influx of Euro-American immigrants, decades of broken treaties and stolen lands, and the U.S. government's forcible removal of Indian peoples.

Magdelaine was also a bridge between the Catholic and Protestant communities. A lifelong, devout Catholic, she opened her home to a Presbyterian mission school and contributed funds to the school when the Reverend Ferry found it a permanent location.

Until 1830 Mackinac Island was without a permanent Catholic priest. Magdelaine faithfully prayed the Angelus, a Catholic prayer liturgy, at six o'clock in the morning, at noon, and at six o'clock in the evening. The bells of St. Anne's Church rang each day to mark these hours.

In the 1920s a new church building was needed, and Magdelaine donated land adjacent to her house. Church records show that, in thanks, the church assigned her pew number one and exempted her from the annual pew rental fees. Magdelaine's request was that she be buried under the altar of the new church house.

In 1830 Fr. Samuel Mazzuchelli, an Italian missionary priest from the Dominican order, was commissioned as the "missionary priest of the whole Northwestern Territory." He was assigned to St. Anne's Church on Mackinac Island.

Upon arriving on the island, Father Mazzuchelli made a temporary home with Madame LaFramboise and assumed responsibility as pastor of St. Anne's Church. Magdelaine gave personal, administrative, and financial assistance to Father Mazzuchelli to establish a school for Catholic children. The school opened, and within a short time twenty-six children were enrolled. One of the teachers, Martha Tanner, had been a student at Reverend Ferry's Presbyterian school. Tanner represented the second generation of island children for whom Madame LaFramboise had helped to provide an education.

Madame LaFramboise took her position as a community leader quite seriously. Much of her wealth was used for her Mackinac Island community. When Schoolcraft visited the island in 1837, he noted that she had provided food and financial assistance for "a poor, decrepit Indian woman" who had been abandoned by her family. After her death, the reading of her will revealed a bequest of $50 for the "most poor of the Island."

Magdelaine raised her granddaughter, Josette Harriet, and remained on the island with her sister, Therese, until her death in 1846 at the age of sixty-six. As she had requested, Madame LaFramboise was buried under the altar of St. Anne's. Many years later, when a basement was added to the church building, her remains were relocated to the churchyard.

Magdelaine's will reflected her interests and loyalties. Her home was left to Josette Harriet Pierce and the remainder of her estate to her son, Joseph, a successful businessman living in Montreal. Small bequests included one hundred dollars given to a niece who was a teacher of Métis children on the island. Historians have noted that, although Madame LaFramboise was wealthy and enjoyed sterling tableware and some imported furniture, in general, her possessions were few and relatively simple.

Magdelaine LaFramboise was a founding mother of the Mackinac Island community. During her lifetime she saw her beloved island grow from a rendezvous site and fishing community to a destination for wealthy adventurers and lovers of natural beauty. She witnessed the establishment of a permanent ministry at St. Anne's Church and the growth, peak, and decline of the great fur trade in North America.

Today, Magdelaine's house still stands on Mackinac Island as the Harbour View Inn. And visitors and residents alike still worship at St. Anne's Church, located next door on land donated by Madame LaFramboise nearly 180 years ago.

Sacajawea
1788–1812 or 1884

♉

Wadze-wipe, Lost Woman of the Lemhi Shoshone

As the men of the expedition dragged their boats up the Beaverhead River, the seventeen-year-old Shoshone girl, her baby secure in a cradleboard strapped to her back, walked along the bank of the river with her French-Canadian husband and the red-haired Captain Clark. The trio had gone but a mile when the girl began to leap and dance in a showing of extreme joy. She turned to Captain Clark and gestured toward a group of Indians approaching on horseback. In her excitement the young girl sucked the fingers of her hand as a sign that the riders were Shoshone, her native tribe. It was seven o'clock in the morning of Saturday, August 17, 1805, when Sacajawea was reunited with her tribe.

The group continued toward the Shoshone camp, where a crowd of Shoshone people awaited their arrival. A young woman burst through the group and warmly embraced the Shoshone girl arriving with the white men. The tender affection between these two young Shoshone women upon their reunion was a scene that touched the hearts of the travel-weary explorers.

The women had been childhood friends, born and raised in what is now Idaho's Lemhi Valley. They had shared the same fate when, as girls, both had been taken prisoner by a raiding tribe of Hidatsa, or Minnetaree.

While Sacajawea was deep in conversation with friends she had thought she would never see again, Captain Clark proceeded on to meet with Captain Lewis and the Shoshone chief Cameahwait. The white men entered a circular tent made of willows, where the chief was seated on a white robe. Cameahwait's hair had been cut short to signify that he was in mourning for deceased relatives. All in the party removed their moccasins and commenced smoking pipes to open the meeting between them. The opening ceremony done, Sacajawea was summoned, as her interpreting services were needed.

She entered the shelter with eyes cast downward in a show of respect, sat down, and started to interpret for the men when a shock of recognition swept over her. Jumping to her feet, she ran to the chief, embraced him, and threw her blanket over him while tears of joy streamed down her cheeks. Chief Cameahwait was deeply moved as well, though he retained the composure expected of one in his position.

Sacajawea and Chief Cameahwait, brother and sister, were reunited. The siblings exchanged conversation, and Sacajawea presented her brother with a lump of sugar, which he later declared was the best thing he had ever tasted. Then, remembering her duty, Sacajawea took her seat and tried to resume interpreting for the council, but, overpowered by her emotions, she erupted into tears frequently throughout the meeting.

When the council had concluded, Sacajawea learned that most of the members of her family had perished. All that remained alive were Cameahwait, another brother who was not then among the tribe, and one young son of her oldest sister. In Shoshone fashion Sacajawea adopted her sister's young son, but he was left in the care of Cameahwait when the expedition left the camp.

Sacajawea, a member of the Lemhi Shoshone tribe, commonly referred to as the Snake[1] Nation in the days of the Lewis and Clark Expedition, was born in Idaho's Lemhi Valley around 1788. Though

[1] The Shoshone called themselves "the people of the grass," but when attempting to convey their name in sign language, the sign for waving grass was interpreted as "snake." The Snake River is named after the misnomer for this tribe.

the Lemhi country was home to this tribe of Northern Shoshone, they traveled widely, following their food sources—digging roots and gathering berries in the mountains and valleys and hunting buffalo on the Plains.

On one such buffalo hunt, the tribe was camped at the Three Forks of the Missouri River in what is now Montana when they were attacked by their mortal enemies, the Hidatsa, also known as the Minnetaree or Gros Ventre. Many Shoshone were killed in the raid while younger children were taken captive. Twelve-year-old Sacajawea and two of her close friends were among those captured to be taken down the Missouri River to the Hidatsa villages of earthen lodges on the Knife River (in what is now North Dakota) to be enslaved, traded, or gambled away.

One of Sacajawea's friends was able to escape her captors and return to the Shoshone. According to the Shoshone the escapee was able to get away by leaping through a stream and was subsequently named *Pop-pank*, meaning "Jumping Fish." The other friend attempted to make her escape by sliding into the water like an otter, earning the name Ponzo-bert, or "Otter Woman." Sacajawea, who had been captured midstream while trying to escape from the Hidatsa, was called *Wadze-wipe*[2], or "Lost Woman," by her people since nothing was known of her ultimate fate. The Hidatsa referred to their captives as *Poo-ey neeve*, or "Maidens of the Grass People."

Otter Woman and Sacajawea lived among the Hidatsa and their neighboring tribe, the Mandan, for the next five years of their young lives. During their captivity the girls were acquired, either through purchase or gambling, by a French Canadian named Toussaint Charbonneau, who lived among the tribes. While living in these Hidatsa-Mandan villages with Charbonneau and Otter Woman, the teenaged Sacajawea, now

---

[2] By some accounts the name Wadze-wipe was given to Sacajawea in later life by the Comanche tribe.

pregnant with her first child, was to have an encounter that would profoundly affect history.

In 1803 President Thomas Jefferson formed an expedition to explore the newly acquired Louisiana Purchase Territory that extended to Montana's western border. The expedition was to establish an American presence in the Northwest and explore a route of travel by water between the Atlantic and Pacific Oceans. Captain Meriwether Lewis, Jefferson's personal secretary, was named to lead the expedition. He, in turn, hired his army friend, Captain William Clark, to share the responsibility for leading the Corps of Discovery. The men of the Corps of Discovery left their quarters near St. Louis on May 14, 1804, and began their journey up the Missouri River.

By late October 1804 they had reached the Mandan villages of present-day North Dakota. Fort Mandan was established to provide winter quarters for the Corps as they prepared for their long journey toward the Pacific Coast. During the winter camp Toussaint Charbonneau approached the expedition leaders and asked to be hired as an interpreter. Charbonneau's reputation was less than stellar, but he knew Hidatsa and sign language; and when the captains learned that his wives were Shoshone, they quickly appreciated the value of having a Shoshone "interpretress" with them. The Shoshone, whom Lewis and Clark referred to as the Snake Nation, were reputed to be rich in horse stock, and the captains planned to obtain horses from them in order to cross the Rocky Mountains. Charbonneau was hired as an interpreter with the understanding that he would bring with him one of his Shoshone wives. Sacajawea was chosen to accompany Charbonneau.

While at Fort Mandan awaiting departure, Sacajawea gave birth on February 11, 1805, to her son, Jean Baptiste Charbonneau. During the difficult birth of Baptiste, the young mother was attended by members of the expedition including Captain Lewis. Lewis wrote in his journal, "About five o'clock this evening one of the wives of

Charbono was delivered of a fine boy. It is worthy of remark that this was the first child which this woman had born, and as is common in such cases her labor was tedious and the pain violent."

Lewis and Jessaume, another interpreter, administered the powdered rattle of a rattlesnake to the young mother, and within ten minutes she gave birth. As was common among the Shoshone, Sacajawea called her first born Pomp, meaning "head," or "leader."

When spring arrived, the expedition prepared to set out through the unexplored wilderness. Captain Lewis recorded the new additions to the expedition: "Our party now consists of the following individuals: interpreters George Drewyer and Taussant Charbono; also a black man of the name of York, servant to Captain Clark, and an Indian woman, wife to Charbono, with a young child."

On April 7, 1805, they began the trip up the Missouri River in six canoes and two large riverboats, called pirogues. The expedition would follow the Missouri to the Rocky Mountains in Montana, where they planned to acquire horses to transport them over the mountains.

Lewis and Clark were expected to study the geology, vegetation, and animal life found along the route and to report their findings to Jefferson. They were also to make contact with and document the various tribes they encountered, while promoting peaceful relations with them. Accordingly, both men kept detailed journals, recording events and findings on a daily basis, and they encouraged their men to do the same.

In order to better observe the environment, the captains made a practice of walking along the riverbanks while the boats proceeded upriver. Captain Clark, Charbonneau, and Sacajawea spent most days walking along the shore together. Clark developed a strong bond with Sacajawea and her baby, whom he referred to as Janey and Pomp.

Sacajawea's knowledge and skill in finding and preparing food for the party became evident early in the journey. Lewis records that the girl located and dug up hordes of wild artichokes that had been stored in the ground by mice. She introduced the group to many native roots and berries, bringing variety to their diet of wild game.

A near crisis occurred one day when the party was hit by a sudden windstorm while Charbonneau was steering one of the larger boats, laden with supplies. The vessel nearly capsized, and supplies spilled overboard. While her husband dropped the tiller and wailed in panic, Sacajawea calmly scooped up as many articles as she could from the river. Without her efforts clothing, navigational equipment, and other necessities would have been lost. According to Lewis,

The loss we sustained was not so great as we had at first apprehended. . . . The Indian woman, to whom I ascribe equal fortitude and resolution with any person on board at the time of the accident, caught and preserved most of the light articles which were washed overboard.

A week later Lewis and Clark honored Sacajawea's valor by naming a river after her. "This stream we called Sah-ca-ger-we-ah or Bird Woman's River after our interpreter, the Snake woman," wrote Lewis.

Beyond the obvious natural hazards the Corps faced, insects, snakes, and dirty food and water threatened their health on a daily basis. By June Sacajawea was stricken with a high fever and excruciating stomach pains. The captains worried about Sacajawea, the baby in her arms, and the effect losing her would have on the future of the entire expedition. Lewis noted that she was the party's "only dependence for a friendly negotiation with the Snake Indians, on whom we depend for horses to assist us in our portage from the Missouri to the Columbia River."

Lewis applied herbal folk remedies to the sick woman, and with one relapse, Sacajawea recovered within two weeks.

When the expedition approached the Great Falls in present-day Montana, it became necessary to drag their canoes around a series of five waterfalls. This journey of 18 miles was to take them ten days. During the overland excursion Captain Clark, Charbonneau, and Sacajawea, with Jean Baptiste, were caught by a flash flood through a creek bed. The trio scrambled to higher ground, Clark pushing Sacajawea, with baby in her arms, up the hill, while Charbonneau, "much scared and nearly without motion," made vain attempts to assist. Wet to their waists, the group eventually reached the hilltop, where they found Clark's servant, York, searching desperately for them. They were safe, but little Baptiste's cradleboard and all of his clothing had been swept away.

The journals often refer to Charbonneau as cowardly and panic-stricken, while commending Sacajawea for her resourcefulness, calm acts of courage, and uncomplaining nature. Lewis's journal refers to an incident when Clark found Charbonneau striking his wife and reprimanded the interpreter severely, ordering him never to hit Sacajawea again. The beating may have been the result of Charbonneau's offering Sacajawea to the men of the expedition, as he was later known to do with other Indian wives. A recorded incident describes Charbonneau, then in his eighties, offering his newly acquired fourteen-year-old Indian wife to the men of his camp. Had this been the case with Sacajawea, as a Shoshone woman she would have found this unacceptable and would have endured a beating rather than submit to such a degradation.

In late July the Corps was in western Montana. Sacajawea began to recognize the country and assure the explorers that they were on the right trail. The captains named a creek she recognized White Earth Creek when she told them that the creek banks were a source of the white earth the Shoshone used to make white paint.

Curiously, the expedition had not encountered any Indians in this territory, though Sacajawea frequently pointed out signs of prior Indian habitation. The leaders began to doubt they would find the Shoshone, from whom they desperately needed horses.

By the time the expedition had reached the Three Forks of the Missouri, they were tired, sick, and losing faith in ever encountering a tribe with horses. Sacajawea brought hope to the men, assuring them that they were near the Shoshone. She explained to them that their present camp was on the very site where her tribe had been camped five years before when the Hidatsa attacked them. She demonstrated her capture and showed them the shallow place where she had been trying to cross the river when she was taken prisoner. She knew the summer camp of the Shoshone was near, and she was clearly familiar with the land and rivers.

Lewis and a small party of men had the first encounters with the Shoshone, all of whom fled Lewis's advances. He was finally able to overtake two women and a child and convince them, with presents and signs of friendship, to take him to their camp. Captain Lewis met with the head chief, Cameahwait, and further gained the trust of the Shoshone by supplying them with deer meat. Some of the subchiefs were still suspicious of the white men, and it was up to Lewis to convince them that Captain Clark's party, pushing their boats up the Beaverhead River, would be peaceful arrivals. He explained that they had a Shoshone woman and child with them. Lewis and some of the Shoshone set out together to ensure a friendly encounter with Captain Clark and the main party.

John Rees, who lived among the Lemhi Shoshone for fifteen years beginning in 1877, provided one account of Sacajawea's naming during this encounter. On the occasion of Sacajawea's reunion with her people, when all were dancing with joy, the Shoshone began making their signs for boat and calling her Sacajawea, or "one who travels with the boat that is pulled." The Shoshone sign for boat, made with a rowing motion of the arms, was misinterpreted by Charbonneau, who told Clark that the name meant "bird woman."

One of the great mysteries of Sacajawea's life is the source and spelling of her name. Traditionally, an Indian was given many names throughout his or her life, and without a written language, all Indian names are subject to interpretation when transcribed into English. Lewis and Clark used very innovative spelling in their journals, spelling both Sacajawea's and Charbonneau's names differently nearly every time they wrote them, though they usually did use a *g* as the middle consonant in her name.

It is generally accepted that *Sacagawea* or *Sakakawea* are Hidatsa words meaning "bird woman," whereas *Sacajawea* is of Shoshone origin and means "boat pusher." Although our government has chosen the Hidatsa version, Sacagawea, for their newly minted dollar coin, this author prefers to use Idaho's Lemhi Shoshone version, Sacajawea.

The Corps spent a week with the Shoshone, making saddles and preparing for their passage through the mountains. Goods that could not be packed on horseback were cached, or hidden, for the return trip. Through Sacajawea Lewis and Clark successfully traded for horses to take them to the Columbia River, and they obtained a guide to show them the route. Sacajawea also informed the leaders of her brother's intention to leave on a buffalo hunt before the expedition was fully equipped and safely underway. Cameahwait was then persuaded to delay his Plains buffalo hunt.

One problem they encountered during their stay with the tribe occurred when an older man claimed that Sacajawea had been betrothed to him by her father prior to her capture. The man already had two wives, and since Sacajawea had a child by another man, her betrothed was easily dissuaded.

Though Sacajawea had been overjoyed during the reunion with her family and tribe, she showed little emotion when leaving them as the expedition continued to the coast. She had made an agreement, through her husband, to stay with the expedition all the way to the Pacific and back. To have remained with her people rather than continue on, as promised, would have been dishonorable. Captain Lewis wrote of her tremendous ability to accept her lot in life and be happy with whatever fate befell her.

Guided by an old Shoshone man, the Corps continued west over Nez Perce trails. Upon reaching the Nez Perce tribe, they branded their horses, left them with the Nez Perce chief Twisted Hair, and continued on by canoe until they reached the Columbia River, which ultimately took them to their final destination.

Sacajawea's and Pomp's very presence with the explorers conveyed their message of being a peaceful expedition, as Clark recorded:

The wife of Shabono our interpreter we find reconciles all the Indians, as to our friendly intentions a woman with a party of men is a token of peace . . . the sight of this Indian woman . . . confirmed those people of our friendly intentions, as no woman ever accompanies a war party of Indians in this quarter.

Rather than attack the party, the Indians they encountered sought to communicate with the leaders of the expedition out of curiosity. During these communications Sacajawea was often the mediator as well as the interpreter. The interpreting was a complicated and time-consuming process, as in the expedition's dealings with the Chopunnish (Nez Perce) tribe, who had with them a captive Shoshone boy. William Clark described the interpreting process:

It was not without difficulty, nor until after nearly half the day was spent, that we were able to convey all this information to the Chopunnish, much of which might have been lost or distorted in its circuitous route through a variety of languages; for in the first place we spoke in English to one of our men, who translated it into French to Chaboneau; he interpreted it to his wife in the Minnetaree language, and she then put it into Shoshonee, and the young Shoshonee prisoner explained it to the Chopunnish in their own dialect.

In November 1805 the Corps of Discovery reached the Pacific Ocean. By Captain Clark's calculations they were now 4,132 miles and 554 days from their original point of departure. The men of the expedition built their winter quarters at Fort Clatsop, where they remained until March 23, 1806. While at Fort Clatsop, repairs were made to clothing and equipment, and trading was conducted with local tribes. Sacajawea sacrificed her own precious blue-beaded belt so that Captain Clark could trade with a local Indian for a fur robe that he desired.

During their winter layover on the Pacific, a whale was discovered washed up on the beach. Lewis and Clark planned to send out a party to retrieve oil and blubber from the giant mammal. Hearing of this great oddity, Sacajawea begged to go with the men to see "the large fish." Although they had been camped only a few miles inland from the Pacific for two months, this was the first time Sacajawea would see the ocean.

In spring of 1806 the Lewis and Clark Expedition began their return journey. When they passed through Sacajawea's homeland, there was no sign of her people, except for a campfire and two horses. She and Charbonneau continued on with the expedition until they returned to the Mandan villages. On Saturday, August 17, 1806, Charbonneau, Sacajawea, and little Jean Baptiste terminated their services with the Corps of Discovery. Clark recorded their departure:

Settled with Touisant Chabono for his services as an interpreter the price of a horse and lodge purchased of him for public service

*in all amounting to $500.33⅓ cents . . . we also took our leave
of T. Chabono, his Snake Indian wife and their son child who
had accompanied us on our route to the Pacific Ocean in the
capacity of interpreter and interpretess. I offered to take his little
son a beautiful promising child who is 19 months old to which
they both himself and wife were willing provided the child had
been weaned. They observed that in one year the boy would be
sufficiently old to leave his mother and he would then take him
to me if I would be so friendly as to raise the child for him in
such a manner as I thought proper, to which I agreed.*

In a letter to Charbonneau written a few weeks later, Clark
reiterated his interest in raising Jean Baptiste and commended
Sacajawea, or Janey, for her invaluable services, expressing regret
that he had not been able to properly compensate her.

William Clark made good on his offer to educate Jean Baptiste,
who even studied in Europe for six years as a young adult.

The second great mystery of Sacajawea's life is that of her
destiny after the Lewis and Clark Expedition. There are two
distinct theories on Sacajawea's fate.

By 1809, as promised, Charbonneau and Sacajawea had brought
Jean Baptiste to Clark in St. Louis. Charbonneau received a land
grant from Clark and made attempts at living a domesticated
life. All failed, as he was always drawn back to the frontier.
He left St. Louis in 1811, leaving Jean Baptiste with William
Clark. The couple next appears in the journals of explorer Henry
Brackenridge, who recorded the presence of Charbonneau and
"his wife, an Indian woman of the Snake Nation, both of whom
accompanied Lewis and Clark to the Pacific."

Charbonneau then became an employee of Manuel Lisa, a fur
trader who built Fort Manuel, just south of the border between
North and South Dakota. John C. Luttig, the clerk at Fort Manuel,
recorded the following on December 20, 1812: "This evening the

wife of Charbonneau, a Snake squaw, died of a putrid fever. She was a good and the best woman in the fort, aged about 25 years. She left a fine infant girl."

By March of 1813 the fort had been abandoned due to attacks by the Sioux, who later burned it. The grave of this unnamed wife of Charbonneau has never been located. The clerk, Luttig, took the baby girl, Lizette, to St. Louis, where he had himself appointed guardian for her as well as for Toussaint, a boy of about ten years of age. Shortly afterward the name William Clark was substituted in the court records as guardian for the two children.

During the mid-twentieth century, a journal kept by Captain Clark between the years 1825 and 1828 was discovered. In it he listed the members of the expedition and what had become of them. Next to the name "Secarjaweau," Clark made the notation "Dead."

The Shoshone people tell a different story. According to the Shoshone, Sacajawea left Charbonneau after a dispute with one of his new Indian wives. She spent time among the Comanche, where she married and had five children. Upon the death of her Comanche husband, she set out to return to her tribe, arriving at Fort Bridger, Wyoming, around 1843. Here she was reunited with her natural son, Baptiste, by then a noted frontiersman and western guide, and her adopted son, Bazil.

This woman, called Porivo, or "Chief," commanded great respect of both Indians and the whites who knew her. She spoke French and had intimate knowledge of the details of the Lewis and Clark Expedition. Although she rarely volunteered information, when asked, she stated that she had traveled with the white men to the big waters in the west and that Baptiste was the baby she had carried on her back during the expedition. She referred to her French husband as "Schab-a-no."

F. G. Burnett, an agent on the Shoshone Reservation at Wind River, Wyoming, in 1871, provides one such account:

I remember very distinctly that one day about 1872 a group of us including Doctor James Irwin, Charlie Oldham, some other white men, and a group of Indians were sitting in a circle with Sacajawea. She was talking about her trip across the mountains, telling her story in the English language. . . . She told that when she was out across the mountains with the Lewis and Clark people, word came to camp one day that a big fish had been found on the great sea, and that she begged the white men to allow her to go down and see the fish. She told about the fish she had seen . . . indicated [the size] by a space that [the whale] was from fifty to sixty feet.

Mrs. James Irwin, wife of another agent on the reservation, interviewed Porivo at length and prepared a manuscript containing her testimony about the Lewis and Clark Expedition. A fire at the agency destroyed this manuscript, but both Dr. and Mrs. Irwin were convinced that Porivo was Sacajawea of the Corps of Discovery.

Porivo lived to be an old woman on the Wind River Reservation, where she died on April 9, 1884, and was buried in the cemetery there. The Reverend John Roberts officiated at the funeral and noted in church records the death of "Bazil's mother." Originally, only a small wooden plank marked the grave, but in 1909 a cement marker was placed on the grave by the Shoshone agent and Porivo's descendants, with the help of a local benefactor. The marker is inscribed:

Sacajawea. Died April 9, 1884. A Guide with the Lewis and Clark Expedition 1805–1806. Identified, 1907 by Rev. J. Roberts who officiated at her burial.

Professor Grace Hebard, of the University of Wyoming, dedicated thirty years of her life to proving that the woman who lay buried on the Wind River Reservation was indeed Sacajawea. Hebard published numerous accounts by both whites and Indians of encounters with Sacajawea during her later life, including those of people who had seen the medal given to her by Lewis and Clark. The testimony makes a compelling case for identifying Porivo as Sacajawea. The Bureau of American Ethnology accepted Ms. Hebard's conclusions.

After Luttig's account of the death at Fort Manuel was published in the 1920s, Dr. Charles A. Eastman, a Santee Sioux, was hired by the Bureau of Indian Affairs (BIA) to determine the true identity of Sacajawea. Bazil, who died in 1886, had been buried with "important papers" provided to his mother by the white leaders. Dr. Eastman exhumed the grave of Bazil in order to obtain these papers. To his dismay a leather wallet was found that contained documents that had so deteriorated as to be unreadable. Still, based on testimony and evidence collected, Eastman reported to the BIA on March 17, 1925, that he believed Sacajawea was the woman buried on the Wind River Reservation in Wyoming.

With Charbonneau's propensity to marry Indian women, either woman could have been another of his Shoshone wives who had knowledge of the expedition. Perhaps modern DNA testing may someday solve this mystery. Until then we must choose which version we find most likely to be true. Sacajawea remains Wadze-wipe, the lost woman of the Lemhi Shoshone.

Jane Timothy Silcott

1842–1895

⚘

Gold Rush Princess

"One night three of us camped in a gorge far up in the mountains. When the moon began to shine we saw a bright light like a star gleaming out from the wall of a cliff. We were afraid. It was like the eye of the Great Spirit. In the morning we went to that place; it was a great shining ball like the white man's glass beads; we tried to dig it out. We could not get it."

Tales of rich veins of gold in the central Idaho mountains, such as the story above as told by a Nez Perce man in Byron Defenbach's *Red Heroines*, were often related by the Nez Perce people. In late 1859 one white man listening to the folklore equated the stories with gold and set out to pursue his fortune. Not knowing the route, he needed an Indian guide to lead him through hostile native territory into central Idaho. As no Indian man could risk the trek without arousing the suspicions of neighboring tribes, an eighteen-year-old Nez Perce woman volunteered to lead the first prospectors to the headwaters of the Clearwater and Salmon Rivers, thus beginning the great central-Idaho gold rush.

Princess Jane of the Nez Perce tribe was born at the mouth of Alpowa Creek around 1842. Her father was the great Nez Perce chief Ta-moot-sin, dubbed Timothy by the Reverend Henry H. Spalding. Timothy's mother was the sister of Chief Twisted Hair, the Nez Perce chief who had cared for Lewis and Clark's horses when they journeyed on to the Pacific via boat. Temar, sister of Old Chief Joseph, was Jane's mother. Old Joseph's son, the famous Nez Perce warrior Chief Joseph, was Jane's first cousin. Chief

Timothy's band was made up of the "lower" Nez Perce, who lived along the riverbanks; the "upper" Nez Perce bands lived above them in the mountains.

The Nez Perce called Jane by many names: The Princess Like the Turtle Dove, The Princess Like the Fawn, and The Princess Like Running Water. Princess Jane was slight of form, with lovely features and regal bearing. She was quiet and shy, while still brave and adventurous.

Chief Timothy was one of the Reverend Spalding's first converts to Christianity and a lifelong friend of the Spaldings. Timothy was sent by Mrs. Spalding to rescue her daughter, Eliza, from the Whitman Mission when she was a hostage there. On November 17, 1839, Timothy and Temar were formally joined in marriage by the Reverend Spalding. Chief Timothy was baptized at the Spalding Mission that same day. In accordance with his faith, Timothy brought his baby daughter to the Spaldings to be baptized and given a Christian name. Mrs. Spalding bestowed the name Jane upon the baby, and she was christened Jane Timothy. Jane's mother, Temar, with baby Jane strapped to her back in a *te-kash*, was baptized that day, May 14, 1843, and took the name Fannie.

Timothy named his village *Alpowa*, meaning "Sabbath Rest." With her family Jane lived between her main home in Alpowa and a tepee at the Spalding Mission. The lower Nez Perce encampment of Alpowa was in a valley below present-day Lewiston, where Alpowa Creek feeds into the south side of the Snake River.

Jane attended the Spalding Mission School, where Eliza Spalding taught her to read, write, and speak the English language. Eliza wrote of Jane sitting in her classroom by her sister's side. At a young age Jane was also taught by Eliza to cook, sew, spin, weave, make soap and candles, and keep house. Jane assisted with keeping the Spalding household.

Chief Timothy was often approached by neighboring chiefs who wished to arrange a marriage between the lovely Princess Jane and their sons. Timothy always deferred to his daughter, stating, "Jane has her own mind; she may choose who she will for her husband."

When she was around fourteen years old, Princess Jane married a man who was half Nez Perce—the son of a Nez Perce mother and white father. There was one son born of this union, who drowned in the Clearwater at a very young age. Her husband died within a few years of their son's death.

Chief Timothy had been a boy when he first encountered white men. On their return journey from the Pacific Ocean, Lewis and Clark and their party had camped at the lodge of Timothy's father on Alpowa Creek. During the visit, Lewis and Clark presented Timothy's father with a flintlock gun, which was passed on to Chief Timothy. According to Nez Perce history, Timothy's actions precipitated the arrival of white missionaries in the Northwest. Chiefs Timothy and Red Bear and their council had selected four Nez Perce men—Chief Black Eagle, Man of the Morning, No Horns on His Head, and Rabbit Skin Leggings—to travel to St. Louis in order to find Lewis and Clark and obtain the white man's "Book of Heaven." The arrival in St. Louis of the four Nez Perce seeking the Bible inspired the great western missionary movement of the early nineteenth century. In this respect Chief Timothy, the Spaldings' first convert, was responsible for bringing the Spalding Mission to the Nez Perce people.

When Chief Timothy heard that Sacajawea[1] had returned to her people, the Shoshone, he called Jane to his side. He asked Jane to ride to the land of the Shoshone to visit the woman he remembered from the Lewis and Clark Expedition. The chief wished to send gifts to the great Shoshone lady. Princess Jane beaded a buckskin dress to bring as a gift of her own. She also brought beaded bags and a shawl as gifts from her father, and set out on horseback, leading a packhorse laden with gifts.

[1] Indian people believed that Sacajawea returned to her people and lived to be an old woman. See Sacajawea chapter, page 197.

The Nez Perce princess found the Shoshone princess among the Shoshone people and presented the gifts to her. In turn Sacajawea gave Jane the buckskin dress she had worn on the Lewis and Clark Expedition. (Some historians dispute that this could have been the dress worn on the expedition, but the Nez Perce believe it to be a true account.) She also gave Princess Jane white glass beads strung on buffalo calfskin, which had been a gift to her from Captain Lewis. Sacajawea told Jane that President Jefferson had given Lewis the beads to present to the Indians as a gesture of peace and friendship.

Jane traveled back to the land of her father with Sacajawea's dress, necklace, her baby's neckpiece, and a lock of her hair. These items, along with a canoe used by Lewis and Clark, were put on display at the Old Spalding Log Cabin Mission Museum in the Spalding National Park until they were destroyed by a flood in 1964.

In 1858 during the Northwest Indian Wars, Lieutenant Colonel E. J. Steptoe brought his troops to Red Wolf's Crossing, near Jane's home, for his ill-fated expedition into the Palouse country. Timothy's fleet of canoes ferried the expedition of 159 men across the Snake River, and the aging chief is reported to have marched with Steptoe as a guide and interpreter. Steptoe's men were attacked in the Palouse country by more than 1,000 members of inland tribes including Palouse, Spokanes, and Coeur d'Alenes. Suffering heavy casualties, the expedition was able to escape during the night by leaving their tents pitched and campfires burning and taking an unguarded route over high plateau terrain, which Timothy had scouted. The chief led the men back across the Snake, and Jane and other Nez Perce women nursed the soldiers' wounds. Jane and her kinswomen gave the exhausted men water and fed them a breakfast of boiled salmon meat. When they were strong enough, the expedition returned to Fort Walla Walla. Colonel Steptoe later recorded accolades for Timothy and his band: "I had vast difficulty in getting the horses over Snake River, which is everywhere wide, deep and strong, and without the help of Timothy's Indians it would have been utterly impossible for us to cross either going or coming."

Two years after the Steptoe battle, in 1860, a party of prospectors sought refuge in Chief Timothy's camp. Captain Pierce, the leader of the group, had heard the stories from the Nez Perce, which led him to believe that there was gold in the mountains of the Clearwater. On a trip Father De Smet made from Fort Boise to the Lemhi in 1844, he had observed, "These Indians roam over wealth that would make nations rich. Where I now sit I can see gold in the rocks." Pierce led his men as far as Alpowa on the Snake River, where he was met by hostile bands of Indians who threatened his life if he went any farther into their country. After several attempts to travel inland were met by armed resistance, Pierce asked Chief Timothy if he could winter near his camp.

Chief Timothy and his family members, including Fannie and Jane, held council with Pierce and his men. Pierce told Timothy of his plans, which he alleged did not include staying on the lower rivers. His plan, as he outlined it, was to follow the Lolo Trail into the land of the buffalo. Timothy told Pierce that all of the surrounding tribes knew of the white men's presence. Through his aid to the Spaldings and Colonel Steptoe, the older chief had raised the ire and distrust of neighboring tribes. He related to Pierce, "My men and I are being watched every day; if one of us were to go with you it would be certain death." At that, Jane spoke out and volunteered to lead the prospectors into the mountains in the spring. She thought that by following the Colville Trail, which was not used by natives at that time of the year, they might avoid trouble on their way north. Jane knew the trail into central Idaho well; she had followed it many times with her people in search of camas roots and on their way to the buffalo country.

Pierce and the men began the journey by traveling up the Alpowa as if they were headed back to Walla Walla. After hiding for a day, the party retraced their steps to the Snake River, where

Timothy's canoes took them across under cover of darkness. Traveling by night and hiding by day, Jane led the group across the Snake and up a ravine to a plateau above. She stayed to the right of the trail, using it as a guide, but taking care not to leave tracks on the path. They followed the present-day Washington/ Idaho state line upland near what is now Moscow, skirted the Thatuna Hills, and crossed the upper Potlatch on to Elk River to Big Island on the North Fork of the Clearwater. They forded the swollen Clearwater and followed several more creeks until they reached Canal Gulch.

One of Pierce's men panned the first gold taken from Canal Gulch. Though the amount panned was worth only 3 cents, this find precipitated the gold rush, which brought thousands of miners stampeding into central Idaho. The prospectors returned the next year with more men and supplies and discovered additional rivers of gold. Since the gold panned was very fine, the prospectors named the creek where they found it *Oro Fino*, or "fine ore." The towns of Orofino, Pierce City, Elk City, Florence, and Warrens sprang up, followed by a rush to the Boise Basin. By March 1861, 500 men were bound for Pierce City.

Princess Jane returned to her father's lodge unaware of the sensation that would be created in the wake of the tidal wave of prospectors soon to arrive in her homeland. Alpowa became a way station for the ever-increasing stream of miners. Lewiston was established at the confluence of the Snake and Clearwater as a supply center for the prospectors. The old Nez Perce prophecy, as told through the mythical creature Coyote (often called "The Trickster" and an important character in Indian mythology), who was constantly saying, *Na-te-tam he-wah-yam* ("the people are coming"), became increasingly true. Tragically, Jane's oldest brother, Edward, was stabbed to death by a Cayuse man in retribution for the Timothy family's services to the white men.

Shortly after leading the Pierce expedition into central Idaho,

Jane met John Silcott, a Harvard-educated man eighteen years her senior who had been sent to construct buildings for the government at Fort Lapwai. The couple was married by the Reverend Henry Spalding at Lapwai. A Lewiston pioneer described Jane: "She was a noted cook and housekeeper and made Silcott a fine wife. She was a good woman."

John and Jane Silcott made their home at the *Tsceminicum,* which means "the meeting of the waters of the Snake and Clearwater Rivers." The Silcotts built and operated the first commercial ferry in Idaho across the Clearwater. The couple often entertained travelers crossing the river. John was noted for his love of cards and drink, and Jane for cooking and caring for their guests.

A middle-aged Jane became plagued with rheumatism and attempted to ease the pain in her joints by applying the white man's medicine. John bought his wife liniment from a Lewiston drugstore for her pain, and she would sit beside her fireplace and rub the balm on her aching joints. But as one old-timer told it, "The attempt to mix the white man's medicine with the red man's open fire met with disastrous results." Jane was fifty-three on January 17, 1895, when sparks from the open fireplace set her clothing ablaze, and she burned to death. Princess Jane was buried at the Tsceminicum, and a marble monument inscribed NOT FORGOTTEN was installed over the grave by her husband. When John Silcott died in 1902, he was buried next to the Nez Perce princess. The graves now rest in a privately owned wheat field and are tended by the people of Lewiston.

A bridge across the Alpowa and a state park west of Clarkston are named in honor of Chief Timothy. Within Chief Timothy State Park lie Silcott Island and the Alpowai[2] Interpretive Center.

[2] The Nez Perce tribe currently uses this spelling; however, the name remains "Alpowa" on maps and in historical references.

The site marks the original Alpowa Nez Perce encampment of the mid-1800s, which later became the now-defunct community of Silcott. All honor Princess Jane's family for playing pivotal roles in the development of Idaho and the Northwest.

Louise Siuwheem
1800–1853

❧

Angel of the Coeur d'Alenes

War cries echoed through the hills, warning of the approach of an enemy tribe. The peaceful Coeur d'Alene encampment was suddenly under attack by avenging warriors from the Spokane tribe. The Spokanes charged the Coeur d'Alenes, encircling them with vastly superior numbers well prepared for battle.

Seeing her tribe outnumbered and realizing her people had no chance to survive such a surprise attack, Louise ran to her tepee and grabbed the large wooden cross she kept there. Holding the cross above her head, the pious woman marched through the encampment, imploring her people to follow her. The parade of chanting Coeur d'Alenes, led by Louise, marched straight at their menacing enemies.

The Spokane warriors could not believe their eyes. The sight of this woman, bearing a cross, dumbfounded them and filled them with fear and awe. The men lay down their weapons and retreated in great haste, vowing never again to challenge the Coeur d'Alenes.

Legend has it that this pious, nineteenth-century Joan of Arc saved her tribe from certain death with her bravery and unwavering Christian faith on more than one occasion.

When a Nez Perce war chief sent an envoy by canoe across Lake Coeur d'Alene to challenge her tribe into battle, the people turned to Louise, a respected tribal leader, for their response. She sent word back to the Nez Perce chief that her people were Christians, not warriors; and, if the Nez Perce stayed on their side of the lake, the Coeur d'Alenes would not fight them, but if they approached, they would all be killed. Thus dissuaded, the Nez Perce chief took his war party and departed.

Although there is no way to verify them, these legends have been passed along throughout the years. Stories state that Coeur d'Alene chiefs respected Louise Siuwheem for her wisdom and bravery and sought her counsel ever after and that Louise's intervention prevented much bloodshed between the Coeur d'Alenes and neighboring tribes. Louise held a position of great respect as the sister of the head chief, Stelaam, an iron-willed ruler whom many, including early priests, found difficult. Louise often acted as an intermediary on her brother's behalf, which may be the root of such stories.

Born around 1800, Louise was the daughter of a chief of the Coeur d'Alene tribe. They called themselves *Schitzu'Umsh,* but early French fur trappers, who found the people to be shrewd traders, sharp or hard-hearted like needles, dubbed the tribe *Coeur d'Alene,* meaning "heart of the needle, or awl." The chief's daughter was given the name *Siuwheem,*[1] or "Tranquil Waters," in the language of her people.

Siuwheem was married when she was a teenager to a member of the Spokane tribe called Polotkin. The couple raised three sons. When her husband became crippled, Louise took on the role of provider for the family as well as nurse to her invalid husband.

Siuwheem's grandfather, the great Chief Circling Raven, had dreamed of a visit by two black-robed angels who descended from heaven to teach his people of a great spirit. This vision was passed on by Chief Circling Raven to his children and grandchildren. In April 1842 Jesuit priest Father Pierre-Jean De Smet, "the Saint Paul of the West," arrived among the Coeur d'Alene tribe. Father

[1] "Sighouin" is the spelling used by Father De Smet and later writers. Father Connolly of the current Sacred Heart Mission spells and pronounces the name "Siuwheem," as it appears on her headstone.

De Smet was the superior of the Rocky Mountain Missions when he met three Coeur d'Alene families who had traveled east on a buffalo hunt. The families had their children baptized by the priest and urged him to visit their tribe. Father De Smet was welcomed by the Coeur d'Alenes, but none received him so joyously as Siuwheem, who saw in him the fulfillment of her grandfather's prophecy.

Father De Smet described his initial impressions of Siuwheem: "Before her baptism, even, she was remarkable for her rare modesty and reserve, great gentleness, and a solid judgment. Her words were everywhere listened to with admiration and pleasure, and her company sought in all families."

Siuwheem and Polotkin were among the first of their people to be baptized. At his baptism Polotkin took the name Adolph, and Siuwheem took the name Louise, meaning "defender of the people." The priest sanctified the union of Adolph and Louise in the eyes of the church by performing an official marriage ceremony.

"Enlightened by a special grace," Father De Smet said of how Louise used her influence to induce many Indian families to follow her to the banks of Lake Coeur d'Alene to hear the priest preach the law of God. After her baptism Louise renounced all material wealth and pledged devotion to the priests, "I will follow the Black Gowns to the end of the world. . . I wish to profit by their presence and their instructions to learn to know the Great Spirit well, to serve him faithfully, and to love him with all my heart."

In 1843 the Jesuits built a mission on the banks of the St. Joe River near the southern end of Lake Coeur d'Alene. During construction of the St. Joseph's Mission, Louise moved her family onto the grounds to be near the missionaries and "The Lodge of the Lord." Father Point became the mission's superior, succeeded by Father Joset in 1845. The Coeur d'Alene Mission was Father Joseph Joset's favorite mission; and, even after being appointed superior of the Missions of the Northwest, Father Joset chose to remain with the Coeur d'Alene people, making his headquarters on their land.

While still caring for the needs of her invalid husband and children, this frail woman, who was often in delicate health herself, spent all available time receiving instruction from the priests and sharing her knowledge and enthusiasm with other members of her tribe. The priests struggled with the Coeur d'Alene language. Father De Smet described his difficulty comprehending and speaking it even after many years working among the tribe. Louise offered the missionaries invaluable help in translating and teaching her people. She was given the position of tribal catechist, head teacher of the catechism, and devoted herself to religious instruction. Thus Louise became known as a great teacher.

In addition to teaching Louise took the position of defender of her religion. She was often at odds with the medicine men of her tribe who, fearing the loss of their own power, tried to disrupt the work of the missionaries. Frequently putting her own safety in jeopardy, Louise tirelessly worked to oppose the powerful medicine men. She boldly intruded upon them, entering their lodges uninvited, in order to lecture them.

One of the leaders of the medicine men was Natatken, a relative of Louise's who staunchly resisted Louise's teaching. Louise persevered, however, until she finally led Natatken and his wife and children directly to the priest to receive the sacrament of regeneration. Natatken took the Christian name of Isidore and became one of the most zealous members of the church, responsible for converting many of his followers to Christianity.

Louise also sought to ensure that once converted, her tribesmen did not revert to unsanctioned practices such as gambling. Chief Emotestsulem, who had been baptized as Peter Ignatius, became consumed by a prior addiction to gambling after his conversion. Upon learning of this Louise walked for two days to find the chief and return him to his duties as a tribal leader. Though it was contrary to tradition for an Indian man to publicly accept criticism and advice from a woman, this woman commanded such respect, even among men and chiefs, that she was able to convince Emotestsulem to renounce his habit and repent. Louise met each challenge with patience, courage, and perseverance.

This gentle woman harbored a special love for the children of the tribe, especially the young girls. Father De Smet wrote of her work among the children:

> *By her motherly vigilance over the behavior of her children, by the simple and persuasive gentleness with which she treated them on all occasions, Louise had inspired them with the most profound respect and entire confidence . . . that . . . a single word from the lips of their good mother, was an absolute order, a law for them, which they accomplished . . . with eagerness and joy.*

It was not uncommon for Louise to take in children whose parents could not care for them. Louise adopted two children who were unwanted because of their severe disabilities. One such orphan was Ignatius, a crippled, blind child who was stubborn, unruly, and a most disruptive member of the family. Though both children she adopted died at early ages, they received the same love and attention that Louise provided her own children, no matter how difficult their needs.

Louise Siuwheem's lodge became a shelter for young girls in need of counsel. She eagerly took them under her wing, offering guidance and instruction. In recognition of her endless work with children, she became known among her tribesmen as the "Good Grandmother."

This Good Samaritan was also an accomplished healer. Father Gazzoli (successor of Father Joset) said that he never arrived to administer to a sick or injured person that Louise was not already there ahead of him. She devoted herself to nursing the sick and dying no matter what time of the day or night she was called.

Although Father De Smet had intended for the St. Joseph Mission to be a permanent settlement, the yearly spring flooding of the St. Joe River raised havoc with the mission's crops. Father Joset decided to build another mission, which was started in 1848, on the banks of the Coeur d'Alene River about 12 miles east of the lake. The new mission was designed by Father Ravalli, who had visions of an elegant Doric-style church and grand mission. Using crude tools and makeshift supplies, the Jesuits and the Coeur d'Alene people set out to build the magnificent mission, a labor that was to take them five years.

Louise's leadership again proved invaluable to the priests when she convinced the tribal members to devote their labor to the construction of the new mission. Building of lodges was not seen as traditional work for Indian men, who scorned it as women's work. Louise offered high praise to those people who labored on the project and public criticism to those who refused to work. In the end more than 300 tribal members participated in the mission's construction.

The natural leader showed great managerial skills in organizing the labor of her people. Women and children were placed on teams and assigned such duties as cutting straw, mixing mortar, carrying water, and weaving grass mats. Built without nails, the church had a framework formed from giant timbers connected by willow bars and woven grass plastered with adobe, which formed walls a foot thick. The facade was later sided with wooden planks. Through the devotion and labor of Louise and her Coeur d'Alene people, the Mission of the Sacred Heart of Jesus was finished in 1853, where it still stands near Cataldo, Idaho.

In 1853 Louise became bedridden by illness, said to be consumption (tuberculosis). That summer she called upon Father Gazzoli to administer last rites. On her deathbed she implored her husband, Adolph, not to return to the home of his people, where there were no priests. Her dying wish was for her children to live good, spiritually rich lives and for those around her to join in one last hymn. Before the singing of the hymn was finished, Louise had passed away.

One of those kneeling beside the bed ran out crying. "'Siuwheem, good Siuwheem is dead.' The cry was taken up and echoed in the valley and the foot of the high mountains which encircle the Residence of the Sacred Heart," described Father De Smet in his writings on the life of Louise Siuwheem. A sudden desolation and grief went through the tribe as they mourned for a beloved mother and grandmother, a faithful friend, teacher, translator, nurse, and social worker who led her people through peaceful times and war times and had lived in great poverty without ever showing her own needs or suffering.

Louise was buried in a plain coffin built by her youngest son and placed into a grave dug by her children. With a prayer and a personal farewell, each person in attendance at her funeral threw a handful of dirt onto the coffin. Her service was performed by Father Gazzoli, who believed Siuwheem to be "the spiritual directress, the guardian angel of her whole tribe."

On August 15 of each year, Coeur d'Alene tribal members make a pilgrimage to the old mission in memory of the good grandmother and the coming of the "Black Robes." Today no one is exactly sure where on the mission grounds Louise's grave lies. In 1985 Louise's great-granddaughter, Blanche La Sarte, and Father Tom Connolly had a monument placed at the old mission to honor Louise.

The Sacred Heart Mission, now more commonly called the Cataldo Mission or Old Mission, has the distinction of being the oldest standing building in Idaho. In 1975 the mission became an Idaho state park, officially titled Old Mission State Park. It stands today as a lasting monument to Louise Siuwheem and her people.

SOURCES

More than Petticoats: Remarkable Nevada Women
Sarah Winnemucca Hopkins
Dat So La Lee

More than Petticoats: Remarkable New York Women
Kateri Tekakwitha

More than Petticoats: Remarkable North Carolina Women
Maggie Axe Wachacha

More than Petticoats: Remarkable Virginia Women
Pocahontas

More than Petticoats: Remarkable Alaska Women
Matilda Kinnon "Tillie" Paul Tamaree
Anfesia Shapsnikoff

More than Petticoats: Remarkable Arizona Women
Lozen
Polingaysi Qöyawayma

More than Petticoats: Remarkable Connecticut Women
Gladys Tantaquidgeon

More than Petticoats: Remarkable Georgia Women
Mary Musgrove Bosomworth

More than Petticoats: Remarkable Indiana Women
Frances Slocum

More than Petticoats: Remarkable New Mexico Women
Nampeyo

More than Petticoats: Remarkable Washington Women
Kick-Is-Om-Lo
Isabel Friedlander Arcasa

More than Petticoats: Remarkable Montana Women
Helen Clarke

More than Petticoats: Remarkable Colorado Women
Chipeta

More than Petticoats: Remarkable Florida Women
Malee

More than Petticoats: Remarkable Michigan Women
Magdelaine LaFramboise

More than Petticoats: Remarkable Idaho Women
Sacajawea
Jane Timothy Silcott
Louise Siuwheem

BIBLIOGRAPHY

Sarah Winnemucca Hopkins

Butruille, Susan G. *Women's Voices from the Western Frontier.* Boise: Tamarack Books, Inc., 1995.

Canfield, Gae Whitney. *Sarah Winnemucca of the Northern Paiutes.* Norman: University of Oklahoma Press, 1983.

Dunlap, Patricia Riley. *Riding Astride: The Frontier Women's History.* Denver: Arden Press, Inc., 1995.

Hopkins, Sarah Winnemucca. *Life Among the Paiutes: Their Wrongs and Claims.* Edited by Mrs. Horace Mann. Boston: Cupples, Upham & Company, 1883.

McClure, Andrew S. "Sarah Winnemucca: [Post] Indian Princess and Voice of the Paiutes" (critical essay). Published by The Society for the Study of the Multi-Ethics Literature in the United States (MELUS), 24.2 (1999), 29–51. Accessed November 2, 2002, from www.findarticles.com/cf_0/m2278/2_24/59211506/print.jhtml.

Miller, Susan Cummins, ed. *A Sweet Separate Intimacy: Women Writers of the American Frontier, 1800–1922.* Salt Lake City: University of Utah Press, 2000.

Moynihan, Ruth B., Susan Armitage, and Christine Fisher Dichamp, eds. *So Much to Be Done: Women Settlers on the Mining and Ranching Frontier.* Lincoln: University of Nebraska Press, 1990.

Schlissel, Lilliam, and Catherine Lavender, eds. *The Western Women's Reader: The Remarkable Writings of Women Who Shaped the American West, Spanning 300 Years.* New York: Harper Perennial, 2000.

Stewart, Patricia. "Sarah Winnemucca." *Nevada Historical Society Quarterly* 14, no. 4 (winter 1971), 23–38.

Zanjani, Sally Springmeyer. *Sarah Winnemucca*. Lincoln: University of Nebraska Press, 2001.

Dat So La Lee

Cohodas, Marvin. "Dat so la lee and the Degikup." *Halcyon, A Journal of the Humanities* (1982), 119–140.

————. "Louisa Keyser and the Cohns: Mythmaking and Basket Making in the American West." *The Early Years of Native American Art History.* Janet Catherine Berlo, ed. Seattle: University of Washington Press, 1992, 88–133.

Hickson, Jane Green. *Dat So La Lee: Queen of the Washo Basketmakers.* Carson City: Nevada State Museum Popular Series, December 1967.

Ross, Christopher. "Dat So La Lee and the Myth Weavers." *Nevada Magazine* (September–October 1989).

Kateri Tekakwitha

Bunson, Margaret R. *Kateri Tekakwitha: Mystic of the Wilderness.* Huntington, Ind.: Our Sunday Visitor Publishing, 1992.

Daughters of St. Paul. *Blessed Kateri Tekakwitha: Mohawk Maiden.* Boston: Daughters of St. Paul, 1980.

James, Edward, ed. *Notable American Women 1607–1950.* Vol. III. Cambridge, Mass.: Belknap Press of Harvard University, 1971.

Liguori online. www.ligouri.org.

The New Catholic Encyclopedia. Vol. II. Washington, D.C.: Catholic University, 1967.

The Position of the Historical Section of The Sacred Congregation of Rites on the Introduction of the Cause for Beatification and Canonization and on the Virtues of the Servant of God, Katharine Tekakwitha, The Lily of the Mohawks. New York: Fordham University Press. Translated in 1940.

Ruether, Rosemary Radford, and Rosemary Skinner Keller. *Women and Religion in America*. Vol. 2: The Colonial and Revolutionary Periods. New York: Harper & Row, 1983.

Sargent, Daniel. *Catherine Tekakwitha*. New York: Longmans, Green and Co., 1940.

Wynne, John J. *Katharine Tekakwitha: Lily of the Mohawks*. New York: The Home Press, 1922.

Maggie Axe Wachacha

Jackson, Gill. "A Profile Maggie Axe Wachacha," *The Cherokee One Feather*, March 26, 1986.

Journal of Cherokee Studies: Fading Voices, Special Edition. Cherokee, NC: Cherokee Communications, 1991.

"Maggie Wachacha Among Five Who Receive N.C. Distinguished Women Awards," *The Cherokee One Feather*, March 25, 1986.

"Maggie Wachacha, 'Beloved Woman,' dies," *The Cherokee One Feather*, February 10, 1993.

Millsaps, Bill (friend of Maggie Wachacha). E-mail and Interview, March and April, 1999.

Mooney, James. *History, Myths, and Sacred Formulas of the Cherokees* (Originally published in 1891 and 1900 by the Bureau of American Ethnology), Asheville, NC: Historical Images (Bright Mountain Books, Inc.), 1992.

Moore, MariJo. "Remembering Beloved Woman Maggie Wachacha," *Asheville Citizen-Times*, September 6, 1998.

Neely, Sharlotte. *Snowbird Cherokees: People of Persistence*. Athens, GA: The University of Georgia Press, 1991.

Perdue, Theda. *Native Carolinians—The Indians of North Carolina*. Raleigh, NC: Division of Archives and History, North Carolina Department of Cultural Resources, 1985.

Welch, Rick, "Maggie Wachacha Honored at Cherokee-Iroquois Conference," *The Cherokee One Feather*, April 19, 1978.

West, Carolyn (great-granddaughter of Maggie Wachacha). Interview, April 6, 1999.

Pocahontas

Adams, Patricia. *The Story of Pocahontas, Indian Princess.* Milwaukee, Wisc.: Gareth Stevens Publishing Company, 1987.

Barker-Benfield, G. J., and Catherine Clinton. *Portraits of American Women from Settlement to the Present.* New York: St. Martin's Press, 1991.

Fishwick, Marshall. "Was John Smith a Liar?" *American Heritage* IX, no. 6 (October 1958): 28–33, 110–111.

Fritz, Jean. *The Double Life of Pocahontas.* Lakeville, Conn.: Grey Castle Press, 1983.

Rountree, Helen C. *Pocahontas's People.* Norman, Okla.: University of Oklahoma Press, 1990.

Watson, Virginia. *The Legend of Pocahontas.* New York: Avenel Publishing Company, 1995.

Woodward, Grace Steele. *Pocahontas.* Norman, Okla.: University of Oklahoma Press, 1963.

Matilda Kinnon "Tillie" Paul Tamaree

Davis, Mary Lee. *We Are Alaskans.* Boston: W. A. Wilde Co., 1931.

DeGermain, Frances Paul. Correspondence with author, September–October 2004.

DeWitt, Marion Paul. Interview with author, September 7, 2004.

Estus, Nana Paul. Correspondence with author, October 5, 2004.

Paul, Frances Lackey. *Kahtahah.* Anchorage, Alaska: Northwest Publishing Co., 1976.

Ricketts, Nancy J. "Matilda Kinnon Paul Tamaree/Kahtahah: Kahtliyudt." *Haa Kusteeyi; Our Culture: Tlingit Life Stories.* Edited by Nora Marks Dauenhauer and Richard Dauenhauer. Seattle: University of Washington Press, 1994.

Sherr, Lynn and Jurate Kazickas. *Susan B. Anthony Slept Here.* New York: Random House, 1994.

Verdesi, Elizabeth Howell and Sylvia Thorson-Smith. *A Sampler of Saints; In praise of our Presbyterian foremothers, no longer forgotten, written to commemorate the Bicentennial of the Presbyterian Church* (U.S.A.). Presbyterian Historical Society, 1988.

The *Verstovian.* "Mrs. William Tamaree Dies at Wrangell." September 1952.

The *Wrangell Sentinel.* "Mrs. William Tamaree, Wrangell Pioneer, Taken by Death." August 22, 1952.

Anfesia Shapsnikoff

Anfesia Shapsnikoff Collection. Box 1, Folders 15, 17, 18. Archives, Alaska and Polar Regions Department, Rasmuson Library, University of Alaska, Fairbanks.

Baranov Museum Web site. "Attu Grass Basket Weaving with Hazel Jones." http://www.baranov.us/events.html.

Hudson, Ray. *Moments Rightly Placed: An Aleutian Memoir.* Kenmore, Washington: Epicenter Press, 1998.

———. Correspondence with author, July 25, 2005.

Letters from Anfesia Shapsnikoff, 1967. Margaret Hafemeister Collection, Archives and Manuscript Department, Consortium Library, University of Alaska, Anchorage.

Neseth, Eunice. Transcript, Oral History Interview at interviewer's home, Kodiak, Alaska, May 21, 1971. Anfesia Shapsnikoff Collection, Archives and Manuscript Department, Consortium Library, University of Alaska, Anchorage.

Oleksa, Rev. Michael. *Six Alaskan Native Women Leaders: Pre-Statehood.* Alaska State Department of Education, January 1991.

Unugulux Tunusangin, *Oldtime Stories.* Unalaska City School District, Unalaska, Alaska.

Lozen

Aleshire, Peter. *Warrior Woman: The Story of Lozen, Apache Warrior and Shaman.* New York: St. Martin's Press, 2001.

Ball, Eve. *In the Days of Victorio.* Tucson: University of Arizona Press, 1970.

Stockel, H. Henrietta. *Women of the Apache Nation: Voices of Truth.* Reno and Las Vegas: University of Nevada Press, 1991.

————. *Chiricahua Apache Women and Children: Safekeepers of the Heritage.* College Station: Texas A&M University Press, 2000.

————. Letter to author, August 6, 2002.

Thrapp, Dan L. *The Conquest of Apacheria.* Norman: University of Oklahoma Press, 1967.

————. *Victorio and the Mimbres Apaches.* Norman: University of Oklahoma Press, 1974.

Polingaysi Qöyawayma

History of the Hopi People. Accessed July 31, 2002, from www .hopi.nsn.us/Pages/History/history.html.

Norwood, Vera, and Janice Monk, eds. *The Desert Is No Lady: Southwestern Landscapes in Women's Writing and Art.* New Haven: Yale University Press, 1987; Tucson: University of Arizona Press, 1997.

Qöyawayma, Polingaysi (Elizabeth Q. White). *No Turning Back: A Hopi Woman's Struggle to Live in Two Worlds, as told to Vada B. Carlson.* Albuquerque: University of New Mexico Press, 1964.

Qöyawayma, Polingaysi (Elizabeth Q. White). Arizona Women's Hall of Fame pamphlet. Phoenix, 1991.

Qöyawayma, Polingaysi (Elizabeth Q. White). Biography included in Native North American pages of the African Americans Publications. Accessed July 31, 2002, from www.nativepubs .com/nativepubs.

Gladys Tantaquidgeon

Fawcett, Melissa Jayne. *The Lasting of the Mohegans,* Part I. Uncasville, Conn.: The Mohegan Tribe, 1995.

———. *Medicine Trail: The Life Lessons of Gladys Tantaquidgeon.* Phoenix: University of Arizona Press, 2000.

Grant, Bruce. *American Indians, Yesterday and Today.* New York: E. P. Dutton & Co., 1958.

Malinowski, Sharon, and Anna Sheets, eds. *The Gale Encyclopedia of Native American Tribes.* Vol. 1. Farmington Hills, Mich.: Gale Research, 1998.

Spencer, Robert F., and Jesse D. Jennings. *The Native Americans.* 2nd ed. New York: Harper & Row, 1977.

Tantaquidgeon, Gladys. *Folk Medicine of the Delaware and Related Algonkian Indians.* Harrisburg, Penn.: Pennsylvania Historical and Museum Commission, 1972.

Voight, Virginia Frances. *Mohegan Chief: The Story of Harold Tantaquidgeon.* New York: Funk & Wagnalls Co., 1965.

Mary Musgrove Bosomworth

Coulter, E. Merton. "Mary Musgrove, Queen of the Creeks: a Chapter of Early Georgia Troubles." *Georgia Historical Quarterly* 11 (1927): 1–30.

Helsley, Alexia Jones. *Unsung Heroines of the Carolina Frontier.* South Carolina Department of Archives and History, 1997.

Johnson, Amanda. *Georgia as Colony and State.* Atlanta: Cherokee Publishing Company, 1970.

Kerber, Linda K. *Women of the Republic: Intellect and Ideology in Revolutionary America.* Chapel Hill: University of North Carolina Press for the Institute of Early American History and Culture, 1980.

Lane, Mills, ed. *General Oglethorpe's Georgia: Colonial Letters 1733–1743,* Vols. 1 and 2. Savannah: Beehive Press, 1975.

Spalding, Phinizy. *Oglethorpe in America.* Chicago: University of Chicago Press, 1977.

Frances Slocum

Bailey, G. S. "The Story of Frances Slocum." The *Morning Republic.* June 19, 1869. Retrieved May 2005 from www.rootsweb.com/~inmiami/fslocum.html.

Dye, Kitty. *Maconaquah's Story: The Saga of Frances Slocum.* Port Clinton, Ohio: LeClere Publishing Company, 2000.

Gilman, Julia. *William Wells and Maconaquah, White Rose of the Miamis.* Cincinnati, Ohio: Jewel Publishing, 1985.

Meginness, John F. *Biography of Frances Slocum, The Lost Sister of Wyoming.* Williamsport, Penn.: Heller Brothers Printing House, 1891. Retrieved June 2006 from http://www.gbl.indiana.edu/archives/miamis21/M78_1a.html.

"Old Bible Owned by Scranton Woman Tells of Capture of [Frances Slocum] Lost Daughter of Wyoming." *Scranton (Penn.) Times,* October 3, 1916. Retrieved August 2005 from www.rootsweb.com/~scwhite/slocum/frances.html.

Peckham, H. H. *Captured by Indians: True Tales of Pioneer Survivors.* New Brunswick, N.J.: Rutgers University Press, 1954.

Phelps, Martha Bennett. *Frances Slocum: The Lost Sister of Wyoming.* 2nd ed. New York: The Knickerbocker Press, 1916.

Winger, Otho. *The Lost Sister among the Miamis.* Elgin, Ill.: The Elgin Press, 1936.

Nampeyo

Dillingham, Rick. *Fourteen Families in Pueblo Pottery.* Reprint edition. Albuquerque: University of New Mexico Press, 1994.

Graves, Laura. *Thomas Varker Keam, Indian Trader.* Norman: University of Oklahoma Press, 1998.

Kramer, Barbara. *Nampeyo and Her Pottery.* Albuquerque: University of New Mexico Press, 1996.

Kick-Is-Om-Lo (Princess Angeline)

"Angeline Is Non-committal." The *Seattle Press-Times*, October 21, 1891.

"Battle of Seattle." The *Seattle Press-Times*, January 30, 1892.

"Chief Seattle and Angeline." *Kitsap County History.* Silverdale, Wash.: The Kitsap County Historical Society Book Committee, 1977.

Conover, C. T. "Just Cogitating: Princess Angeline Was Familiar Figure in Seattle," The *Seattle Times*, November 11, 1956.

———. "Just Cogitating: Angeline Was Best-Known of Chief Seattle's Children." The *Seattle Times,* December 15, 1957.

———. "Just Cogitating: Angeline Wanted to Be Buried among Tillicums." The *Seattle Times*, December 21, 1958.

———. "Just Cogitating: Princess Angeline Was Noted Sight in Old Seattle." The *Seattle Times*, July 19, 1959.

Dorpat, Paul. "Princess Angeline's Shack." The *Seattle Times*, May 13, 1984.

Duncan, Don. "Gentle Reign of Angeline." Don Duncan's Driftwood Diary, The *Seattle Times*, June 28, 1970.

"Gift Recalls Local History." *Capitol Hill Times*, September 17, 1958.

"Poor Old Angeline, Only Living Child of the Great War Chief Seattle." *Seattle Post-Intelligencer*, August 2, 1891.

Princess Angeline—Obituary. *Seattle Post-Intelligencer*, May 31, 1896.

"'Princess Angeline' to Be Given Friday Afternoon in Frederick & Nelson Store Auditorium." The *Seattle Times*, May 8, 1930.

"A Princess Prophecies." The *Seattle Press-Times*, March 31, 1892.

Riley, Lori Jackson. "Grandmother and Princess Angeline." *In Incidents In the Life of a Pioneer Woman*. The State Association of The Daughters of the Pioneers of Washington, 1976.

"The Royal Family." The *Seattle Press-Times*, April 7, 1892.

Sayre, J. Willis. *This City of Ours*. Seattle, 1936.

"Seattle's Princess." *Seattle Mail & Herald*, October 26, 1901.

"She Was Very Ancient." The *Seattle Press-Times*, October 21, 1891.

Isabel Friedlander Arcasa

Anderson, Eva. "Silico Saska Was Entiat's Indian." *Wenatchee World*, circa 1955.

Arcasa, Isabelle [sic] and Robert H. Ruby. "No Wrath Like That of an Indian Chief Scorned." *Columbia Magazine*, Fall 1987.

Barham, Melvin. "Isabel Arcasa Keeps Indian Heritage Alive." *Wenatchee World*, November 23, 1980.

Brown, John A. and Robert H. Ruby. "Isabel Arcasa, a Centennial Centenarian." *Columbia Magazine*, Fall 1989.

Connolly, Tom, S.J. Manuscript prepared from interview taped with Isabel Arcasa, May 5, 1979.

Connolly, Tom, S.J. "Stories about Isabel Arcasa." *Colville Tribal Tribune*, December 1, 1989.

Greene, Bernice. "Interview With Isabel Arcasa." October 18, 1977, October 25, 1977, Manuscripts from North Central Washington Museum collection, Wenatchee, WA.

Greene, Bernice. "The Oldest Colville Indian in the West! Isabel Arcasa Celebrates 100th Birthday." *Colville Tribal Tribune*, December 1, 1989.

Schmeltzer, Michael. "Our Pioneers Are Part of the Present." *Spokane Chronicle*, May 26, 1983.

Special thanks to: Maybelle and Sheila Gendron, daughter and granddaughter of Isabel Arcasa.

Father Tom Connolly, S.J., of Sacred Heart Mission, DeSmet, Idaho.

Father Patrick Twohy, S.J., of Swinomish Spritual Centre, La Connor, Washington.

Mark Behler, curator, North Central Washington Museum, Wenatchee, Washington.

Jessica Sylvanus, Research Assistant, Okanogan County Historical Society, Okanogan, Washington.

Helen P. Clarke

Clarke, Helen P. Certificate of Death, Montana Bureau of Vital Statistics.

Clarke, Helen P. "Sketch of Malcolm Clarke." In *Contributions to the Historical Society of Montana*. Vol. 2. Helena: State Publishing Co., 1896.

Ewers, John C. *The Blackfeet: Raiders on the Northwestern Plains.* Norman: University of Oklahoma Press, 1958.

Farr, William E. *The Reservation Blackfeet, 1882–1945.* Seattle: University of Washington Press, 1984.

Halligan, Rev. Father. Eulogy for Helen P. Clarke, March 7, 1923.

Hanna, Warren L. *Stars Over Montana.* Glacier National Park, Mont.: Glacier Natural History Association, 1988.

"Malcolm Clark's Daughter Was Treasure State Heroine," Montana Newspaper Association, December 11, 1939.

"Maligned by a Newspaper," The *Montana Daily Record*, September 26, 1903.

Rowell, Agnes Sherburne. "Malcom Clarke, Fur Trader, Was a Power Among Blackfeet Indians," *Great Falls Tribune,* May 15, 1932.

Turvey, Joyce Clarke. "Helen Piotopowaka Clarke." In History of Glacier County. Glacier County Historical Society, 1984.

Chipeta

Benjamin, Peggy H. "The Last of Captain Jack, a Fresh Appraisal of the Ute Subchief Who Touched Off the Meeker Massacre and Met a Violent Death." *Montana, the Magazine of Western History,* vol. 10, no. 2, Spring 1960, 22–31.

Churchill, Caroline Nichols. *Active Footsteps.* Colorado Springs, CO: Mrs. C. N. Churchill, 1909.

Leckenby, Charles H. *The Tread of Pioneers.* Steamboat Springs, CO: Pilot Press, 1944.

Osborn, Katherine M. B. *Southern Ute Women: Autonomy and Assimilation on the Reservation, 1887–1934.* Albuquerque: University of New Mexico, 1998.

Perkin, Robert L. *First Hundred Years: An Informal History of Denver and the Rocky Mountain News.* New York: Doubleday, 1959.

Pettit, Jan. *Utes: The Mountain People.* Boulder, CO: Johnson Books, 1990.

Reagan, Albert B., and Wallace Stark. "Chipeta, Queen of the Utes." *The Utah Historical Quarterly,* vol. 6, 1933, 103–111.

Smith, P. David. *Ouray, Chief of the Utes.* Ouray, CO: Wayfinder Press, 1986.

Sprague, Marshall. *Massacre: The Tragedy at White River.* Boston: Little, Brown, 1957.

Trimble, Stephen. *The People: Indians of the American Southwest.* Santa Fe, NM: School of American Research Press, 1993.

Wommack, Linda. *From the Grave: A Roadside Guide to Colorado's Pioneer Cemeteries.* Caldwell, ID: Caxton Press, 1998.

Malee Francis

Covington, James W. *The Seminoles of Florida.* Gainesville, FL: University Press of Florida, 1993.

Croffut, W. A., ed. *Fifty Years in Camp and Field: Diary of Major-General Ethan Allen Hitchcock,* USA. Freeport, NY: Books for Library Press. First published in 1909, reprinted in 1971.

Davis, T. Frederick. "Milly Francis and Duncan McKrimmon: An Authentic Florida Pocahontas." Florida Historical Quarterly, Vol. XXI, 1943.

Foreman, Grant, ed. *A Traveler in Indian Territory: The Journal of Ethan Allen Hitchcock.* Norman, OK: University of Oklahoma Press, 1930.

Georgia Journal. Milledgeville, Georgia. Nov. 3, 1818, Sept. 29, 1818, Oct. 13, 1818, Dec. 22, 1818.

Kersey, Harry A., Jr. "Private Societies and the Maintenance of Seminole Tribal Society, 1899–1957." *Florida Historical Quarterly,* Vol. LVI, No. 3, Jan. 1978.

Long, Ellen Call. *Florida Breezes: Florida New and Old.* Gainesville, FL: University of Florida Press, 1962. (Facsimile reproduction of 1883 edition.)

Mahon, John K. *History of the Second Seminole War, 1835–1842.* Gainesville, FL: University Presses of Florida, 1992.

Peithman, Irvin M. *The Unconquered Seminole Indians.* St. Petersburg, FL: Great Outdoors Publishing Co., 1957.

Seminole Tribe of Florida. *History Where We Come From.* www .history.com. Accessed Feb. 20, 1999.

Wright, Leitch J. *Creeks and Seminoles.* Lincoln, NE: University of Nebraska, 1986.

Magdelaine LaFramboise

Kinzie, Juliette (Mrs. John). Wau-Bon, *The Early Day of The Northwest.* Chicago: D.B. Cooke & Co., 1857.

Métis Women in the Fur Trade at Mackinac. www.rootsweb
.com/.

Widder, Keith R. *Historic Women of Michigan*, chapter 1. Lansing,
Mich.: Michigan Women's Studies Association, 1987.

Bernard, Jacqueline. *Journey Toward Freedom: The Story of
Sojourner Truth.* New York: Norton, 1967.

Douglass, Frederick. *The Life and Time of Frederick Douglass.*
Hartford, Conn.: Park Publishers, 1881. Mineola, N.Y.: Dover
Publications, 2003.

McLoon, Margo. *Sojourner Truth: A Photo Illustrated Biography.*
Mankato, Minn.: Bridgestone Press, 1997.

Painter, Nell Irvin. *Sojourner Truth: A Life, a Symbol.* New York:
W.W. Norton, 1996.

Robinson, Marius. *The Salem Anti-Slavery Bugle*, June 21, 1851.

Truth, Sojourner, and Olive Gilbert. *The Narrative of Sojourner
Truth.* Boston: For the Author, 1875. Oxford, England: Oxford
University Press, 1994.

Sacajawea

Anderson, Irving W. "Sacajawea?—Sakakawea?—Sacagawea?"
We Proceeded On, Summer (1975). Reprinted by The Lewis &
Clark Trail Heritage Foundation. On-line. www.lewisandclark
.org.

Beal, Merrill D., Ph.D. and Merle W. Wells, Ph.D. *History of Idaho.*
Vol II. New York: Lewis Historical Publishing Company, Inc.,
1959.

Bergon, Frank. *The Journals of Lewis and Clark.* New York: Viking
Penguin, Inc., 1989.

Clarke, Charles G. *The Men of the Lewis and Clark Expedition.*
Glendale, Calif.: The Arthur H. Clark Company, 1970.

Defenbach, Byron. *Red Heroines of the Northwest.* Caldwell, Ida.:
The Caxton Printers, Ltd., 1935.

Flandrau, Grace. *A Glance at the Lewis and Clark Expedition.* Great Northern Railway, 1927.

Hebard, Grace Raymond. *Sacajawea, a Guide and Interpreter of the Lewis and Clark Expedition.* Glendale, Calif.: The Arthur H. Clark Company, 1933.

Howard, Harold P. *Sacajawea.* Norman: University of Oklahoma Press, 1971.

Rees, John E. "The Shoshoni Contribution to Lewis and Clark." *Idaho Yesterdays,* Summer (1958): Vol. II, No. 2.

Thwaites, Reuben Gold. *Original Journals of the Lewis & Clark Expedition,* 1804–1806. New York: Dodd, Mead & Co., 1904.

Jane Timothy Silcott

Bailey, Robert G. *River of No Return.* Lewiston, Ida.: R.G. Bailey Printing Company, 1935.

Defenbach, Byron. *Red Heroines of the Northwest.* Caldwell, Ida.: The Caxton Printers, Ltd., 1935.

Drury, Clifford Merrill. *Henry Harmon Spalding.* Caldwell, Ida.: The Caxton Printers, Ltd., 1936.

———. *Where Wagons Could Go.* Lincoln, Nebr.: University of Nebraska Press/Bison Books, 1997. First published as First White Women Over the Rockies. Vol I. Glendale, Calif.: Arthur H. Clark & Co., 1963.

Evans, Pauline. *The Old Spalding Log Cabin Mission, and the Story of Princess Jane.* Unpublished manuscript. Pullman, Wash.: Washington State University Libraries, 26 November 1935.

Louise Siuwheem

Bradley, Rt. Rev. Cyprian, O.S.B. and Most Rev. Edward J. Kelly, D.D., Ph.D. *History of the Diocese of Boise 1863–1952.* Boise: Roman Catholic Diocese of Boise, Caldwell: The Caxton Printers, Ltd., 1953.

Chittenden, Hiram Martin and Alfred Talbot Richardson. *Life, Letters and Travels of Father Pierre-Jean De Smet, S.J. 1801–1873.* New York: Francis P. Harper, 1905.

De Smet, Rev. P. J., S. J. *New Indian Sketches.* New York: D. & J. Sadlier & Co., 1865.

Dozier, Jack. "The Light of the Coeur d'Alenes." The *Spokesman-Review,* 15 July 1962.

Hultner, Vi. "The Good Grandmother of the Coeur d'Alenes." The *Spokesman-Review,* 7 December 1952.

Hutton, May Arkwright. *The Coeur d'Alenes or A Tale of the Modern Inquisition in Idaho.* Fairfield, Wash.: Ye Galleon Press, 1985. First published, Wallace, Ida./Denver: Self-published/May Arkwright Hutton, 1900.

LaVeille, E., S. J. *The Life of Father De Smet, S. J.* New York: P. J. Kenedy & Sons, 1915.

Point, Rev. Nicolas, S. J. *Biographies of the Coeur d'Alene.* Unpublished manuscript. DeSmet, Ida.: Sacred Heart Mission, circa 1892.